IMAGES
of America

FEDERAL RESERVE BANK OF BOSTON

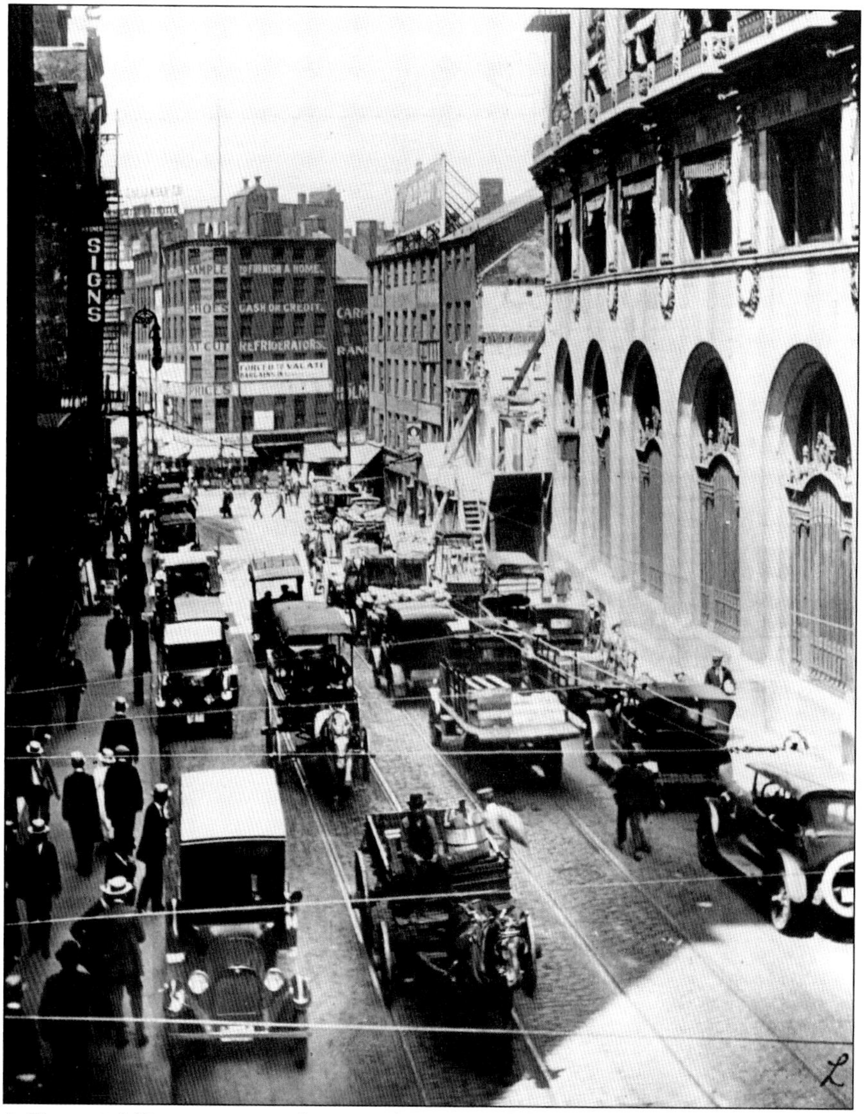

Boston's Financial District is seen here at the time of the Federal Reserve Bank of Boston's opening. An 1872 fire had devastated the area, causing $73 million in damages. During the rebuilding, Congress and Federal Streets were widened and much of the rubble was used to fill in Atlantic Avenue, where the bank would eventually make its home. The Fed would impact the face of the district on more than one occasion. (Courtesy of the Federal Reserve Bank of Boston Archives.)

ON THE COVER: An internal audit is no one's idea of a good time, but, nonetheless, it is a necessity. Here, the "watcher," Raymond Whiteman (standing), keeps a keen eye on a cash audit in 1951. At the time, bank departments were usually segregated by gender (if not by law, by custom), but the first female auditor was hired in 1944. In addition to their internal duties, the auditing staffs of the 12 Federal Reserve Banks served rotating three-year assignments assisting Fed Bank examiners in the examination of large member banks, including the New York Fed, and the Federal Reserve Board of Governors, in Washington. (Courtesy of the Federal Reserve Bank of Boston Archives.)

IMAGES
of America

FEDERAL RESERVE BANK OF BOSTON

Diane Shephard for the
Federal Reserve Bank of Boston
Foreword by Eric S. Rosengren

ARCADIA
PUBLISHING

ISBN 978-1-4671-2089-0

Published by Arcadia Publishing
Charleston, South Carolina

Printed in the United States of America

Library of Congress Control Number: 2013943959

For all general information, please contact Arcadia Publishing:
Telephone 843-853-2070
Fax 843-853-0044
E-mail sales@arcadiapublishing.com
For customer service and orders:
Toll-Free 1-888-313-2665

Visit us on the Internet at www.arcadiapublishing.com

To all employees, past and present, of the Federal Reserve Bank of Boston

CONTENTS

FOREWORD

As you browse the pages of this book, you will see that the Federal Reserve Bank of Boston has always been about more than just monetary policy. Over the past century, we have contributed to local communities, the region, and the nation through our high-quality research, regulatory oversight, and financial services, and through our commitment to leadership and innovation.

As part of the nation's central bank, we aim to promote sound growth and financial stability in New England and the nation. We have tried to do that in a variety of ways, including fostering policies that help the economy, bringing local business leaders and elected officials to the same table, working to ensure that the financial system is providing safe and reliable services for all citizens, and making sure that the region has access to the currency it needs, especially when disaster strikes.

I believe that serving the public well means not only learning from our past, but also continuing to push forward on the issues that matter in our region and the nation as a whole. Currently, our focus is on issues such as the regulation of money-market mutual funds, mobile payments standards and security, capital requirements for banking institutions, and unemployment. We are also working to improve the lives of lower-income families and jump-start the economies of the region's struggling smaller cities.

Over the past 100 years, the heart and soul of this institution has truly been the dedicated men and women who have walked these halls. It is through their tireless efforts that the bank continues to make a difference. I would especially like to thank Diane Shephard and David Greene for their hard work on this book. We hope you enjoy this look back on our history.

—Eric S. Rosengren
President and Chief Executive Officer
Federal Reserve Bank of Boston

ACKNOWLEDGMENTS

The author would like to thank David Greene and Barbara DeBiase, her stalwart companions in Boston Fed time line making, a job that made *this* job so much easier; Joyce Hannan, for her encouragement and support for this project and her general patience with a person who often requires a lot of it; Patricia Geagan, the assistant vice president, for her continued support of the bank's archives program; and director of research Geoff Tootell and the entire Economic Research Information Center for their general awesomeness.

Unless otherwise noted, all images are from the archives of the Federal Reserve Bank of Boston.

Introduction

From Alexander Hamilton to Ben Bernanke, the United States has had a lengthy and complex relationship with the concept of a centralized national bank. What Jefferson decried as "the graveyard of our liberties," Hamilton pointed to as "necessary and proper." As president, even James Madison, as bitter a foe of the First Bank of the United States as any man, discovered the difficulty of conducting a war and managing a growing economy without a central bank; he signed the charter for the Second Bank of the United States in 1816.

When Andrew Jackson effectively killed the Second Bank in 1833, the nation continued for close to 80 years without a comparable institution. This set the tone for a dialogue that often pitted the "moneyed interest" (usually read as "East Coast") against "the people," in terms more likely to produce hard feelings and misunderstandings than solutions. It was a period marked by repeated financial panics, depressions, and wildly, often catastrophically, fluctuating business cycles culminating in the devastating panic of 1907, which saw the New York Stock Exchange lose 50 percent of its value. When the total collapse of the American financial system could only be averted through the intercession and manipulation of private individuals such as J.P. Morgan and other New York City bankers, the need to strengthen the government's power and control in such situations became clear. How it was to be accomplished, however, was anything but clear.

In response to the panic of 1907, the Aldrich-Vreeland Act established a National Monetary Commission to study ways that other nations, particularly in Europe, avoided the kind of economic extremes that plagued the United States. The passage, on December 23, 1913, of the act establishing the Federal Reserve System was the culmination of the National Monetary Commission's work.

The act provided for a board of governors in Washington, DC, and 12 independent district banks in cities across the nation, including in Boston, which was designated as District A-1. The duties of the Federal Reserve System, known popularly as the Fed, are fourfold: conduct the nation's monetary policy; supervise and regulate the nation's banks; maintain the stability of the financial system and contain the risks inherent in financial markets; provide financial services, including payment systems, to the US government, the general public, financial institutions, and foreign governments.

The 12 Fed banks occupy a unique position in the political landscape of the United States as what are somewhat inelegantly termed quasi-governmental entities. While the Federal Reserve Board of Governors in Washington is an independent agency of the US government, the individual banks themselves are private, nonprofit corporations whose stock is owned by the member banks of each district, although this stock does not confer the rights typically associated with that of commercial, for-profit endeavors.

Since opening for business on November 16, 1914, the Federal Reserve Bank of Boston has been an integral part of the economic life of the entire New England region, with the exclusion of

Fairfield County, Connecticut (concerning that oddity, more later). From the outbreak of World War I, almost simultaneous with the bank's own birth, through the technological challenges of the century date change in the year 2000 and the dark days of the September 11 attacks, the Boston Fed has played a prominent role in providing stability and strength to the region.

Beyond its financial role, however, as vital as that has been, the story of the Boston Fed is also the story of Boston and all of New England for the past 100 years. The transformation of the local economy, the changing face of the area's population and its workforce, the march of technology, the emerging roles of women and minorities—all are reflected in microcosm in the history of the bank, its employees, and the people and institutions that it serves.

As the Fed approaches its centennial year, it looks back upon an era of our nation's history unprecedented in both the challenges and triumphs it has faced. It has faced its own unique pressures as well, as its supporters and its critics are nearly equal in number, and it looks ahead to take these lessons as building blocks to its future service.

The pages that follow are not a comprehensive or scholarly history of the Boston Fed, nor would such even be possible in this format—as vital as it is, monetary policy is just not very photogenic. This volume instead largely focuses on two particular threads of the Fed's story. One is the people who have made the Boston Fed the respected organization and the good neighbor it is widely viewed as in the New England community. This includes the variety of vital, groundbreaking, and, occasionally, downright baffling work they have devoted themselves to over the years. The other is the impact that the bank has had on the city of Boston and its development over the years, through construction that has changed the face of the city on more than one occasion. It is fortunate that these projects were so well documented photographically.

An additional word about the photographs is necessary. To current employees accustomed to the diversity that the bank values so highly today, some of these historical photographs may be a bit jarring. The sea of white faces in so many images is not an editorial decision on the part of the author, be assured. It is a true representation of the workforce as it was for many years: minorities were few or nonexistent and the role of women was limited to very specific departments and positions. The late Dan Aquilino, a former executive vice president, recalled that the ultimate reward for a woman who excelled at any position at the bank was to be appointed as a secretary, whether office skills were her area of expertise or not. Without attempting to disguise anything, certain decisions had to be made about which images were appropriate to show and which were not. This choice must be a subjective one on the author's part; thus, images of charm classes for female employees have been included but blackface minstrel show acts have not. The acknowledgement of their existence is perhaps sufficient. In this, the bank was no worse than other institutions of the time, but one may still wish it had found a way to be better than the times, however unfair that may be to ask. Finally, the photographs only take us up to 2001. The volatile decade that has followed is left for those future observers with a greater opportunity for placing events in their proper perspective.

One

Beginnings

While not everyone approved of the fledgling Federal Reserve System, nearly every city wanted to be selected as a reserve city. The Reserve Bank Organization Committee was lobbied hard from all corners. Boston bankers were more beloved by the rest of the country than New York bankers, but that was not saying very much. There existed some sentiment that a New York Fed that served the entire northeast region would at least save the nation from having to endure them both, but not much in the way of serious opposition was ever mounted against Boston's claim. This may be attributed in part to the extremely well-organized nature of the city's banking interests at the time.

The Boston Clearing House Association had been formed in 1856, the second in the nation after New York's, giving the city's bankers a ready-made forum for discussion and organized action. It was the Clearing House that called meetings, met with the Reserve Bank Organization Committee, nominated individuals for membership on the Federal Reserve Bank of Boston Board of Directors, and generally orchestrated the city's successful bid to gain one of the 12 district banks. With New York, Philadelphia, and Richmond, Virginia, also gaining approval, Baltimore was left as the odd city out as far as the East Coast districts were concerned, a matter that excited much comment in that city at the time, not all of it highly flattering to Boston.

The map of Federal Reserve districts, with four on the East Coast and only one, in San Francisco, on the West Coast, made more sense in 1914 than it does today, although perhaps only marginally so. Westward expansion of the nation's population had been going on for about 200 years and was not showing any signs of stopping in the early 1900s. The gaps were filled in to a certain degree by branch offices; Boston and Philadelphia were the only districts that never required additional branches.

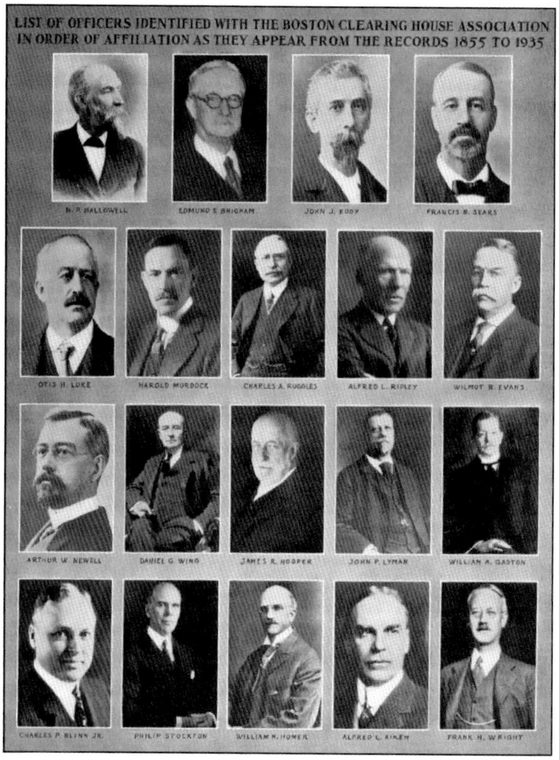

The Boston Clearing House, established in 1856, was the most influential financial organization in Boston prior to the establishment of the Federal Reserve System, and its members led the move to bring a reserve bank to the city. The cast of leading characters in the two institutions was often the same. Alfred Aiken, the Boston Fed's first governor (bottom row, second from right) moved directly to the Clearing House following his tenure at the bank.

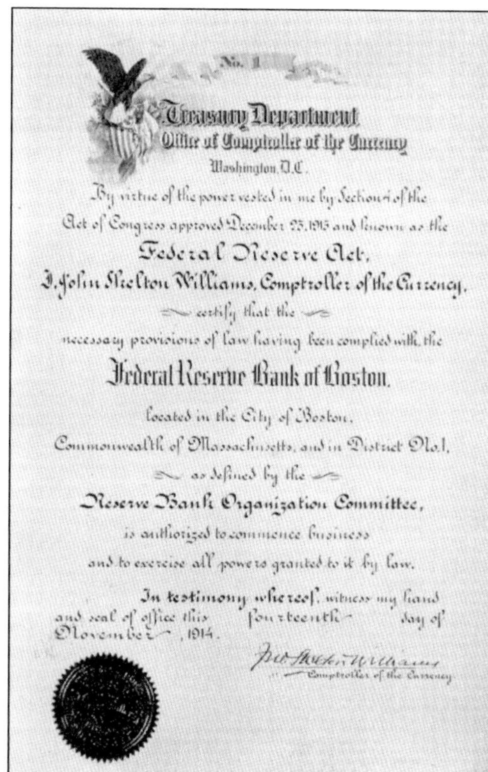
No. 1

Treasury Department
Office of Comptroller of the Currency
Washington, D.C.

By virtue of the power vested in me by Section 4 of the Act of Congress approved December 23, 1913 and known as the

Federal Reserve Act,

I, John Skelton Williams, Comptroller of the Currency,

certify that the

necessary provisions of law having been complied with, the

Federal Reserve Bank of Boston,

located in the City of Boston,

Commonwealth of Massachusetts, and in District No. 1,

as defined by the

Reserve Bank Organization Committee,

is authorized to commence business

and to exercise all powers granted to it by law.

In testimony whereof, witness my hand and seal of office this fourteenth day of November, 1914.

Comptroller of the Currency

All 12 Federal Reserve Banks had their formal charters signed on November 14, 1914, and opened for business on November 16. Many local bankers had hoped for a later date. According to one, "It is in no spirit of petty criticism that I state that Secretary [William] McAdoo's sudden decision to inaugurate the Federal Reserve System on November 16, after a poll of banking sentiment at Washington had indicated a preference for November 30, is at best a trifle ill-advised. Most banks are equipped only with a governor and a board of directors, and it will be a herculean task to assemble competent bank staffs within a fortnight."

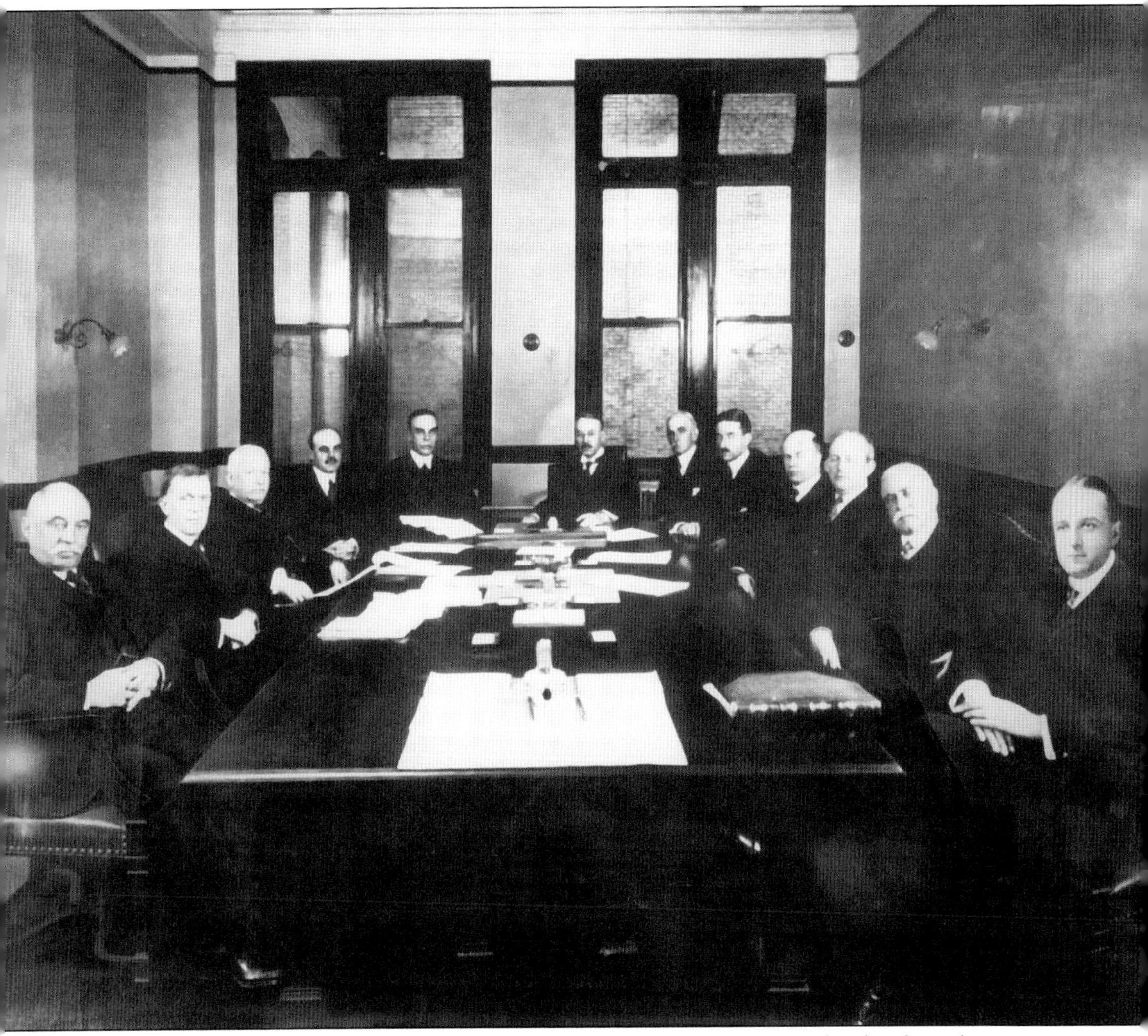

The first Board of Directors of the Federal Reserve Bank of Boston poses for this formal portrait at the temporary State Street quarters. Three directors in three separate classes comprise the full board. Class A directors represent the banking institutions of each district, Class B directors represent the interests of industry, agriculture, and consumers, and Class C directors are appointed by the Federal Reserve Board. Alfred Aiken, the president of the Worcester National Bank, was appointed the first governor, and Frederick H. Curtiss was appointed as the first Federal Reserve agent. At the inception of the Federal Reserve System, there was some uncertainty as to which of these positions would assume active leadership, but, according to Joseph H. Taggart, the author of an early history of the Boston Fed, Aiken and Curtiss quickly reached an accord and worked together "without friction."

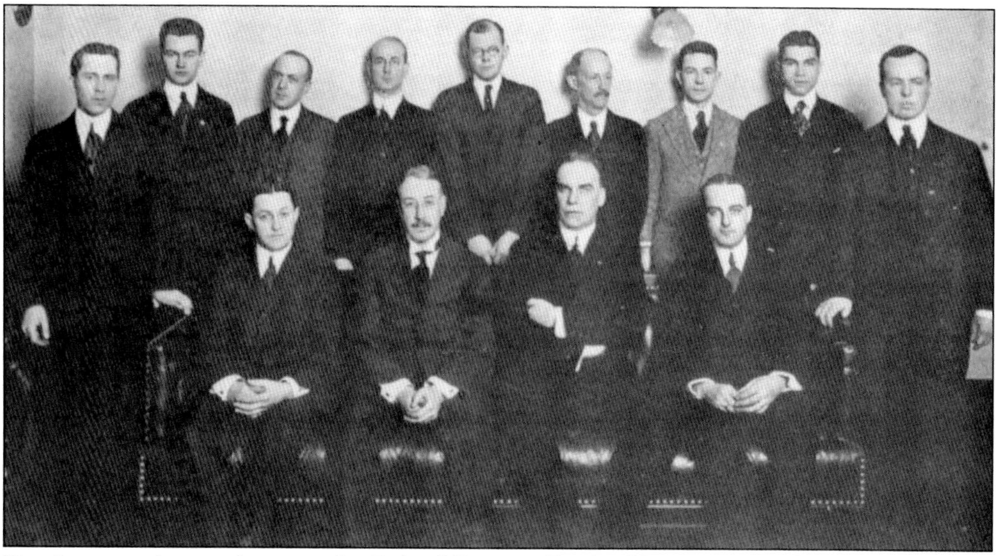

Despite some dire predictions, the Federal Reserve Bank of Boston opened fully staffed, with three officers and 14 clerks. According to Frederick Curtiss, "First deposit of reserves, amounting to about $14,500,000, was received at the Sub treasury. A force composed of a few clerks in the Sub treasury, augmented by a number of employees loaned for the occasion by some of the Boston banks, began to count this money at 8.00 o'clock on the morning of November 16 and finished work at 1:30 A.M. on November 17 . . . The initial comparison indicated a difference of $55. After searching for this amount until 4.00 o'clock in the morning of the 17th, with no results, Governor Aiken decided to charge the difference to profit and loss. Thus the employees received their first taste of night work."

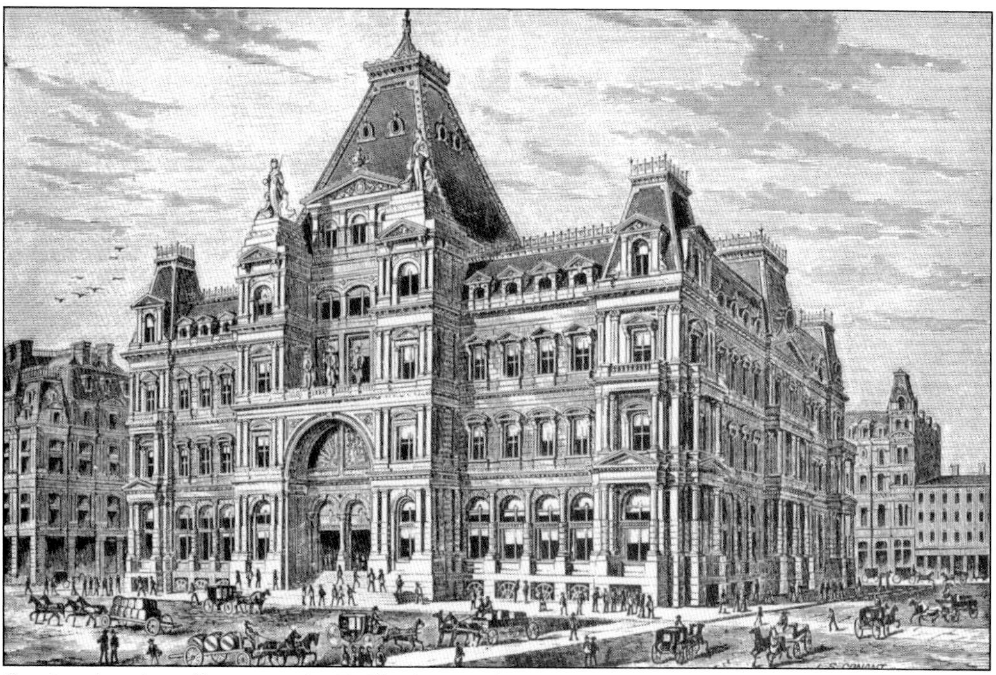

On that first day of business, the Fed had no vault space of its own; it was rented from the United States Sub-Treasury, which was then located in the Post Office Building.

Two

Tests and Trials

Before the Boston Fed could even open its doors, the world was confronted with the first truly modern war, conducted on a scale that was almost unimaginable, as all major European powers were engaged in the struggle. The United States did not enter the hostilities officially until 1917, but there was no avoiding the turmoil that rocked the financial world. Business in New England's textile mills—the area's dominant industry—was stalled, and interest rates were high, making borrowing expensive. Nonetheless, the Fed had to make its way and prove its usefulness.

In 1916, the reserve banks were made the fiscal agents of the US government. In addition, Boston took over the New England Department of the Boston Clearing House, clearing checks for the so-called country banks, meaning all institutions outside of Boston and Cambridge. The entire relevant staff of the Clearing House moved en masse to the Fed's employ. The staff was further enlarged when the United States entered the war, and the Federal Reserve System was given charge of the Liberty Loans, which raised the enormous amounts of cash the government required for the effort.

The successful conclusion of hostilities did not bring immediate stability to the financial world, and the 1920s were a time of wildly fluctuating conditions. The bank had its own problems to contend with unrelated to broader issues, as its expanded staff outgrew its rented facilities and was forced to lease space wherever it could, as close to the Financial District as possible. Realizing the need for a permanent solution, a building committee was formed in 1920.

The high-flying 1920s were famously brought back to earth with the stock market crash of 1929, and the Federal Reserve System was once again confronted with a catastrophe that had no precedent and was amenable to no easy solution. The role of the Fed would be refined through various legislative acts, most significantly the Banking Act of 1933, which established the Federal Open Market Committee as a key tool of the nation's monetary policy.

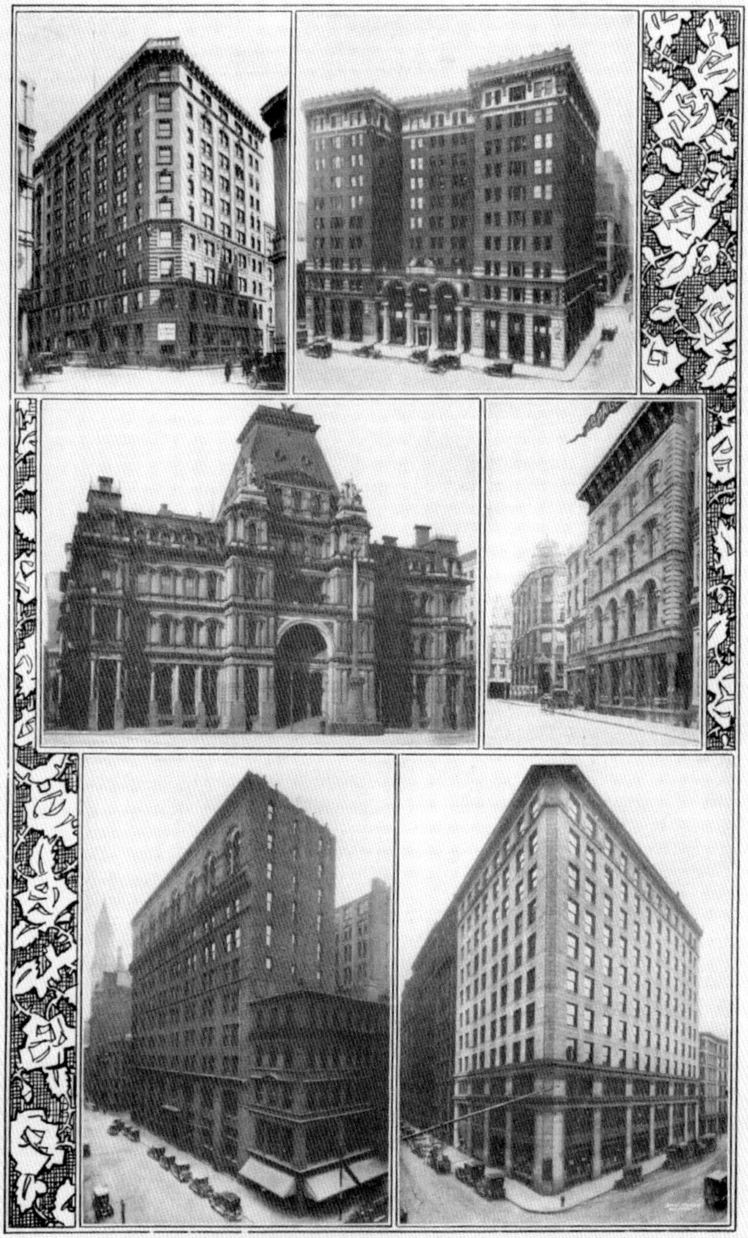

BUILDINGS FORMERLY OCCUPIED BY VARIOUS DEPARTMENTS OF THE FEDERAL RESERVE BANK OF BOSTON

Reading from upper left to right

1 Converse Building, 101 Milk St. *Courtesy of Boston Herald*
2 Board of Trade Building, 131 State St.
3 Post Office Building, Post Office Sq.
4 John C. Paige Building, 20 Kilby St.
5 Exchange Building, 53 State St.
6 India Building, 50, 66, 84 State St.

Until 1922, the bank occupied various rented spaces in the Financial District. These included, as seen here, the Converse Building, at 101 Milk Street; the Board of Trade Building, at 131 State Street; the Post Office Building, at Post Office Square; the John C. Paige Building, at 20 Kilby Street; the Exchange Building, at 53 State Street; and the India Building, at 50, 66, and 84 State Street.

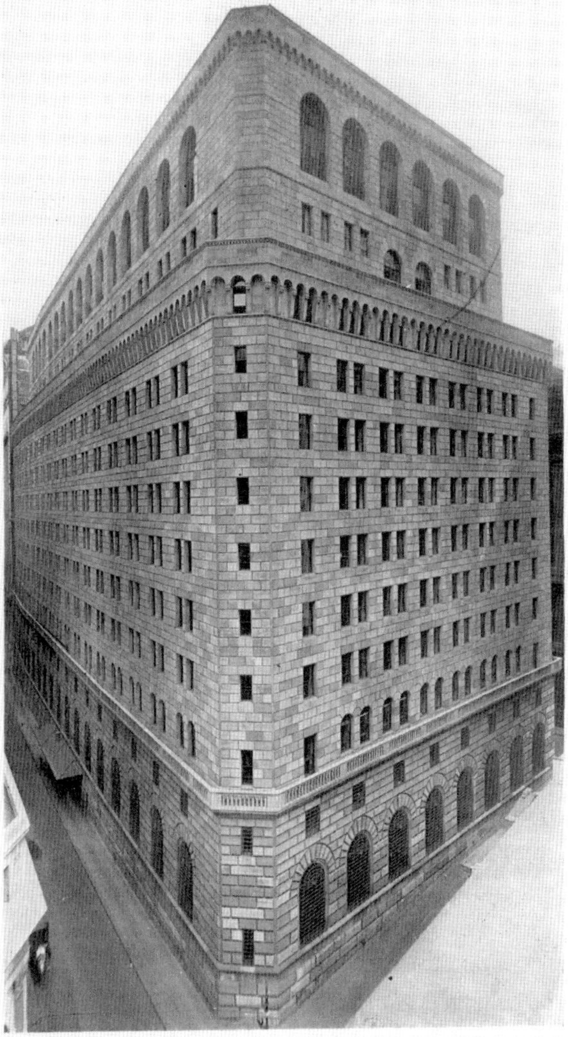

FEDERAL RESERVE BANK, NEW YORK CITY.
York & Sawyer, Architects.
A. B. Trowbridge, Consulting Architect.
Meyer, Strong & Jones, Inc., Consulting Engrs.

ARCHITECTURE AND BUILDING. Plate 135.
Built by Marc Eidlitz & Son, Inc.; limestone furnished by Michael Cohen & Co.; sandstone from the Briar Hill Stone Co.'s quarries and furnished by Arlando Marine; miscellaneous iron—Thomas A. Williams, Inc.; LaFarge non-staining cement used; flooring—Indiana Flooring Co.; structural steel made by American Bridge Co. and erected by Post & McCord; special bronze wall pockets—Universal Electric Stage Lighting Co., Inc.; Newman grille clocks and Eco-electrical recorders—Detex Watchclock Corp.; vault—York Safe & Lock Co.—advertisement.

Bankers in Fairfield County, Connecticut, were unhappy with their inclusion in the First District, feeling that their interests more closely coincided with those of New York City than New England. For a number of years, in fact, there was a sentiment that the entire state would be better served by District B-2 than by A-1. The *Boston Herald* did not think much of the argument, facetiously reporting, "Massachusetts, Rhode Island, Vermont, Maine and New Hampshire are decadent. There is nothing left for them but the raising of potatoes and the showing of scenery . . . It damages an aggressive and progressive state like that of the wooden nutmeg to be associated in the popular mind with a group of other states now on the decline." Nonetheless, in 1916, the Federal Reserve Board of Governors granted the county its wish, leading to the oddity of five states and one state minus one county comprising the Boston Fed's territory.

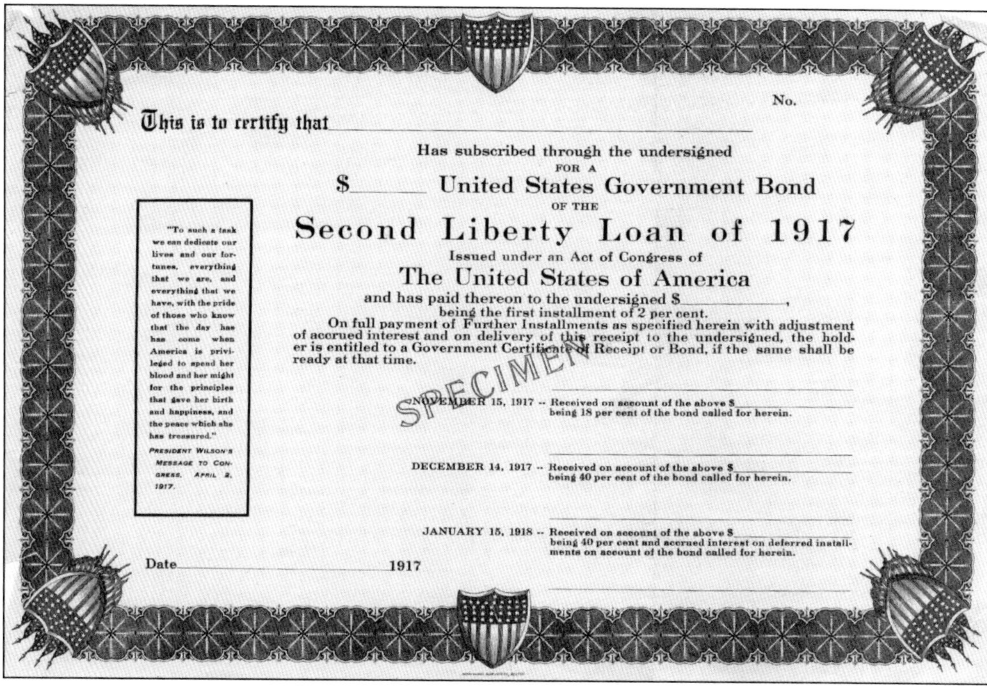

No.

This is to certify that ____________________

Has subscribed through the undersigned
FOR A
$______ United States Government Bond
OF THE
Second Liberty Loan of 1917
Issued under an Act of Congress of
The United States of America
and has paid thereon to the undersigned $__________,
being the first installment of 2 per cent.

On full payment of Further Installments as specified herein with adjustment of accrued interest and on delivery of this receipt to the undersigned, the holder is entitled to a Government Certificate of Receipt or Bond, if the same shall be ready at that time.

SPECIMEN

"To such a task we can dedicate our lives and our fortunes, everything that we are, and everything that we have, with the pride of those who know that the day has has come when America is privileged to spend her blood and her might for the principles that gave her birth and happiness, and the peace which she has treasured."

PRESIDENT WILSON'S MESSAGE TO CONGRESS, APRIL 2, 1917.

NOVEMBER 15, 1917 -- Received on account of the above $__________ being 18 per cent of the bond called for herein.

DECEMBER 14, 1917 -- Received on account of the above $__________ being 40 per cent of the bond called for herein.

JANUARY 15, 1918 -- Received on account of the above $__________ being 40 per cent and accrued interest on deferred installments on account of the bond called for herein.

Date__________________1917

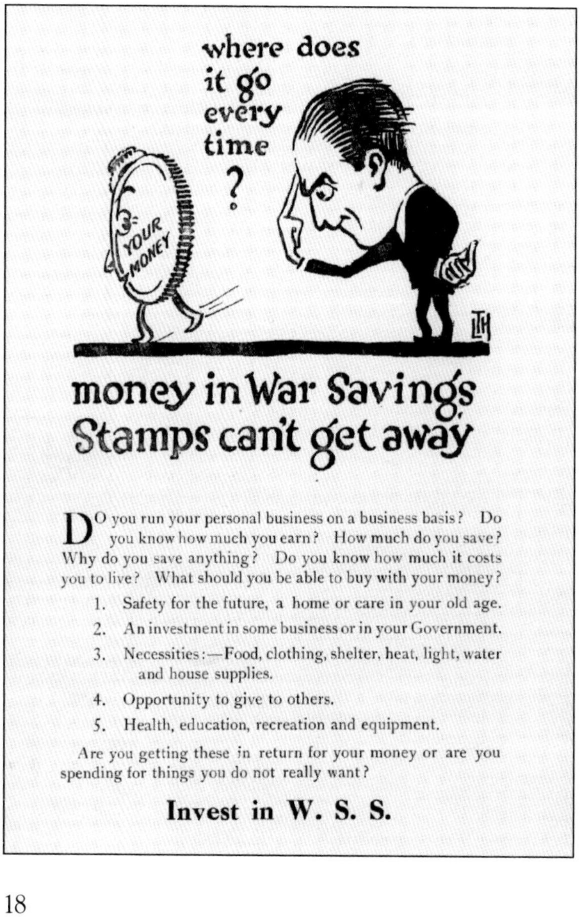

When the United States entered World War I in 1917, the nation found itself ill prepared for the fight. To rapidly raise the unprecedented sums needed for America's own efforts and to bolster American allies, a series of loans was conceived wherein even Americans of modest means could support the war effort. A central Liberty Loan committee was formed at each of the 12 Federal Reserve Banks to oversee the sale and distribution of these bonds and stamps in each district. The Liberty Loans' administration proved to be such a large undertaking that the workforce at the bank grew from 70 in 1916 to 617 by 1919, when the Victory Loan was floated. Bonds and stamps continued to be promoted even after the war as a tool of savvy financial planning.

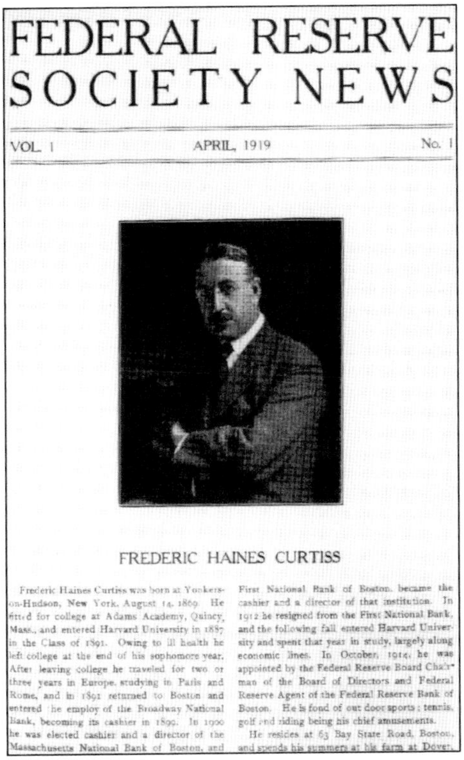

FEDERAL RESERVE SOCIETY NEWS

VOL. 1 APRIL, 1919 No. 1

FREDERIC HAINES CURTISS

Frederic Haines Curtiss was born at Yonkers-on-Hudson, New York, August 14, 1869. He fitted for college at Adams Academy, Quincy, Mass., and entered Harvard University in 1887 in the Class of 1891. Owing to ill health he left college at the end of his sophomore year. After leaving college he traveled for two or three years in Europe, studying in Paris and Rome, and in 1891 returned to Boston and entered the employ of the Broadway National Bank, becoming its cashier in 1890. In 1900 he was elected cashier and a director of the Massachusetts National Bank of Boston, and First National Bank of Boston, became the cashier and a director of that institution. In 1912 he resigned from the First National Bank, and the following fall entered Harvard University and spent that year in study, largely along economic lines. In October, 1914, he was appointed by the Federal Reserve Board Chairman of the Board of Directors and Federal Reserve Agent of the Federal Reserve Bank of Boston. He is fond of out door sports; tennis, golf and riding being his chief amusements.

He resides at 63 Bay State Road, Boston, and spends his summers at his farm at Dover,

The Federal Reserve Society was formed for the stated purpose of fostering "a feeling of cooperation and service in the bank." The society was comprised of all employees. Over the years, it has sponsored social events and charitable events and published a newsletter, seen here, which served as an invaluable resource in researching the experiences of Boston Fed employees through the years.

The society established a welfare department in 1919. Volunteers acted as go-betweens when conflicts arose and visited sick employees, but, it was assured, "only to ascertain whether we can be of any service and not that we feel any doubt as to the sincerity of the report." Female employees were given assistance in securing respectable and affordable lodging, and several lounges (pictured) were set aside at each of the bank's buildings where "the girls may seek peace and quiet in case of illness." It seems that male employees were expected to manage both their health and their respectability on their own.

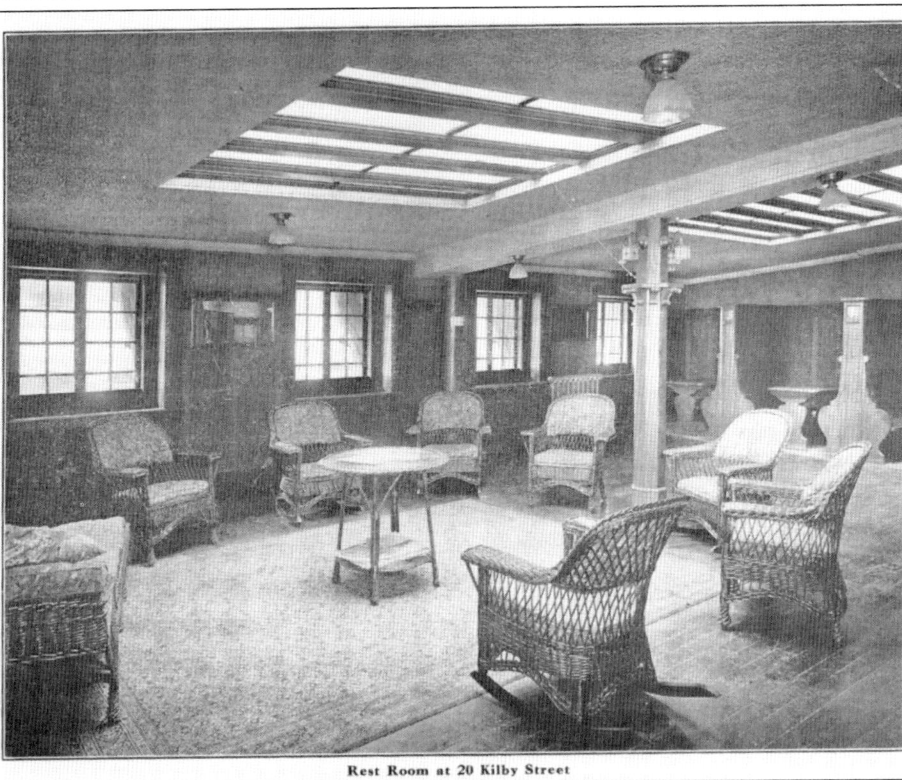

Rest Room at 20 Kilby Street

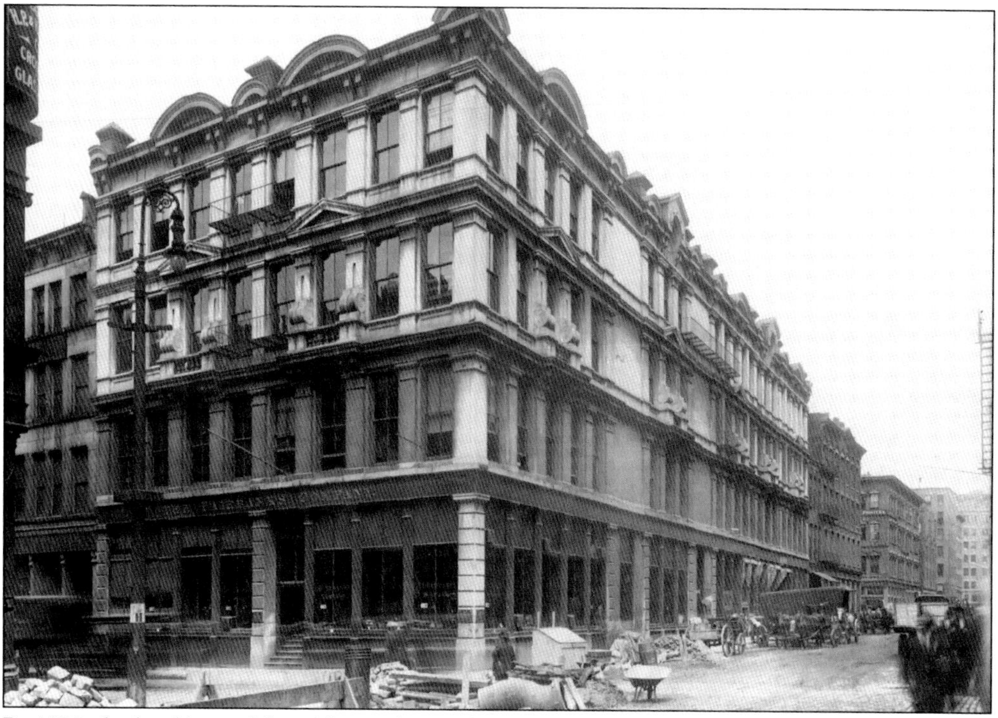

By 1920, the bank's need for additional space had grown acute. A site was initially purchased on Milk Street, adjacent to the New England Life Insurance building, with an eye to developing and occupying it in conjunction with that organization. The plans ultimately fell through, and the bank sold the property back to New England Life for $1.15 million and purchased this building, bounded by Pearl, Franklin, and Oliver Streets, for $1.5 million.

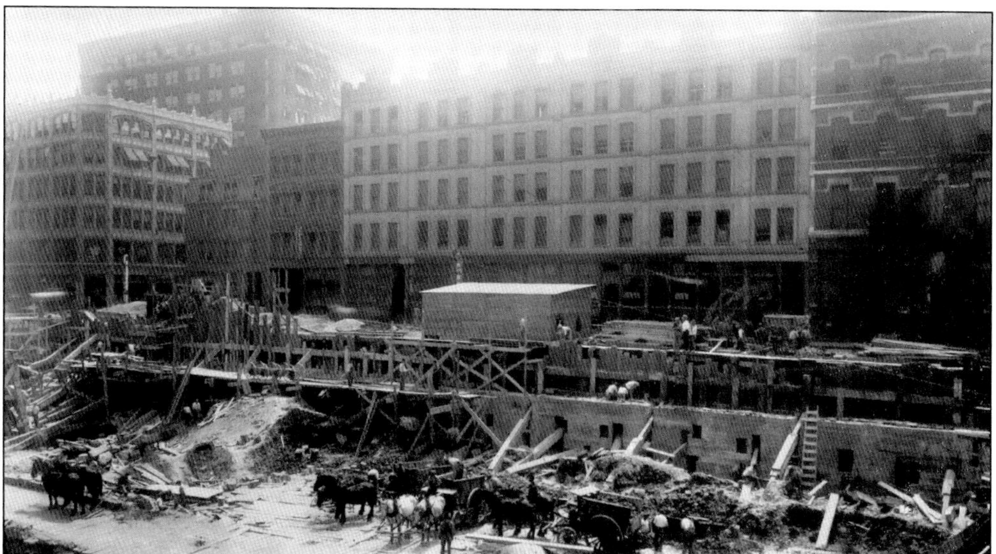

Demolition at the new bank site commenced on March 1, 1920. Among the design suggestions not acted upon was one that called for revolving turrets on either side of the main entry manned by armed guards. Larger-than-life equestrian statues were also scrapped since the connection to banking was not readily apparent.

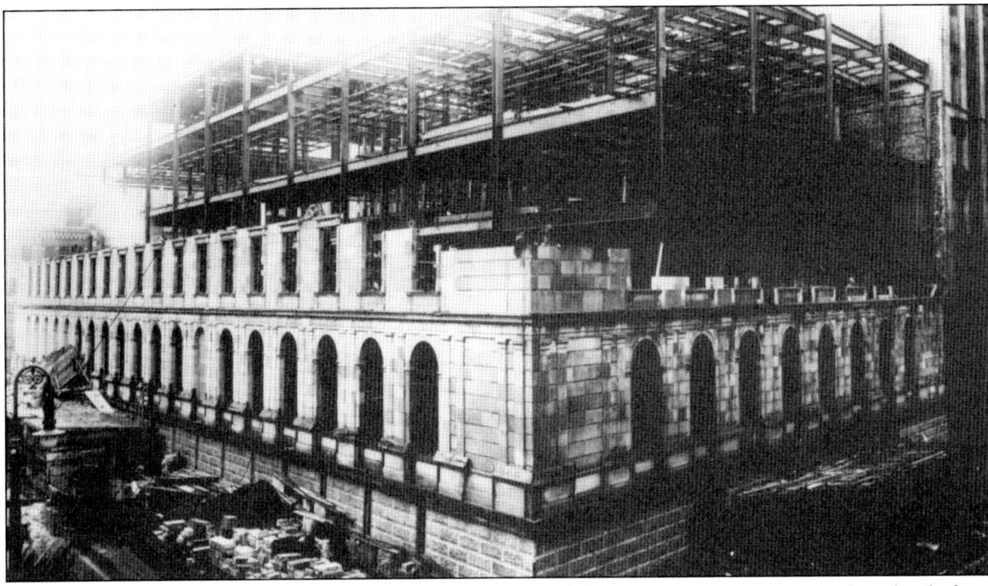

As is so often the case, delays in construction pushed the projected occupancy date back from September 1921 to April 1922. Labor issues were the primary cause of delay, as a wage dispute between workers and the supervising contractor led to a three-month strike early in 1921. Nonetheless, work had progressed sufficiently by December for the Auditing, Bookkeeping, and Supply Departments to move in.

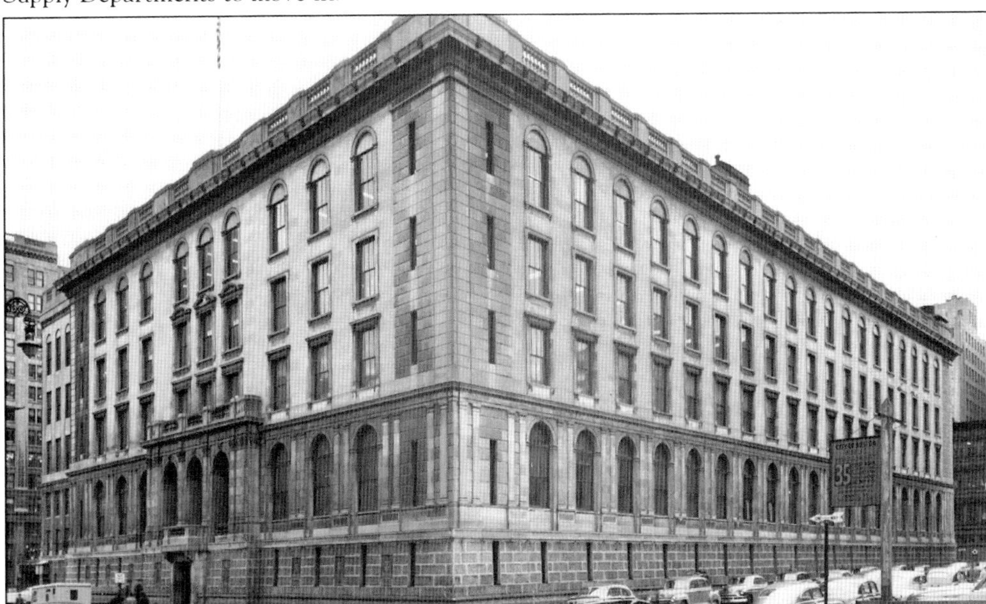

Designed by R. Clipston Sturgis in the Renaissance Revival style, the bank's new quarters officially opened on March 20, 1922. Boston was one of several reserve banks to construct a new building in the early 1920s, a fact that did not meet with universal approval. According to the *Report on the Committee on Relations with the Federal Reserve System*, one unnamed First District bank declared that its reluctance to join the system was partly owing to the fact "that the managers of the System have been unnecessarily extravagant in its operation, especially in the buildings that have been erected."

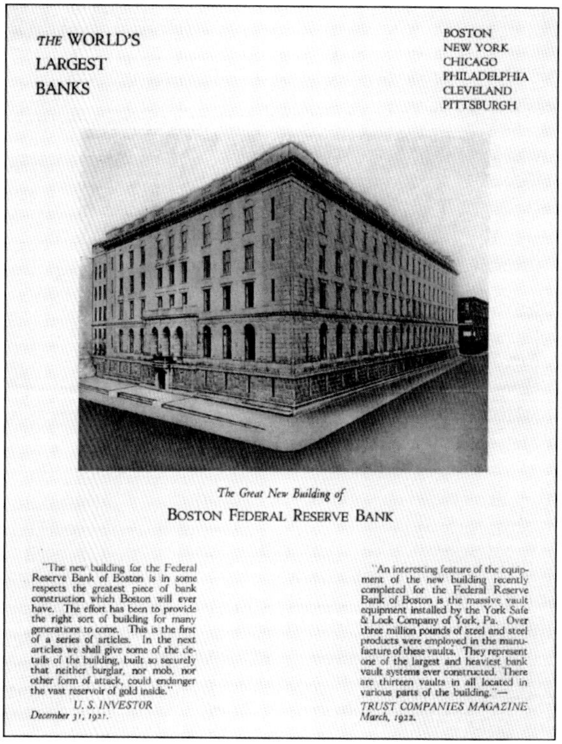

The bank has rarely lent its name to commercial advertisements. In fact, the only two occasions on record were connected with the completion of the Pearl Street building. York Safe & Lock Company used its connection with the new Boston Fed, "the greatest piece of bank construction which Boston will ever have," to tout the quality of its vaults, which were "built so securely that neither burglar, nor mob, nor other form of attack, could endanger the vast reservoir of gold inside." There never were vast reservoirs of gold inside, but that did not mean the vaults would not have been satisfactorily mob-proof had such reserves ever needed a place to stay.

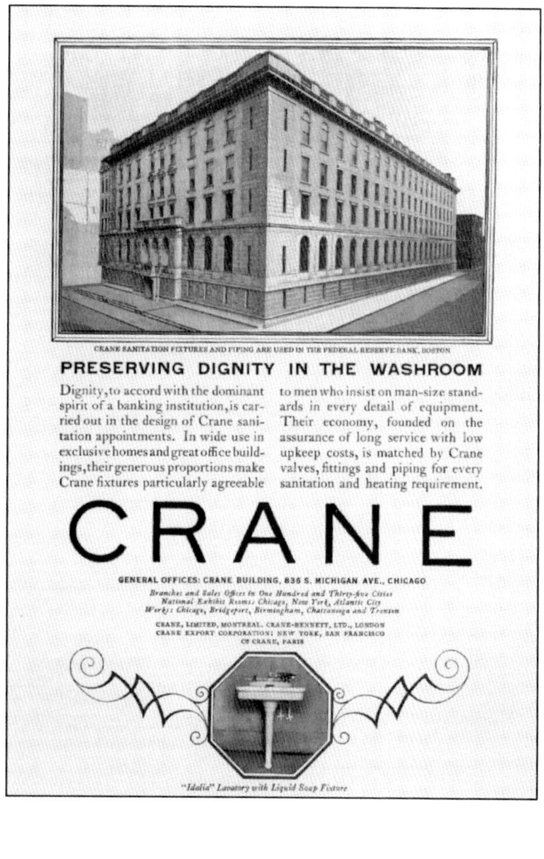

A less likely advertising angle was found by the Crane Company, a manufacturer of plumbing "valves, fittings and piping for every sanitation and heating requirement." Crane's fixtures, the advertisements assured, were "particularly agreeable to men who insist on man-sized standards in every detail of equipment."

A formal reception for the opening of the new building was held on April 17–18, 1922. Society member Gerald Harrison was moved to verse—and, perhaps, a bit of hyperbole—by the occasion, writing, "The Members' Court was all agleam; A gorgeous palace in a dream . . . With glass o'erhead and massive walls, where kings might romp at festive balls." History has not preserved any record of romping kings during the Fed's tenure, although lesser nobles have possibly romped through the building in its present incarnation as a luxury hotel.

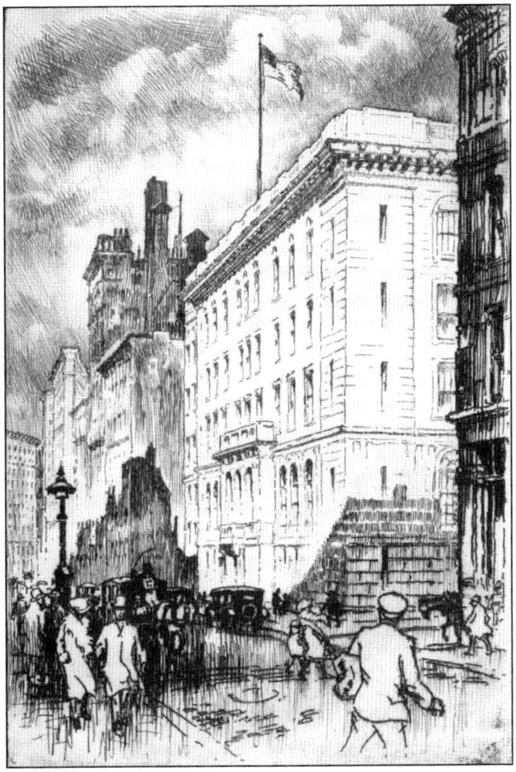

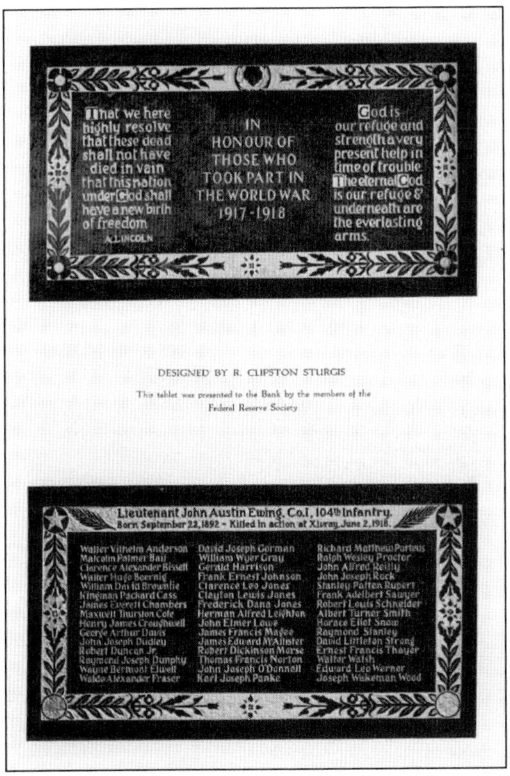

R. Clipson Sturgis, the architect of the new building, also designed the memorial tablet that was placed in the Members' Court in honor of the bank's World War (optimistically, it had not been assigned a number yet) veterans, including the lone casualty, John A. Ewing, who was killed by a German shell in the French town of Xivray. This tablet and a later one dedicated to World War II servicemen and women were removed to the present building in the 1970s and preserved.

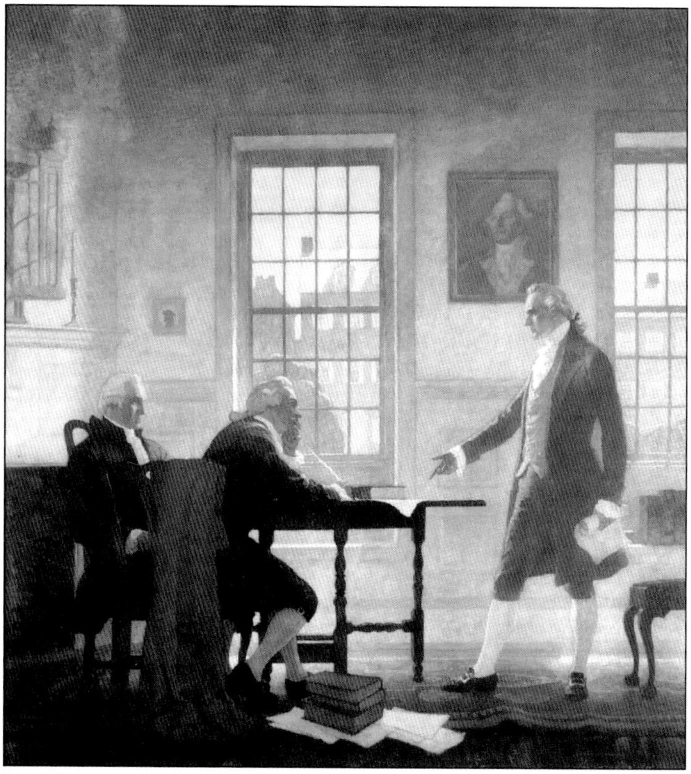

These two magnificent murals by N.C. Wyeth adorned the walls of the junior officers' room at 30 Pearl Street. At left, Alexander Hamilton presents his plan for the First Bank of the United States to George Washington and Robert Morris. Below, Abraham Lincoln confers with Secretary of the Treasury Salmon P. Chase during the dark days of the Civil War. The murals have been preserved by the present owner of the building, the Langham Hotel, and are still on view to the public. (Both, courtesy of the Langham Hotel.)

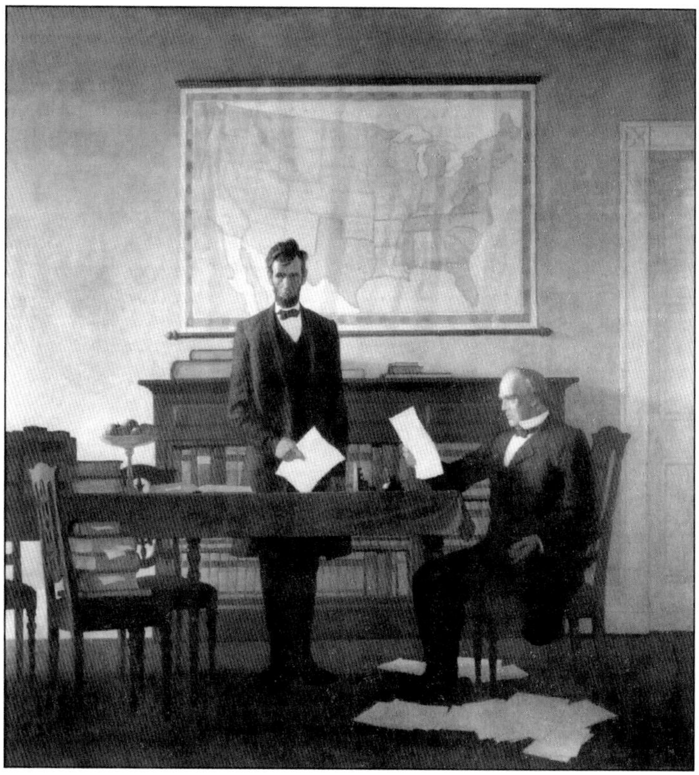

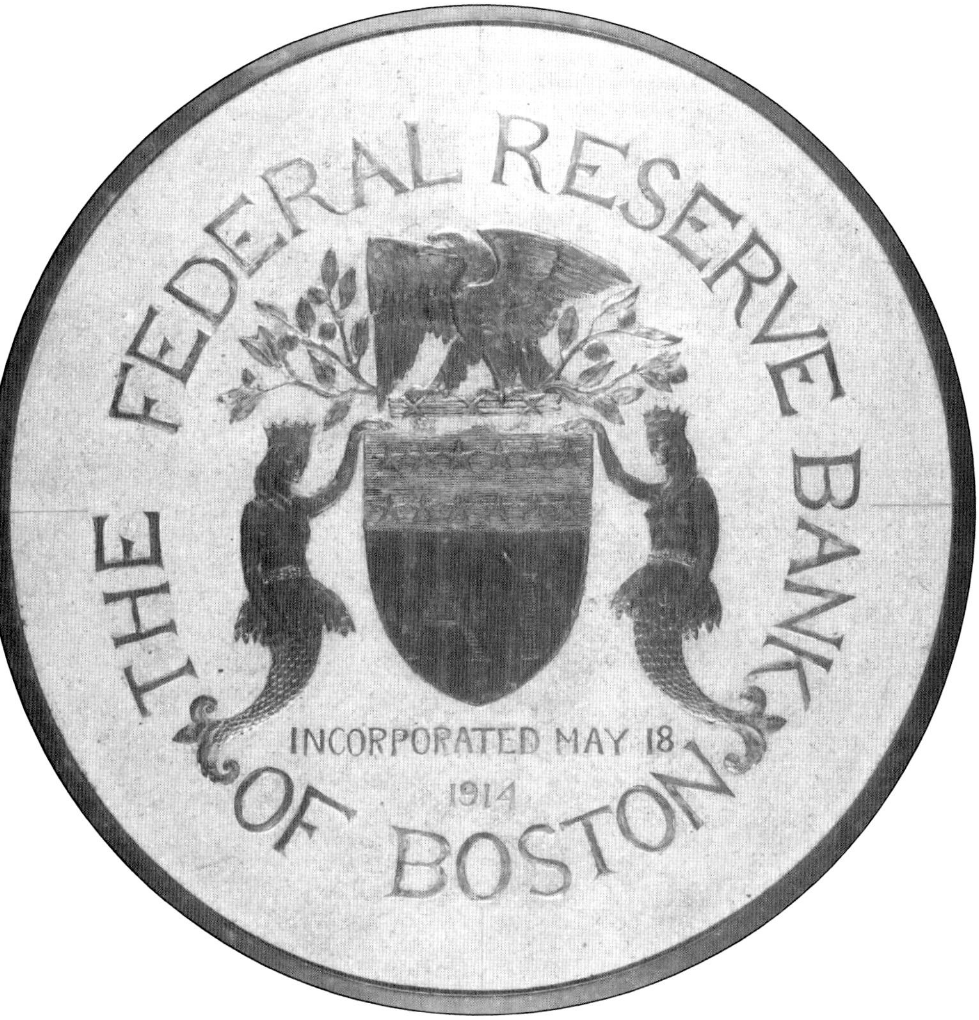

The 40-foot-by-70-foot Members' Court was designed, as its name implies, "for the convenience of officers of member banks for personal conferences and the keeping of their Boston appointments," according to the *Federal Reserve Society News*. The floor was adorned with this unusual version of the bank's seal, replete with merpeople whose significance has long since been obscured. Recent renovations at the Langham Hotel revealed the intact seal under layers of carpet. (Courtesy of the Langham Hotel.)

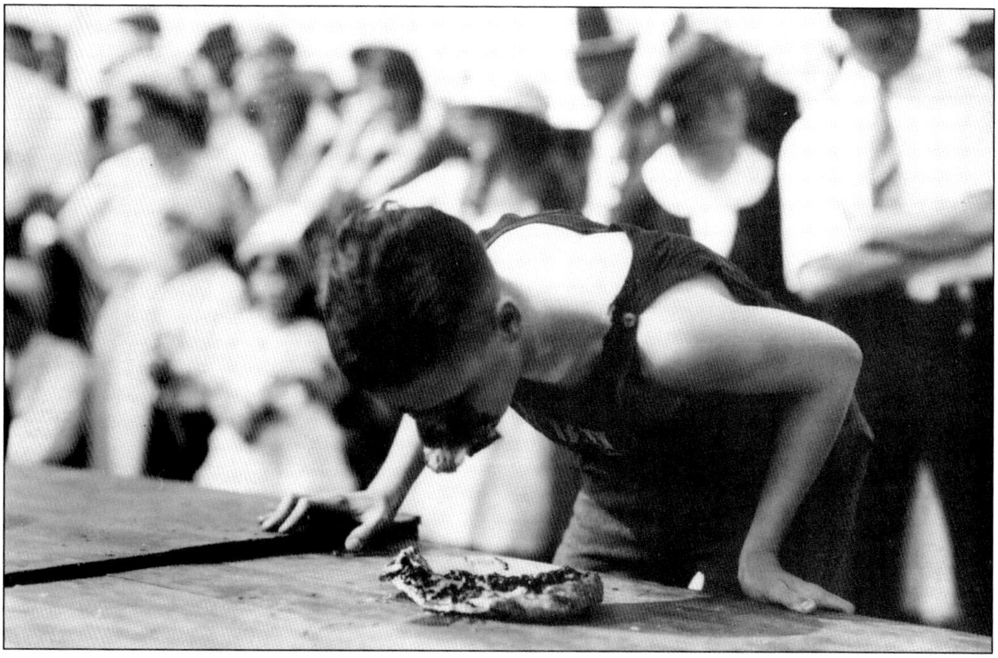

The Federal Reserve Society held the first of its annual summer outings on June 7, 1919, at Riverside Recreation Grounds, on the Connecticut River in Agawam, Massachusetts. Among the activities were a pie-eating contest (above), a fat man's race, and a tug-of-war match against representatives of the New York Fed (below), who, it seems, were victorious. Prizes included a gold pencil, a box of cigars, a Gillette safety razor, and a pair of silk stockings.

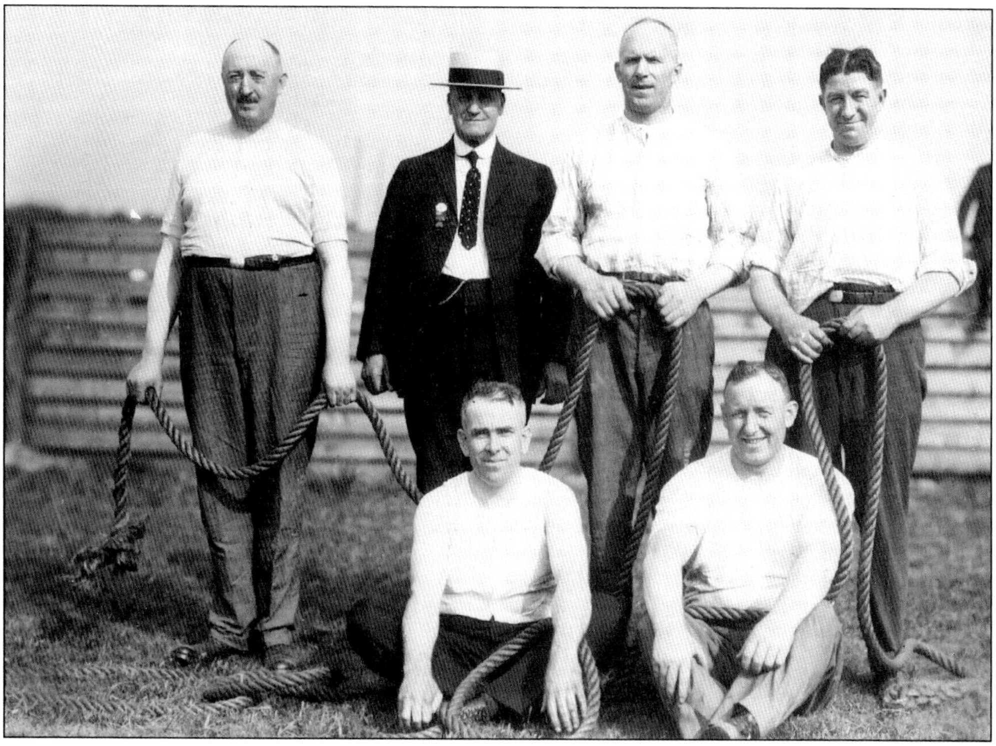

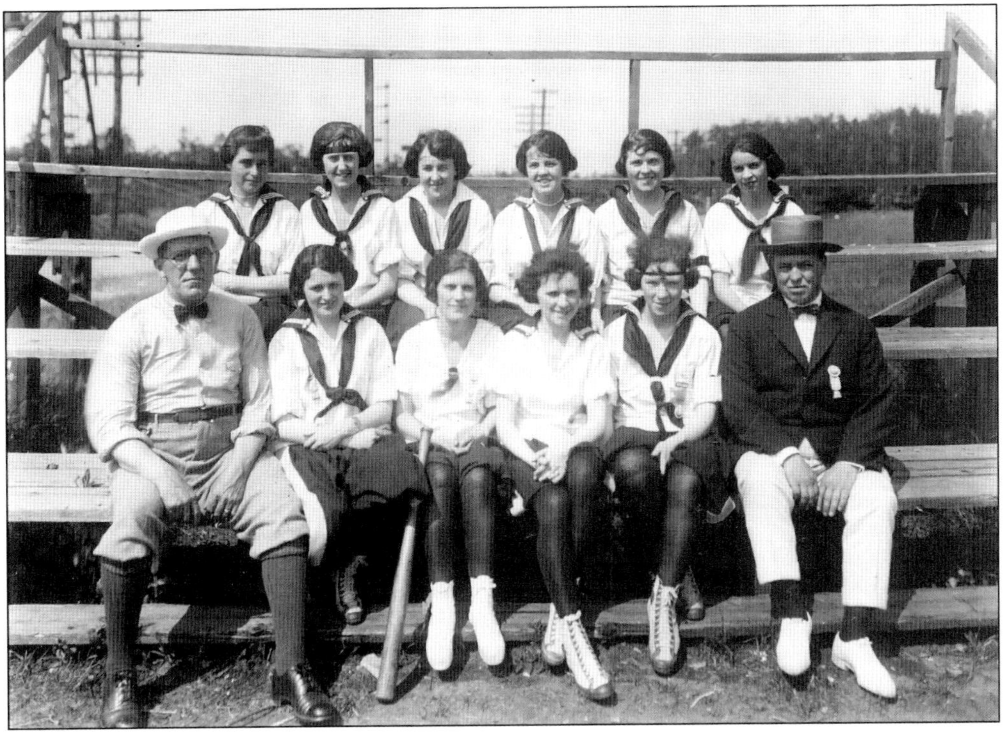

At the Federal Reserve Society's annual outing in July 1922, the ladies' basketball team (there being no ladies' baseball team at the time) made a rare appearance on the baseball diamond in a matchup against the victorious "single men's" team that appeared to have been played more for fun than competition. The *Federal Reserve Society News* reported, "Here is where the girls might teach the men something. Instead of making third by the conventional route, Evelyn [Hiltz] ran across the diamond just behind the umpire and was on third before the pitcher had time to wind up."

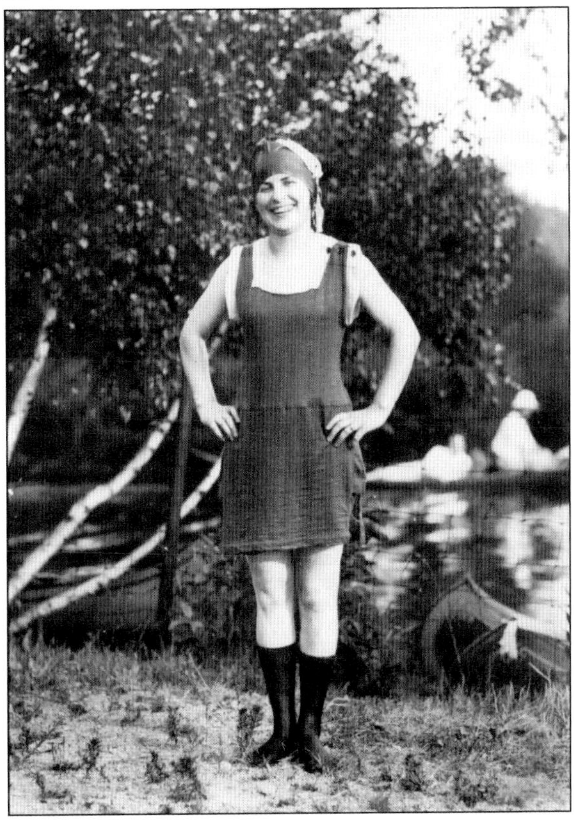

The more daring of the bank's female athletes, including Margaret Cunningham of the Money Department, entered the swimming contest. Her attire may have been shocking to her contemporaries because of its scanty nature, but it surprises a modern viewer because it was made of wool.

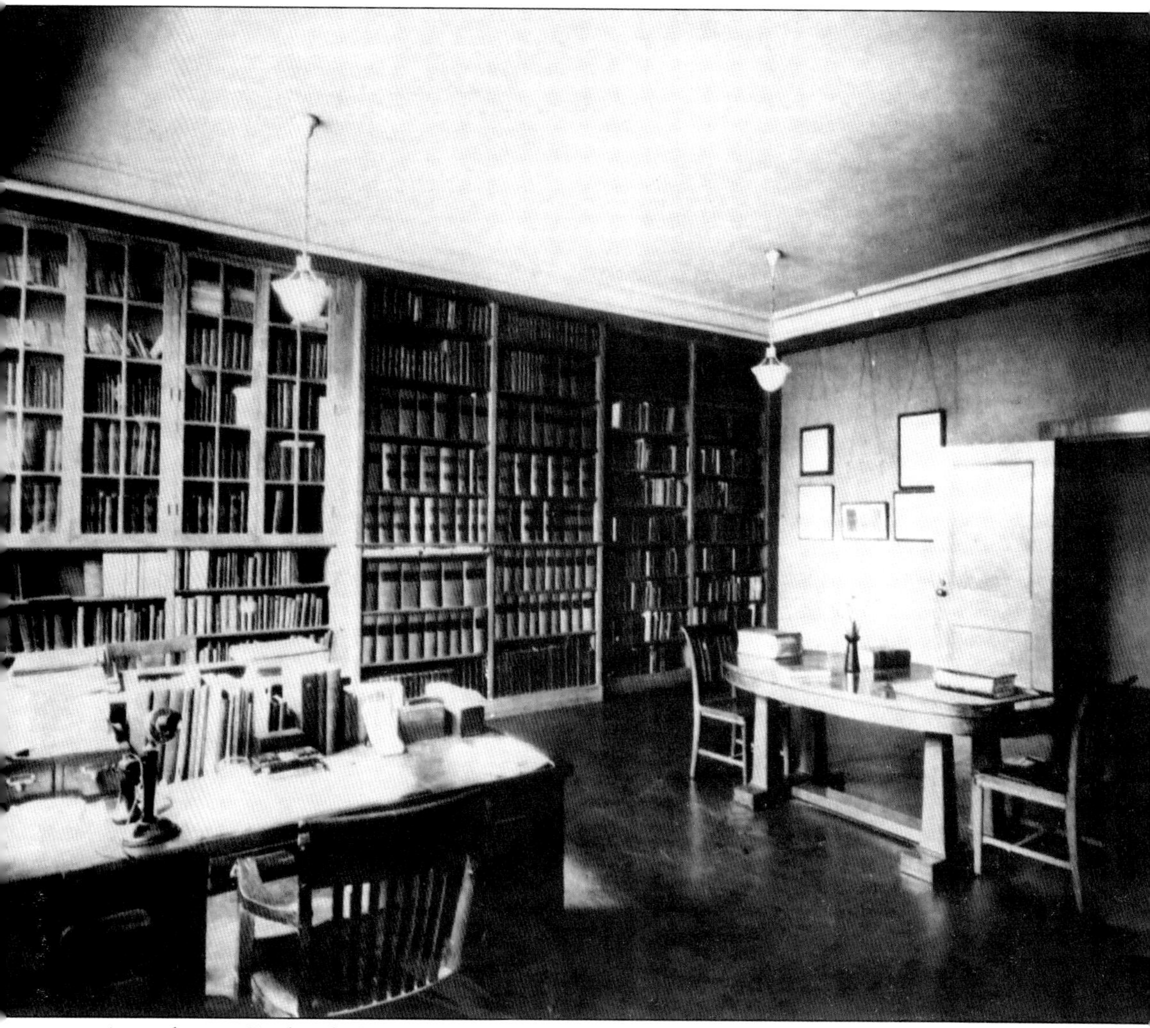

According to Frederick Curtiss, "One of the most important functions of the librarian at the Federal Reserve Bank of Boston is the reading and digesting of articles appearing in periodicals and the principle daily papers. The result is mimeographed and furnished to the officers and department heads in the form of brief paragraphs every day, usually by 11 A.M. and usually on a single sheet so that it can be read in a very few minutes." In addition to several hundred volumes specifically pertaining to matters of economics, the bank's library, seen here, also lent works of popular fiction to employees.

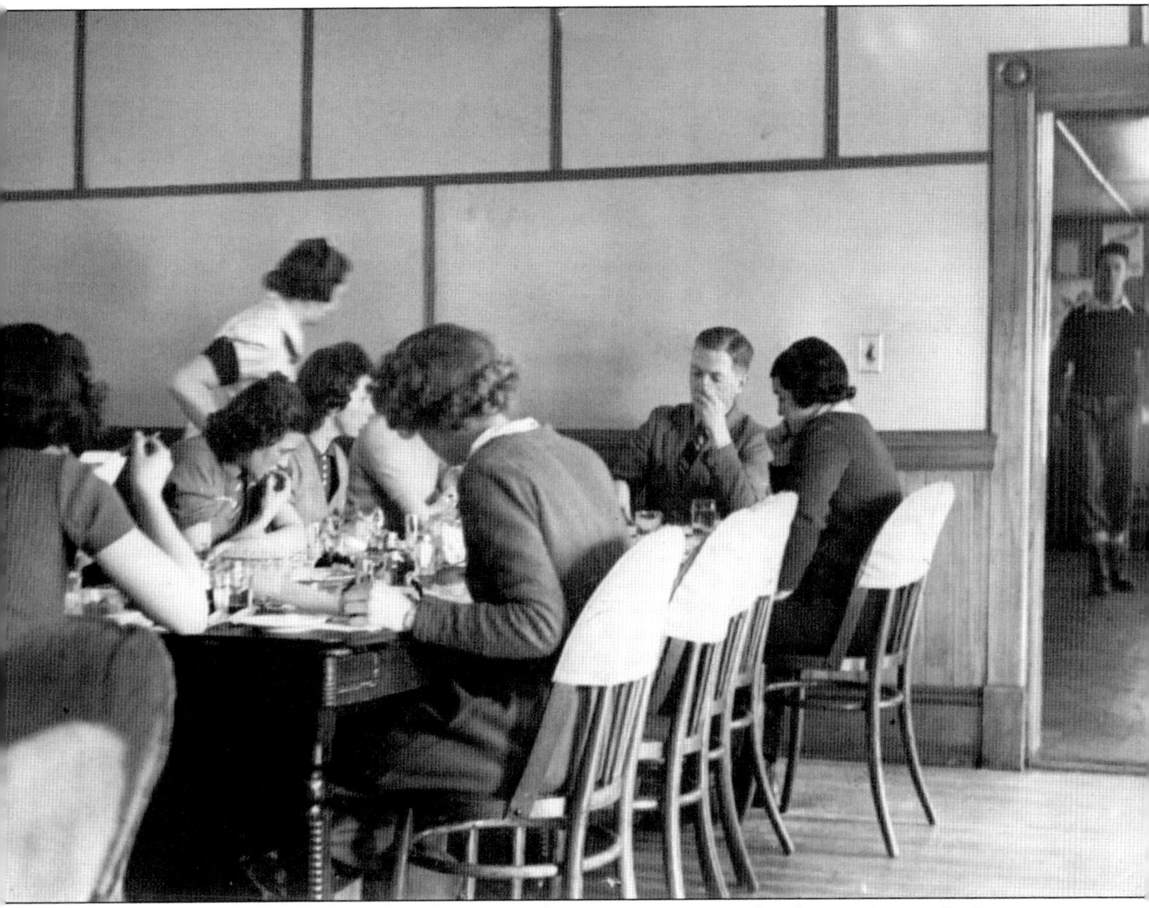

Bank employees made do without anything glamorous in terms of in-house dining facilities in their rented quarters, so the cafeteria in the new building was a major point of interest upon its opening. The *Federal Reserve Society News* enthused, "And now at noon you ride up to our cafeteria and notice that it is located convenient to the rest rooms. Miss Eastman greets you with a smile and as you push your tray along the rail you have the satisfaction of knowing that your food has been prepared in the only kitchen in New England which is electrically equipped throughout."

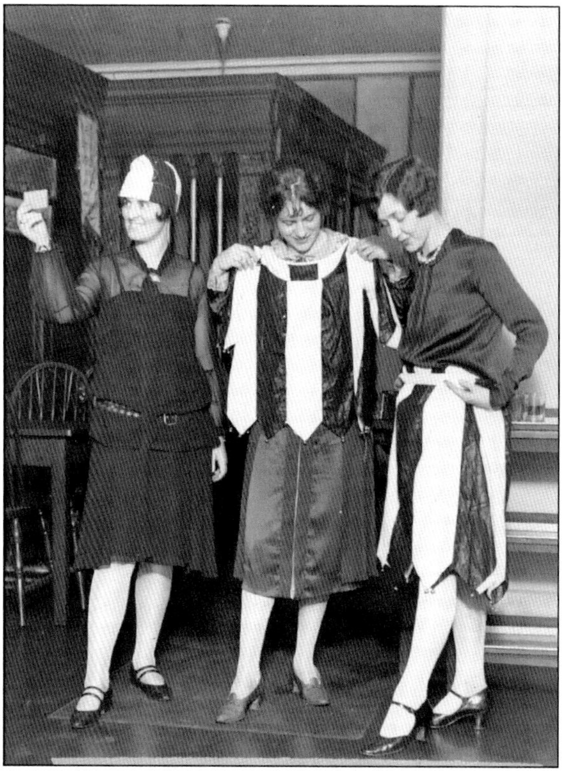

These ladies are perfect examples of that most iconic of all Roaring Twenties creatures: the Flapper. They are presumably headed off to some frolic, as the caption on the back of the photograph simply says, "Friday, Five 'o'clock."

The mock trial below was conducted by the society in April 1925 to a surprisingly large crowd of 500 friends and relatives of the employees. This being the height of Prohibition, a favorite target of jokes in the society's publications, the defendant was charged with "unlawfully facilitating the transporting of anti-Volstead liquor." These standard amateur theatrics were made somewhat remarkable by the prominent role played by William Paddock, who went on to become the president of the bank and was rumored to go months, if not years, without cracking a smile. Paddock is the gentleman in the back right wearing the judge's wig.

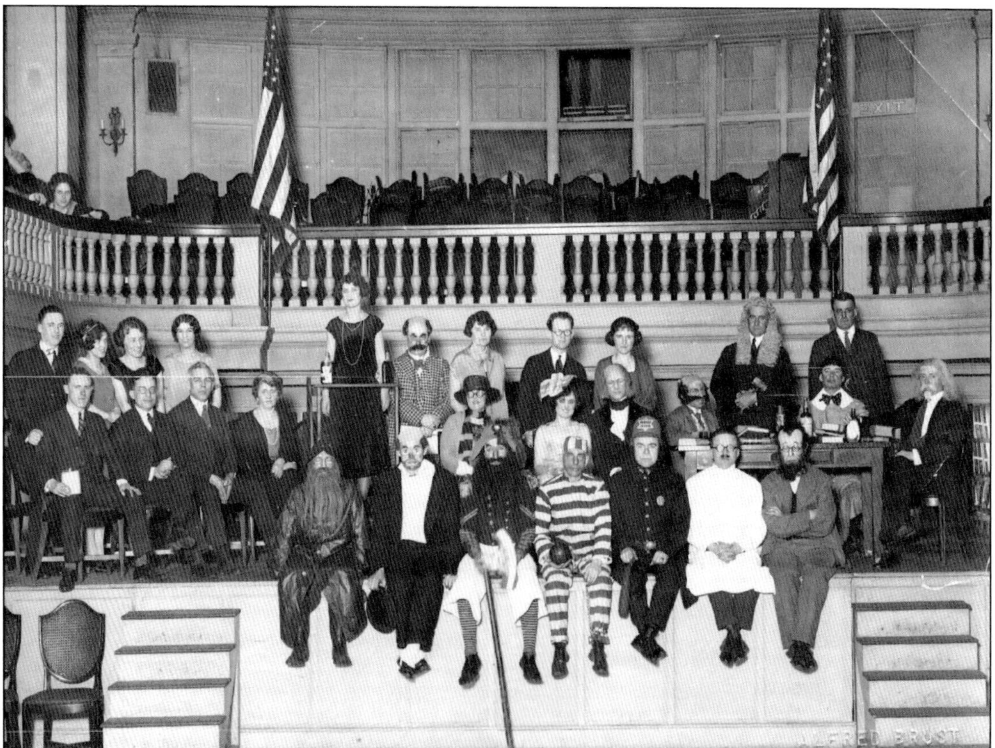

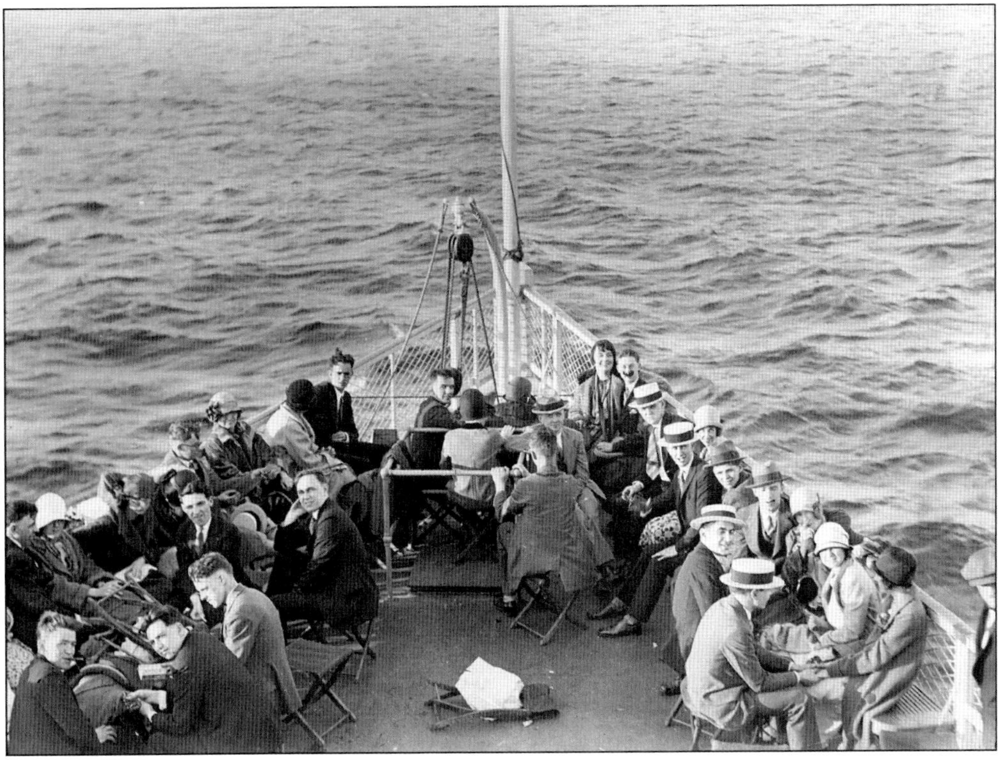

Another society event was described as a "moonlight cruise," though apparently conducted in broad daylight. The time of day was probably not as important as the amount of open sea between the boat and the Twenty-first Amendment.

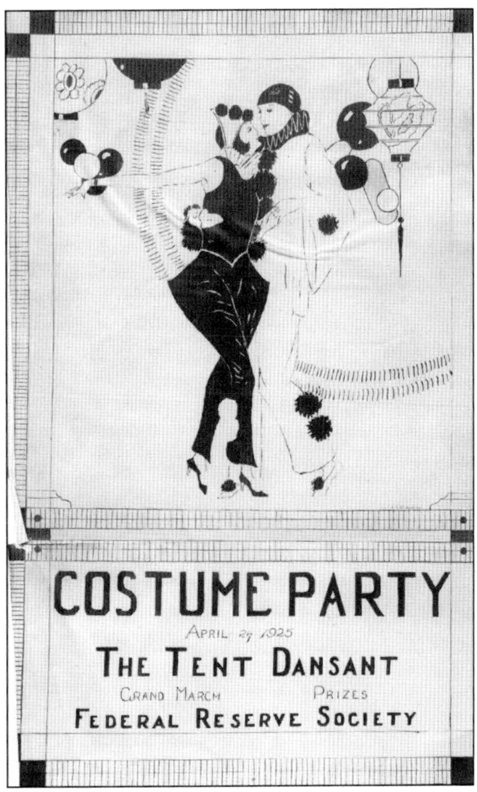

The society members capped off the same week as the previous events, in April 1925, by throwing themselves this costume party.

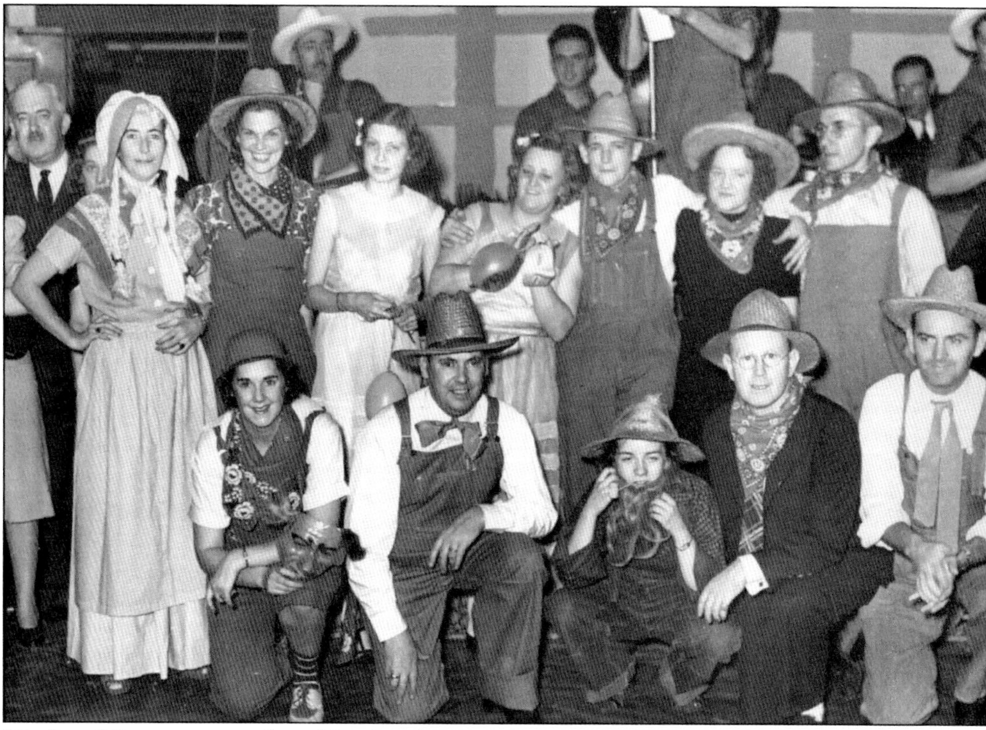

The Bond Department gathered for this photograph in September 1938. The event is not specified, but those pictured are certainly not wearing normal business attire, and "Casual Friday" was not yet a well-established practice.

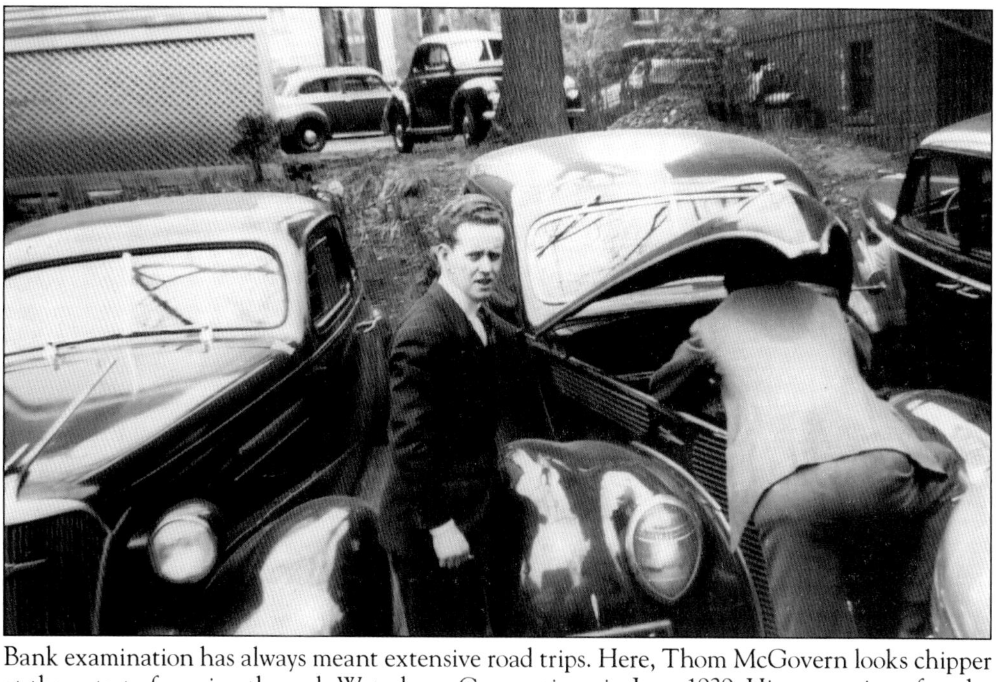

Bank examination has always meant extensive road trips. Here, Thom McGovern looks chipper at the outset of a swing through Waterbury, Connecticut, in June 1939. His expression after the return trip was not recorded.

Three

World War II

As the 20th century seemingly careened from one disaster to the next, the world again found itself embroiled in a struggle of even greater magnitude than the earlier war, which some had optimistically declared the "war to end all war." World War II would impact the Boston Fed even more than World War I, as over 150 male and female staffers served in the armed forces and four lost their lives. As in so many industries, with the departure of a large number of young men, the bank saw increased numbers of women in its workforce and an expansion in the roles they played. In fact, the bank made a concerted effort to hire what the Personnel Department called "war brides"; the wives of employees in active service were hired whenever possible.

The war was not the only event effecting changes at the Boston Fed; bank technology was also beginning to take giant leaps forward. In 1942, the Transit Department installed new machinery for check handling, nicknamed "IBMs." Even more noteworthy was the fact that the machines were kept in tune by a "girl mechanic." In addition, tabulating machines were introduced, microfilming of checks began, magnetic separators with "fingertip control" were purchased for counting pennies more quickly and efficiently, and general ledger posting became fully automated.

With peacetime came an end to austerity measures and the return of diversions that had been put aside for the duration of the war. The Federal Reserve Society was revived and boasted 100-percent employee membership. With it came regular galas, field days, and sports competition, all well attended. Bank employees were offered new benefits as well, including health insurance through Blue Cross and Blue Shield and an employee credit union.

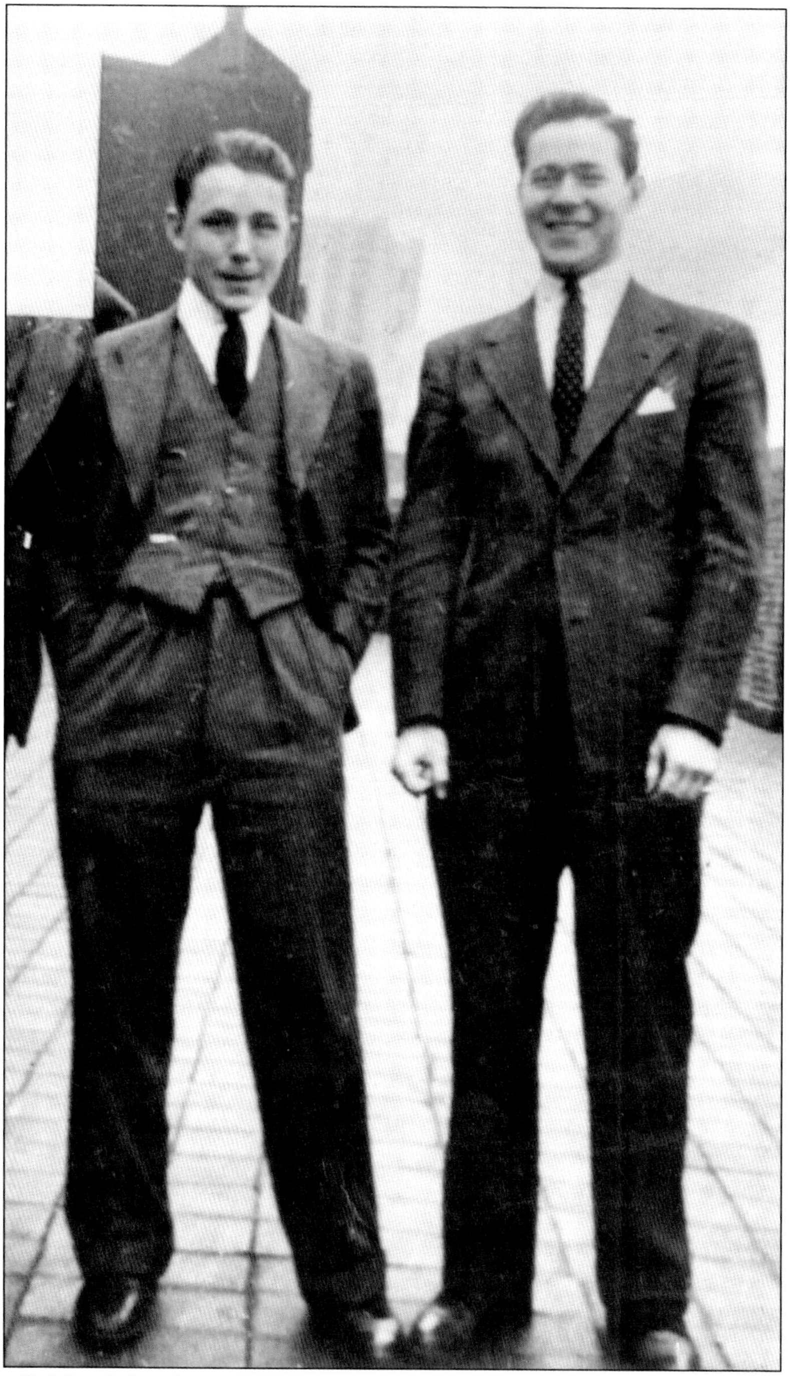

The Boston Fed family lost four members to combat casualties in World War II. In this photograph, snapped just prior to America's entry into the hostilities, Gene Belli (left) and Sumner Roberts take a break on the roof of the old building. Belli died when the USS *Meredith* was sunk in the South Pacific, and Roberts was shot down in a bombing mission during the North Africa campaign. Also lost were Leo C. Donahue, who was killed in the Battle of Leyte in the Philippines, and Charles W. Shannon Jr., whose plane crashed in a training exercise.

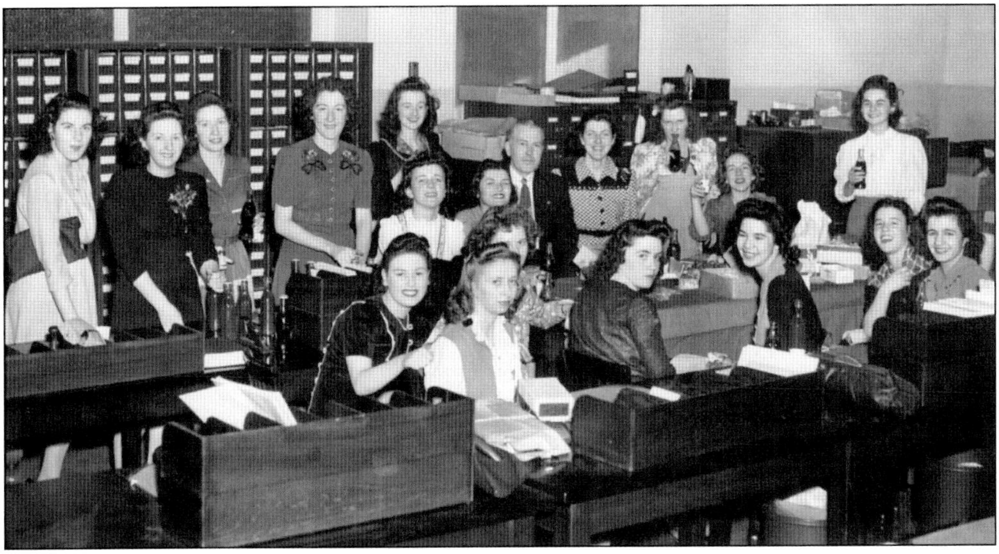

The issuing division of the Bond Department was largely a female enterprise, with the exception of supervisor Lew Pingree, who is seen here with his "girls" in 1943. More than 25 employees typed as many as 500 bonds each on a daily basis following the country's entry into World War II in 1942. In 1944, the Department of the Treasury instituted a policy whereby war bonds could be redeemed at all incorporated banks and trust companies, to the great relief of the bank's Fiscal Agency Department. By the war's end, over 86 million Americans—half the total population—had purchased at least one bond.

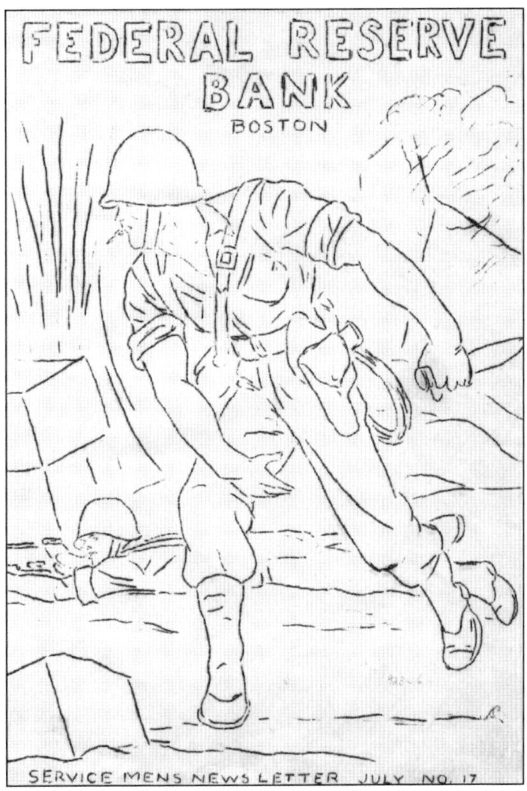

The Federal Reserve Society ended the publication of its newsletter in 1922. A smaller sheet called *Chatter* made irregular appearances through 1927, but nothing else along those lines was attempted again until 1942, when the *Servicemen's Newsletter* made its debut. As the name suggests, it was instituted to create a news exchange between the bank and its employees serving in the armed forces in World War II. With the stringent wartime restraints that were in place, the *Servicemen's Newsletter* was a bare-bones affair of mimeographed sheets, with anywhere from 10 to 30 single-sided pages. This was the first newsletter published under the auspices of the bank itself, as opposed to the Federal Reserve Society.

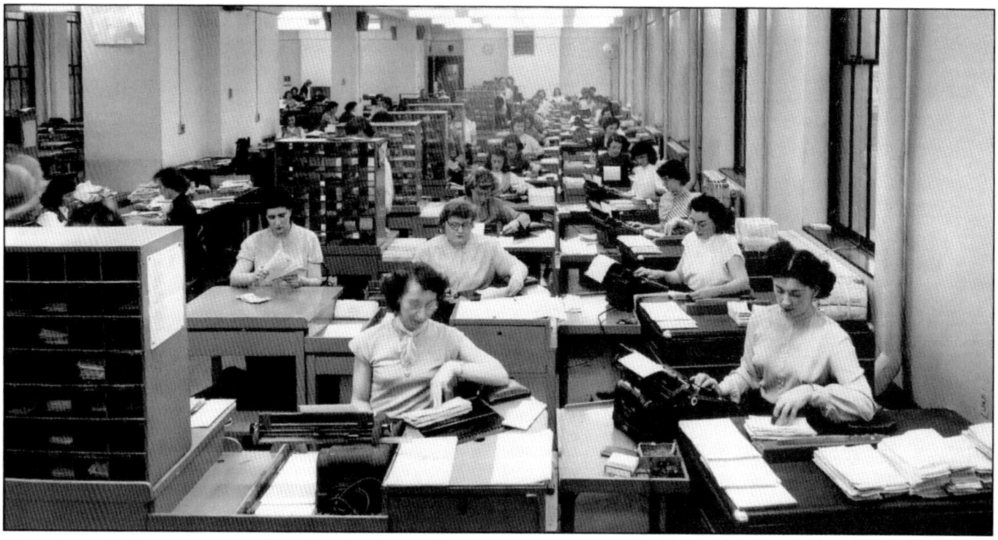

The Transit Department handled all checks and cash items deposited through the Boston Fed, as well as all items returned unpaid. In 1941, the department had converted to a system of punch cards and electric tabulating equipment, but, in 1944, it reverted back to an adding machine method with "modern desks and new adding machines."

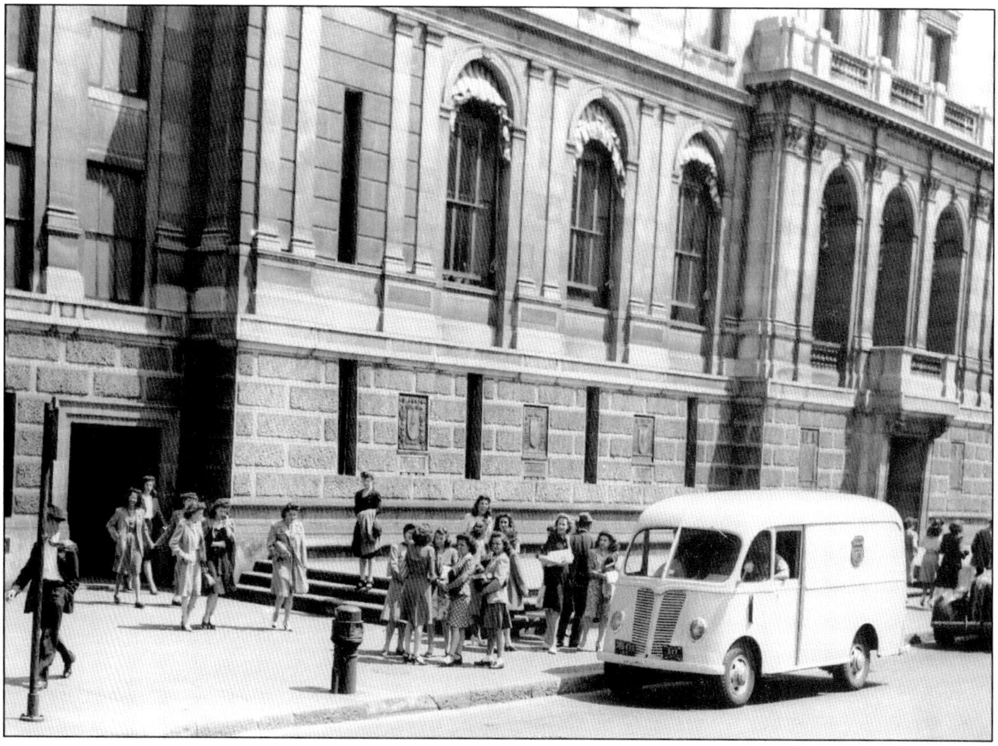

This photograph shows the day's end at Pearl Street in 1945. The predominantly female workers reflect the toll that military enlistments had taken among the younger male employees. It should be noted, however, that the bank's women were also well represented in the armed forces, with over 35 enlisted in the Women's Army Corps (WAC) and the Women Accepted for Volunteer Emergency Service (WAVES).

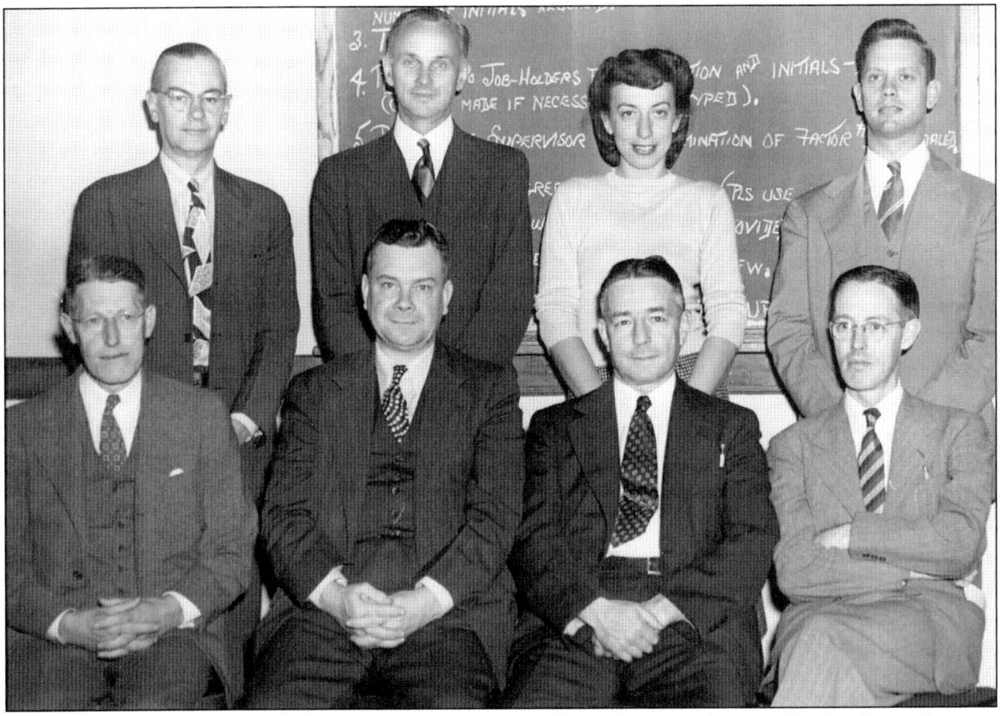

Everyone enjoys job evaluation time. The staff pictured here have not been tasked with conducting a standard evaluation, however, but instead with—according to the announcement by bank president Laurence Whittemore—"a technique for determining the relative worth of jobs," which cannot have taken much of the pressure off.

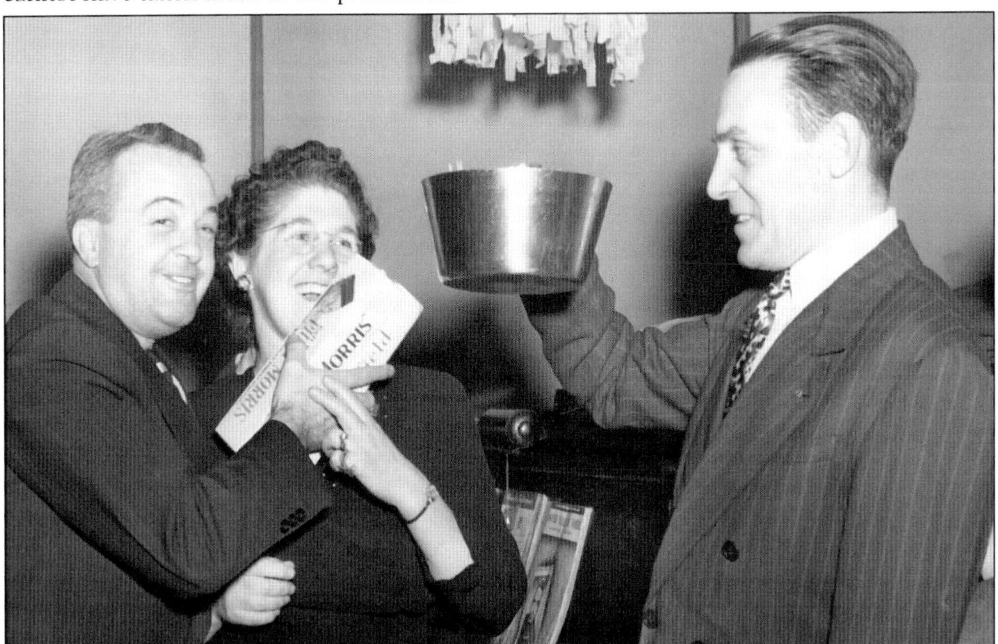

For Halloween 1946, a door prize of a carton of cigarettes was apparently appreciated by most employees.

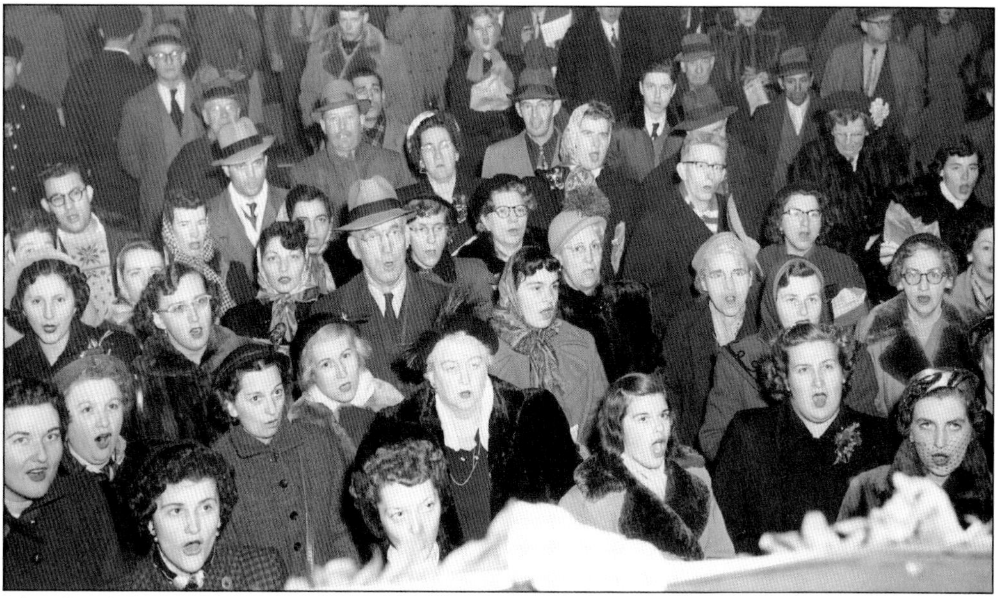

The glee club was a popular extracurricular activity for employees, who are seen here serenading holiday shoppers at North Station in 1947. The group also made several appearances on the fledgling WBZ-TV Channel 4's early broadcasts, at least one of which was recorded on a vinyl LP.

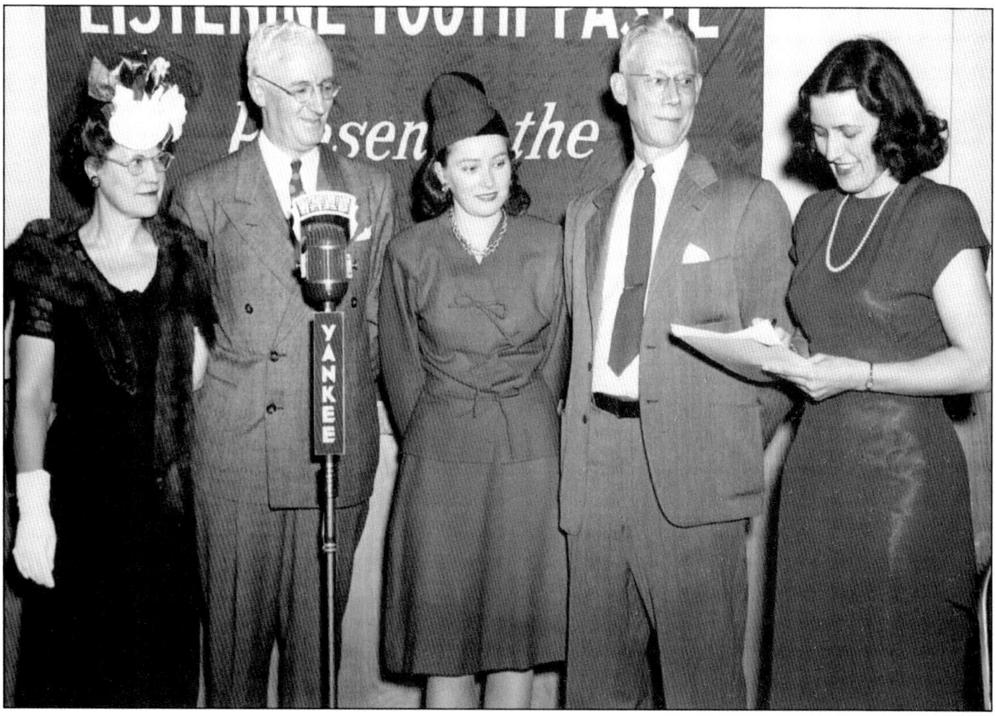

The Boston Fed fielded a team for the WNAC radio program *A Quiz of Two Cities* in March 1947. From left to right, Evelyn Hiltz, Eddie Stevens, Betty Marshall, and Elliot Boardman competed against an unidentified team from Providence. The contest ended in an unsatisfactory tie when Boardman failed to identify the longest among a rod, a furlong, and a half mile for the win. Judging from Hiltz's hat, she may have been under the impression the show would be televised.

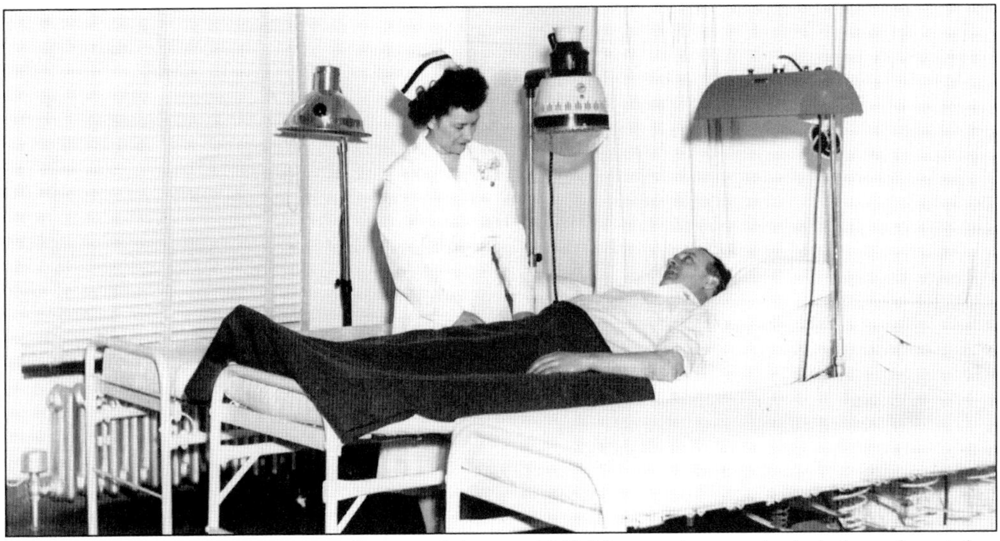

The Medical Department received a remodeling in 1949. New equipment included an ultraviolet-ray lamp, which was handy for those not getting enough radiation naturally, and an infrared lamp "used in case of colds, muscular pains, arthritis, etc." Here, nurse Barbara Cole administers to Bill Doyle of the cafeteria staff in what was likely a staged photograph.

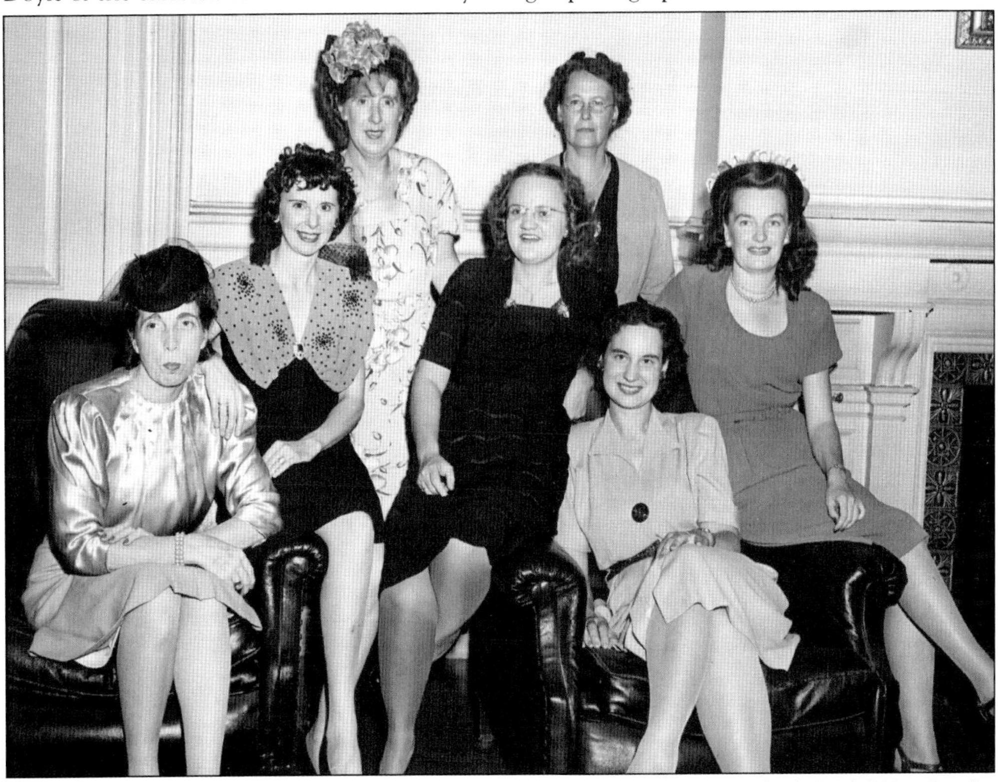

The war's end saw the reorganization of the Federal Reserve Society, which had fallen by the wayside in light of more pressing concerns. The annual dinner was the premier social event of the new calendar, and the initial revival of the event drew a crowd of 1,100 Fed employees and their guests to the Hotel Statler on January 7, 1946.

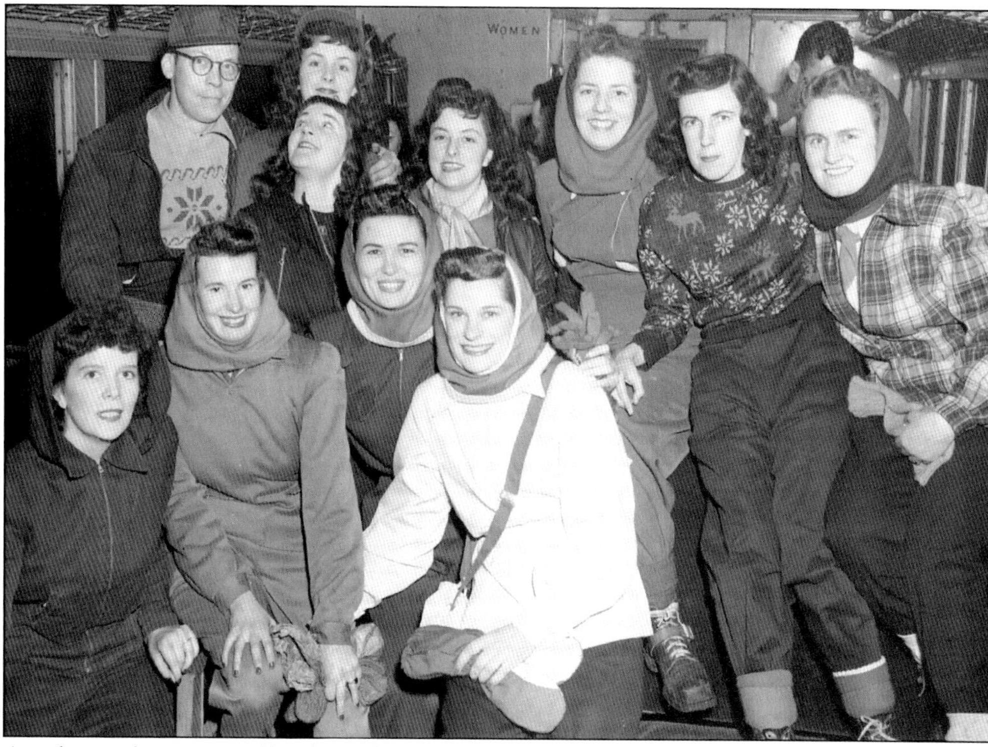

Another tradition revived by the Federal Reserve Society following the war was the annual Snow Train, a trip to North Conway, New Hampshire, in the White Mountains, for a weekend of skiing, ice-skating, and dancing. The train excursions continued until the 1960s, when the completion of Interstate 93 made the White Mountains much more accessible by private transportation.

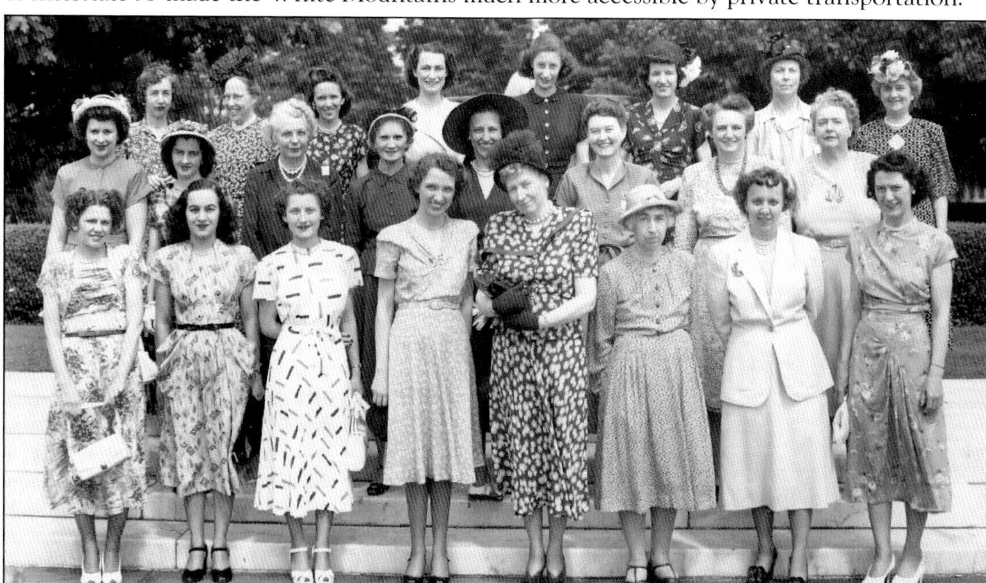

The librarians of the Federal Reserve System pose for this group photograph while attending the Special Libraries Association conference in Washington, DC, in June 1948. Boston's longtime head librarian Marion Eaton is third from the right in the first row.

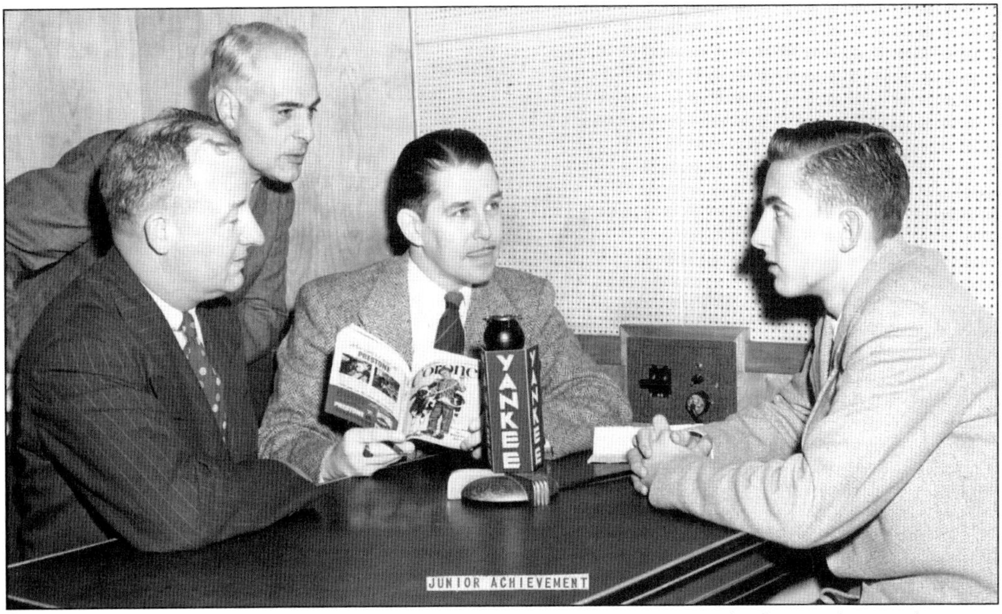

The Boston Fed participated in the Junior Achievement program, which was designed to give young people hands-on experience in a variety of business settings. Here, Jack Schlaikjer (far left), the vice president and general counsel of the Boston Fed, participates in an interview for WNAC radio in 1948.

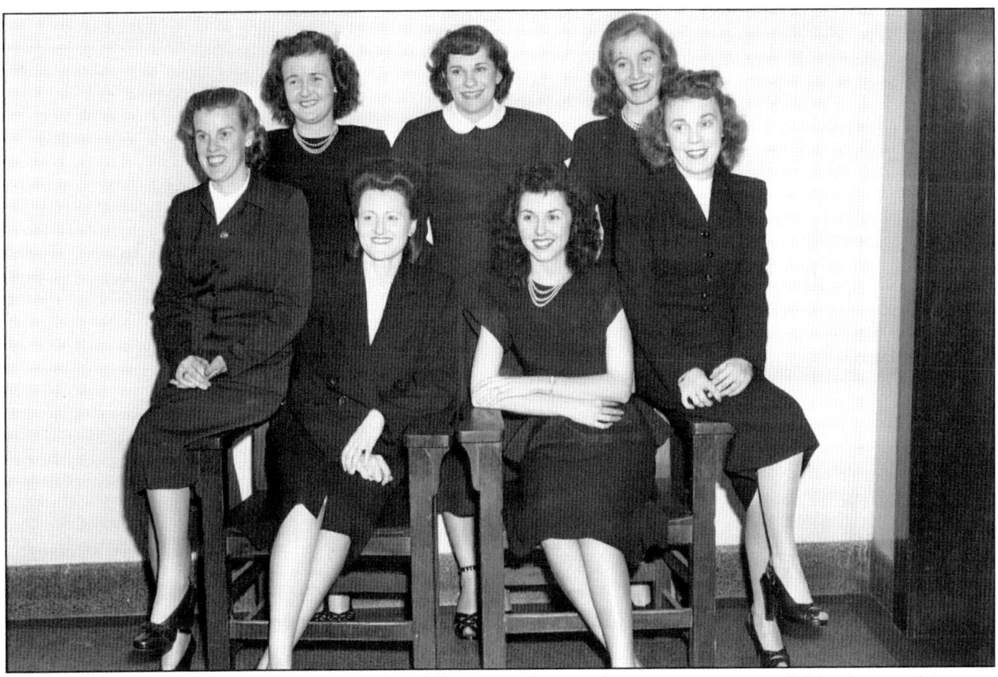

A charm show was held in 1948 and, oddly enough, no charming men could be located in any bank department. Fortunately, the ladies made up the difference. According to the *Newsletter*, "These girls were selected as models as they possess plenty of charm, personality, and to coin a word—ZING!" The evening was mostly devoted to a fashion show featuring styles from local department stores.

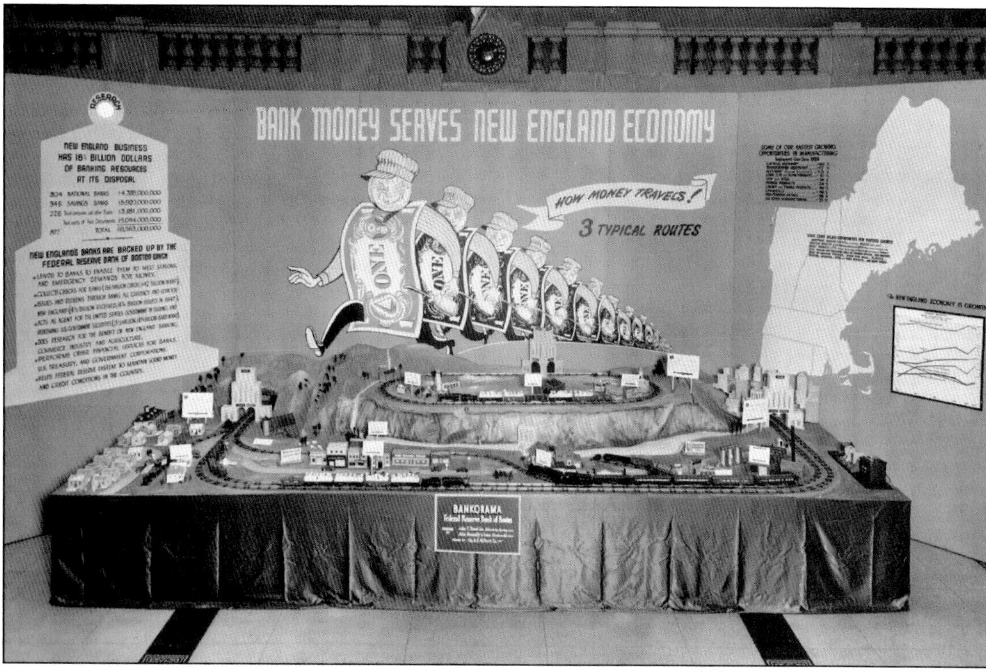

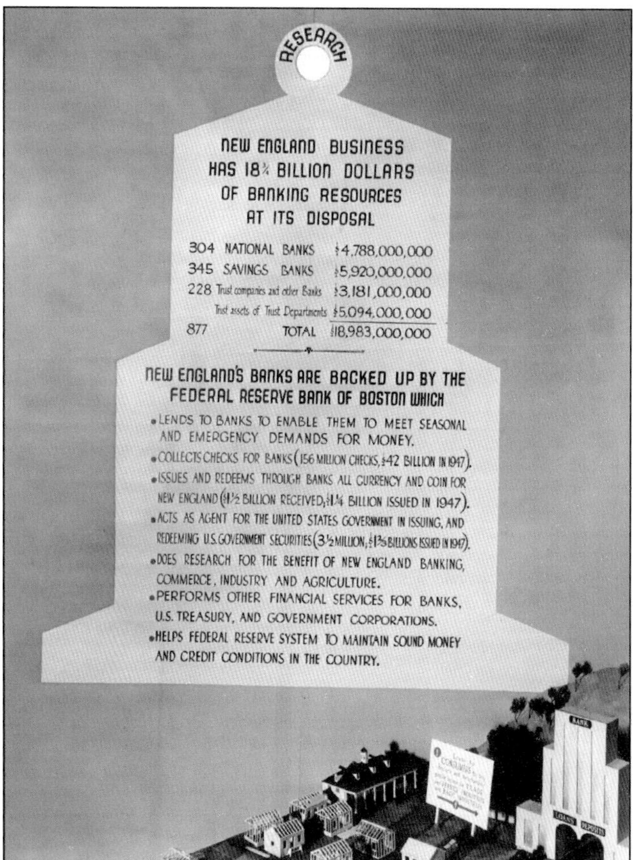

The Bankorama, an educational display installed in the Members' Court in 1947, explained the bank's duties and functions through the unexpected medium of model trains. "Three scale-model trains carrying miniature bags of money, emerge from the loan portals of the banks, and after travelling through their respective important circuits, re-enter the deposit portals." The Bankorama may or may not have been the most efficient illustration of "how bank money serves the New England economy," but it was a popular exhibit at the bank and the several banking conferences it traveled to.

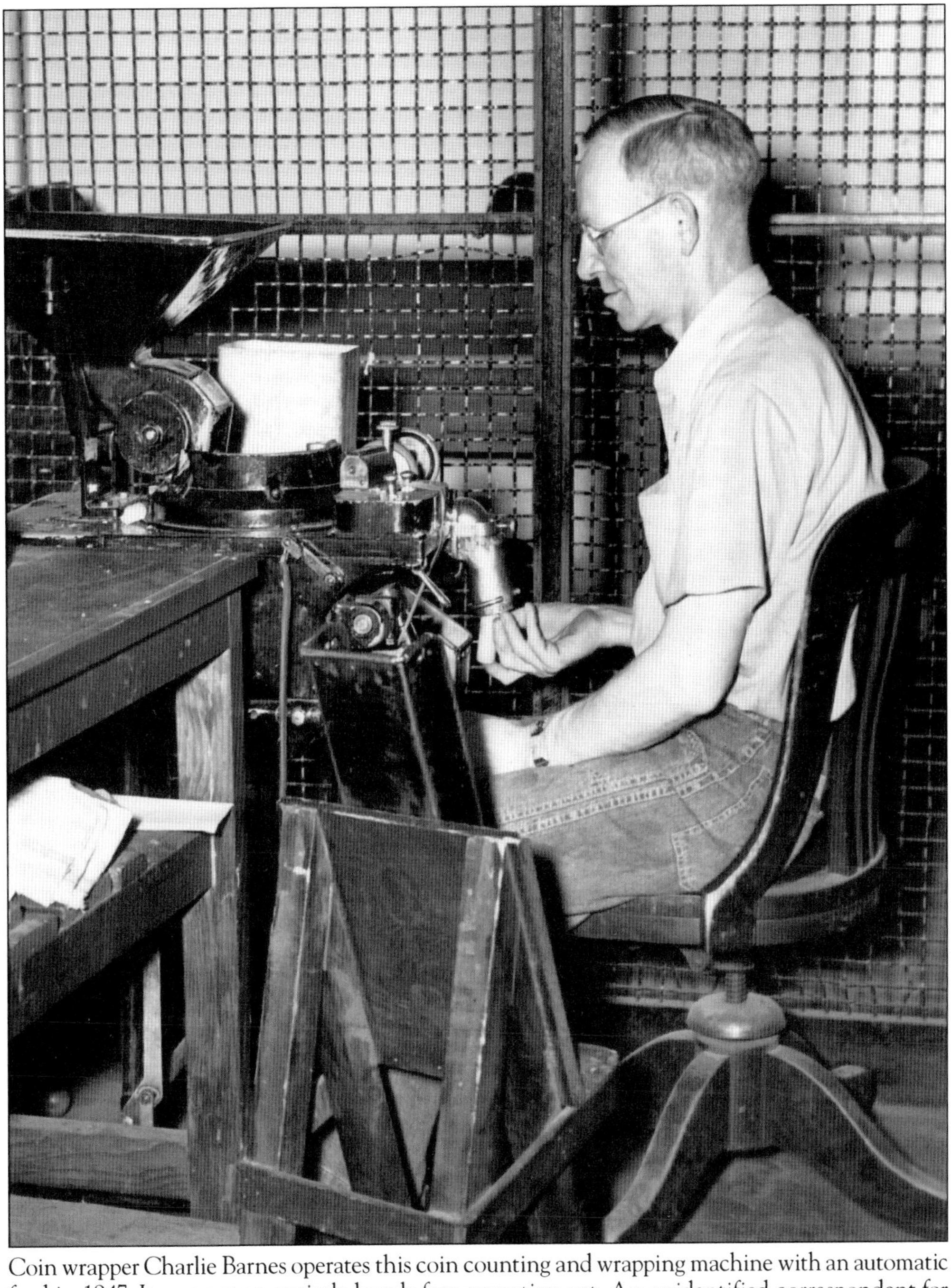

Coin wrapper Charlie Barnes operates this coin counting and wrapping machine with an automatic feed in 1947. It was not an entirely hands-free operation yet. An unidentified correspondent for the *Newsletter* reported that the Money Department had 120 employees equipped "adequately to cope with our heavy volume of business. The New England recreational district as well as Horse and Dog Tracks and the various holidays all add up to the volume of work processed by our Dept." The correspondent added, "With our Saturdays off, however, we all should be in better physical condition to maintain the high standards of efficiency set by the Money Dept." Having Saturdays off was an innovation in 1947.

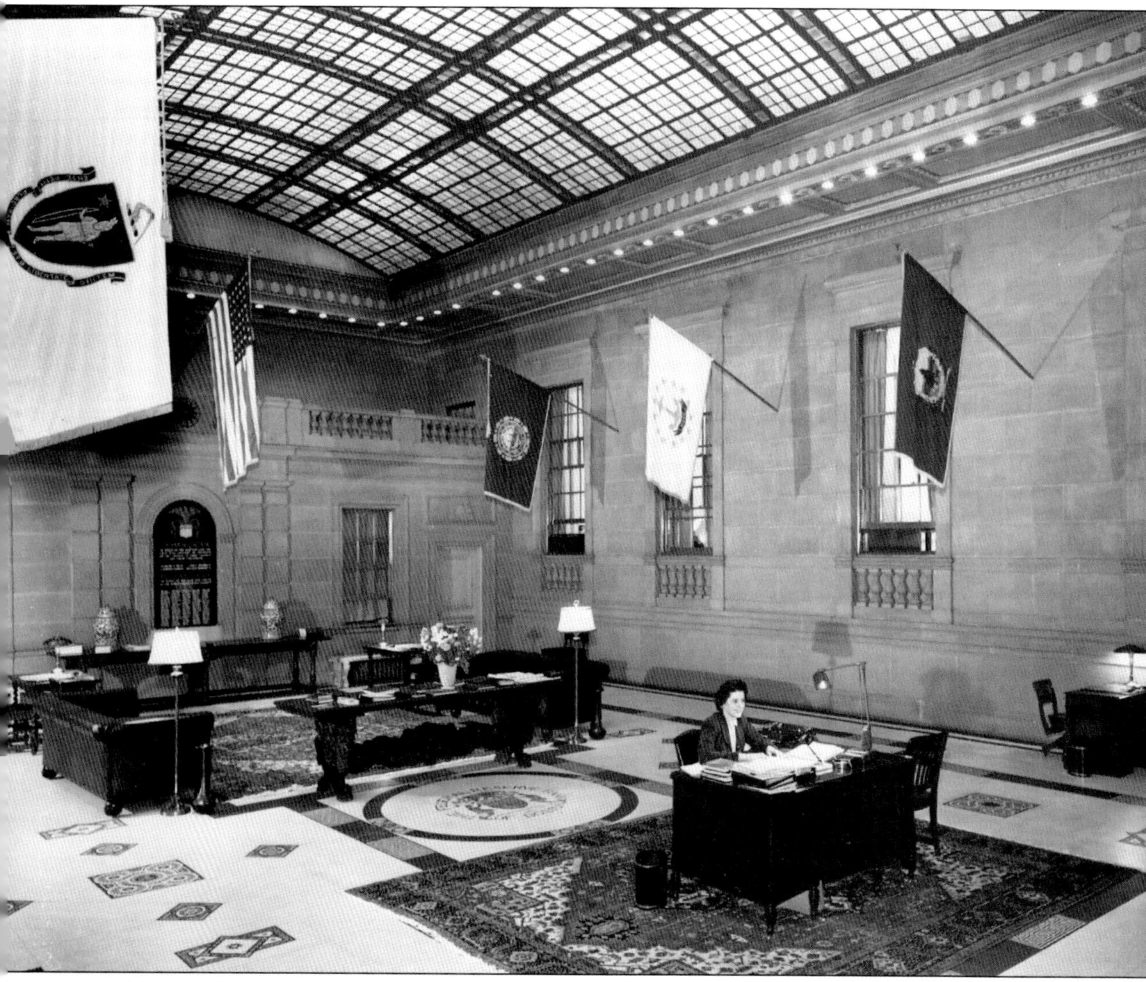

Although designed to be a meeting place for officials of member banks, the Members' Court was not widely used as such, perhaps because of its somewhat cold formality. Indeed, over the years, it acquired the nicknames of "the icebox" and "the morgue," which did not add to its popularity. In 1946, "in keeping with a program for the establishment of a more understanding and closer relationship between [the Fed] and its members," Mary Hardyman was appointed as a general receptionist, through whose "cordiality and service" it was hoped members would feel the bank's interest in their problems.

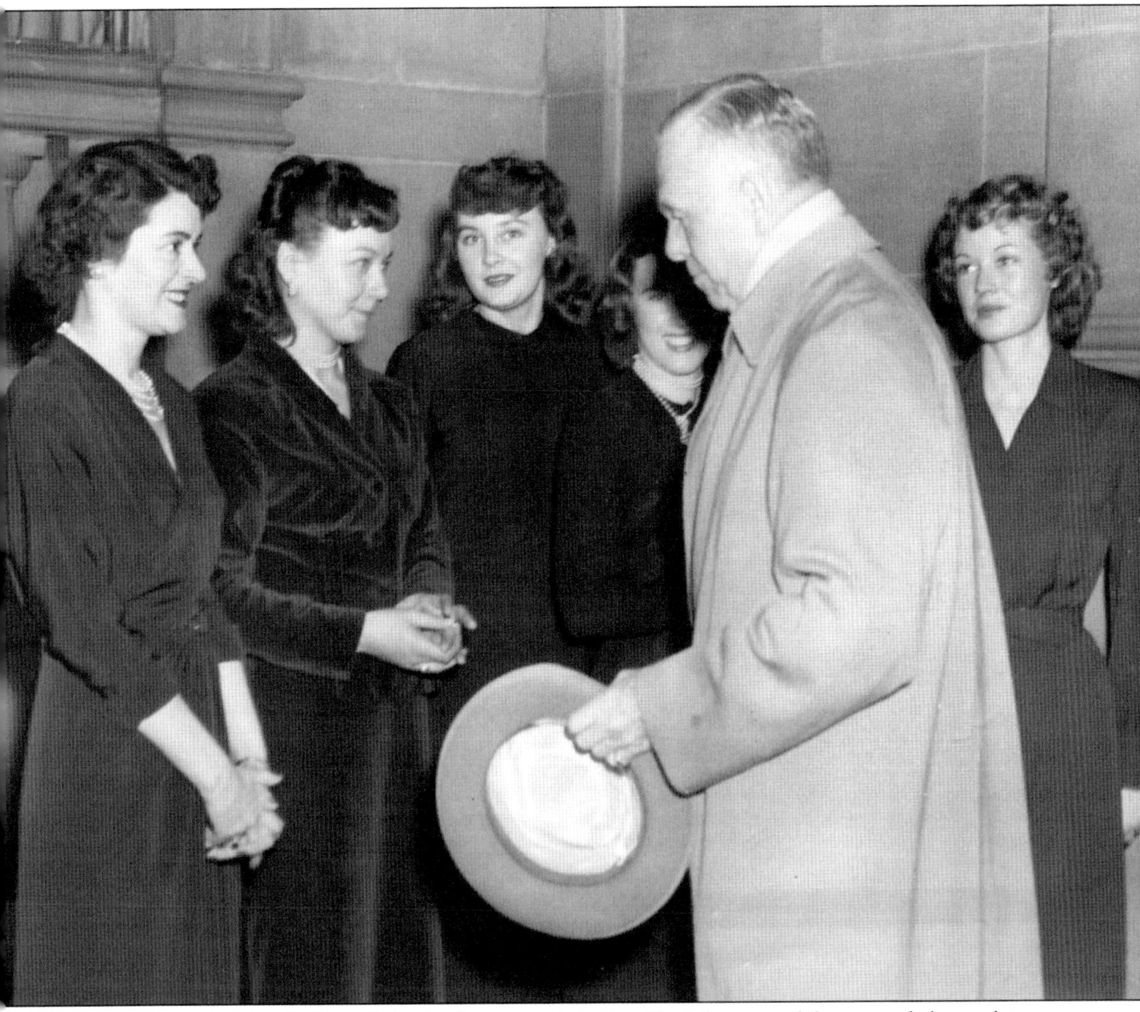

Gen. George C. Marshall (right), the former chief of staff of the armed forces and the architect of the Marshall Plan, paid a visit to the bank in January 1950 in his role as national chairman of the American Red Cross. The Boston Fed was one of many businesses and organizations that loaned employees to the Red Cross for the duration of its annual drive.

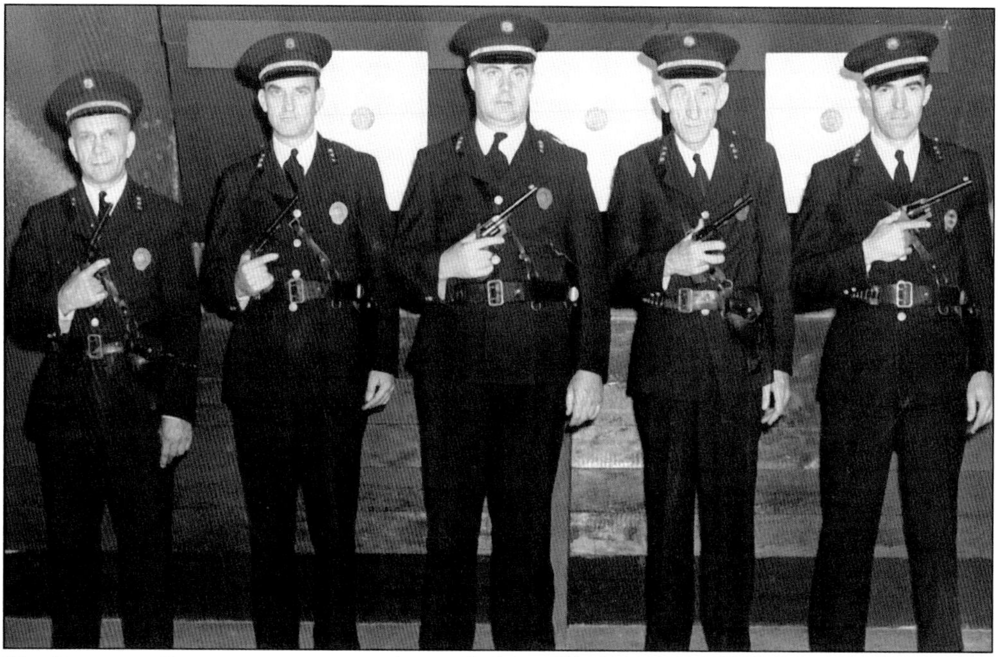

The Protective Department, as it was then called, handily beat the Wakefield Police Department in a revolver team match held on November 4, 1946. Herb "Tobey" Tobin (second from right) was one of the original guards who joined the bank in 1919. In the *Newsletter*, he was said to be "still a crack shot."

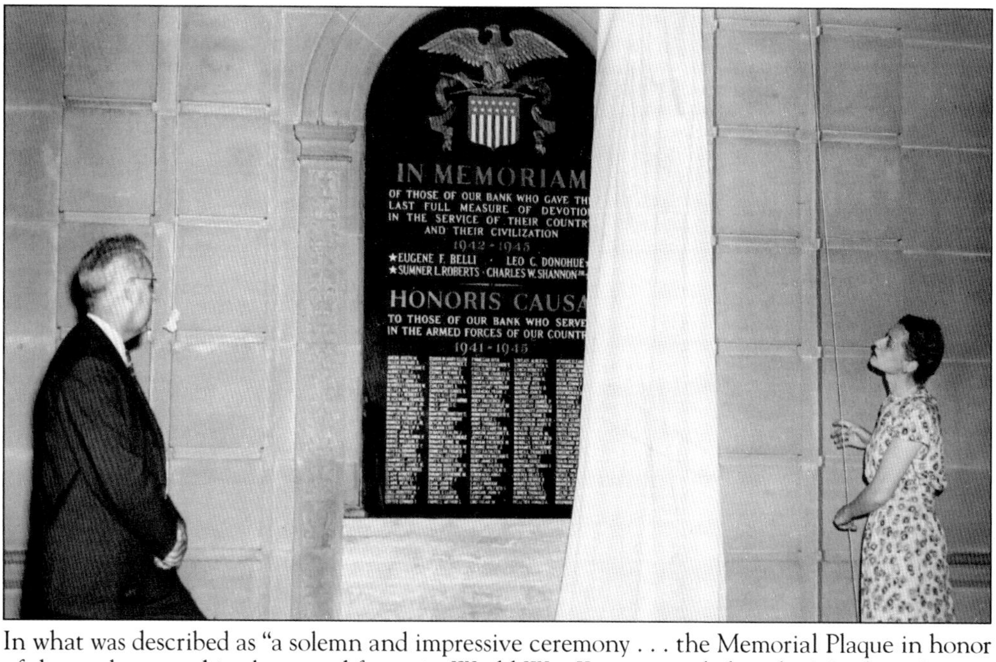

In what was described as "a solemn and impressive ceremony . . . the Memorial Plaque in honor of those who served in the armed forces in World War II was unveiled in the Members Court." Bank president Laurence Whittemore was assisted at the event by Isabelle Dabrowski of the Bond Department, who had served with the Navy in the South Pacific. Over the course of the war, more than 150 Fed employees served in the military.

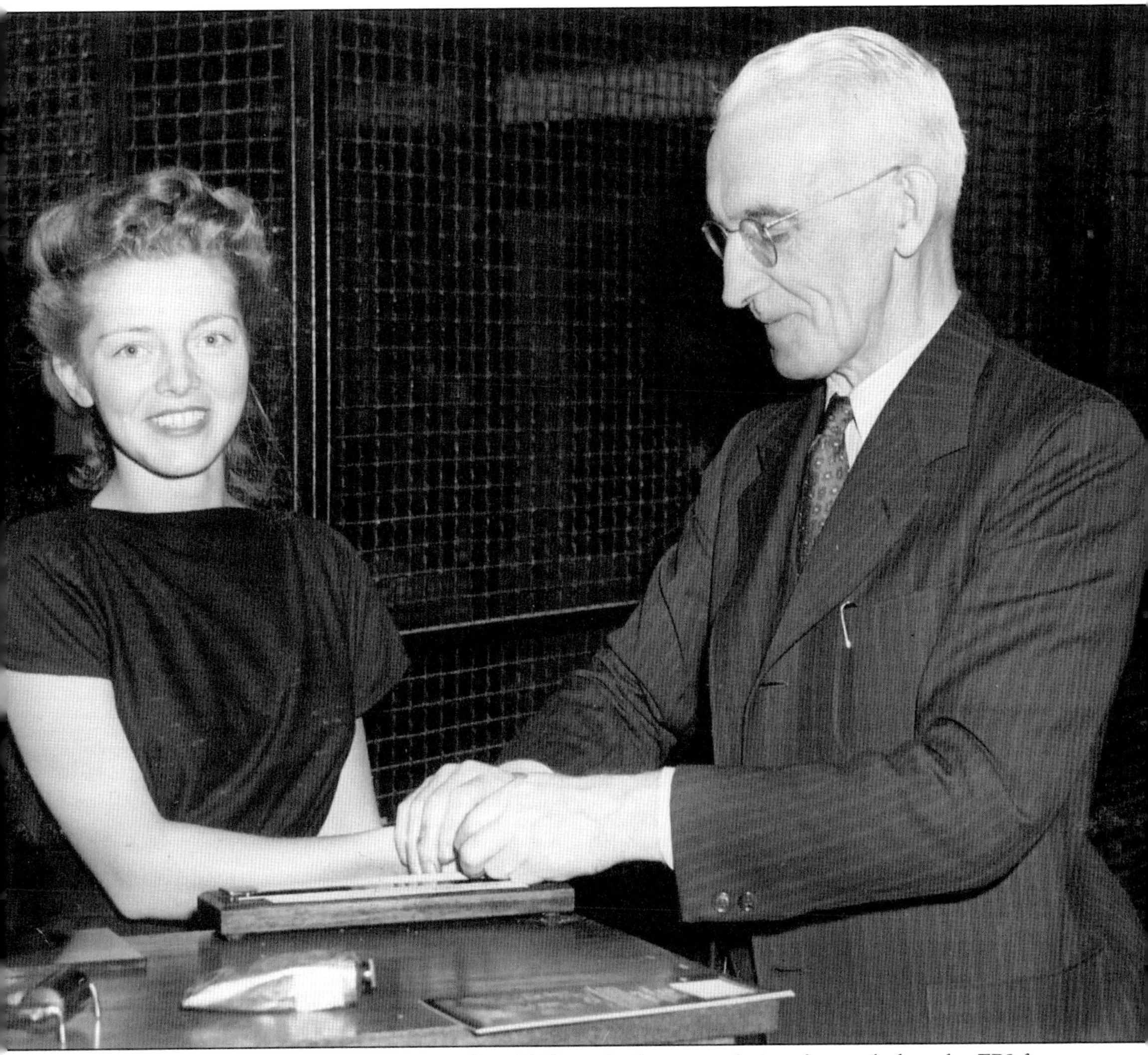

Bank-wide fingerprinting was instituted in 1947, with the prints being forwarded to the FBI for, as employees were told, their protection in cases of accident, death, or amnesia. The case of a woman found murdered in the nearby Blue Hills Reservation around that time and promptly identified thanks to proactive fingerprinting policies was pointed out in support of the practice, although that was possibly not as comforting a notion as it was meant to be.

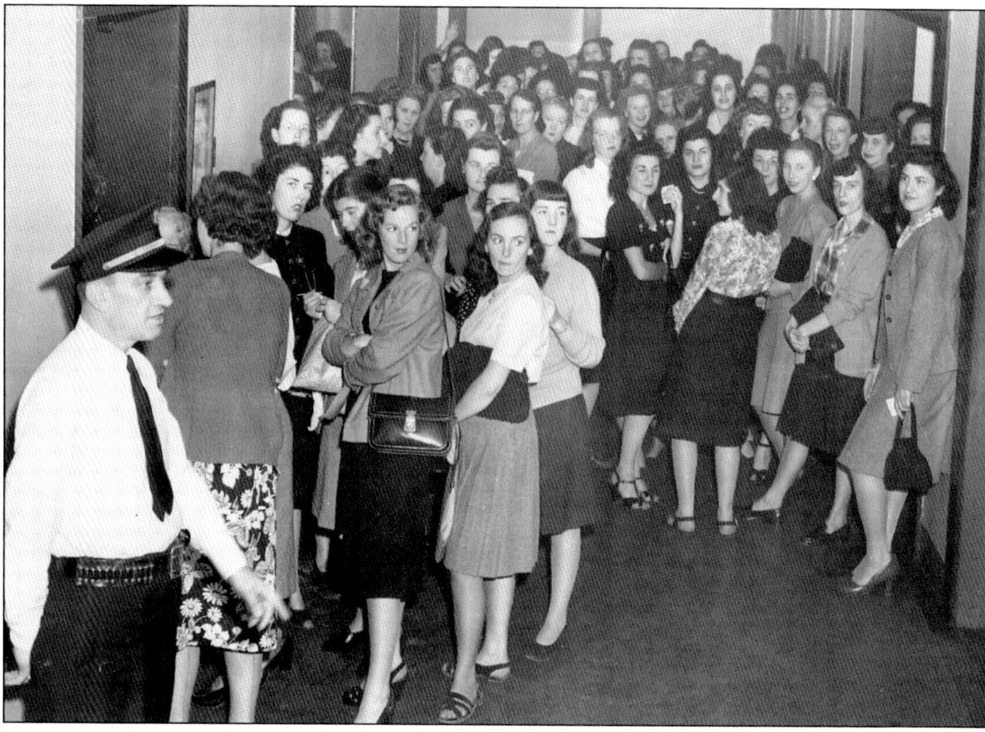

Indicative of the erudition and culture typical of Boston Fed employees, crowds eagerly await the opportunity to hear Marion R. Rudkin deliver what the *Newsletter* called "another of her entertaining and fascinating book reviews" in September 1947. Rudkin reviewed *The Money Man* (appropriately enough), *Kings Blood Royal*, and *Inside the U.S.A.* The "audience regretfully dispersed, with the thought in the minds of many, that these reviews were too brief."

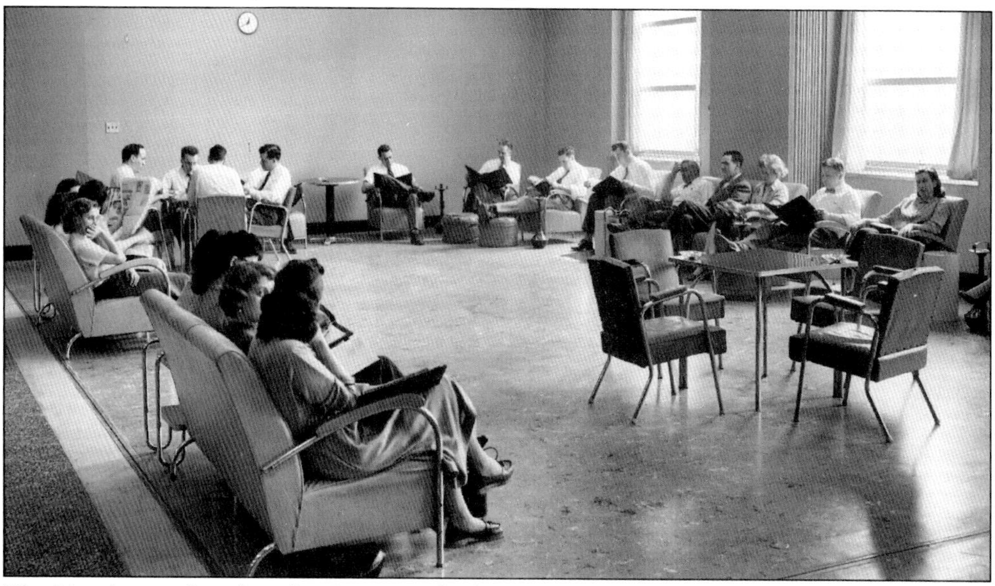

The *Newsletter* referred to this "attractively decorated and completely equipped new lounging room" as "another indication of the Bank's constant effort to make conditions as pleasant as possible for the members of the Bank staff."

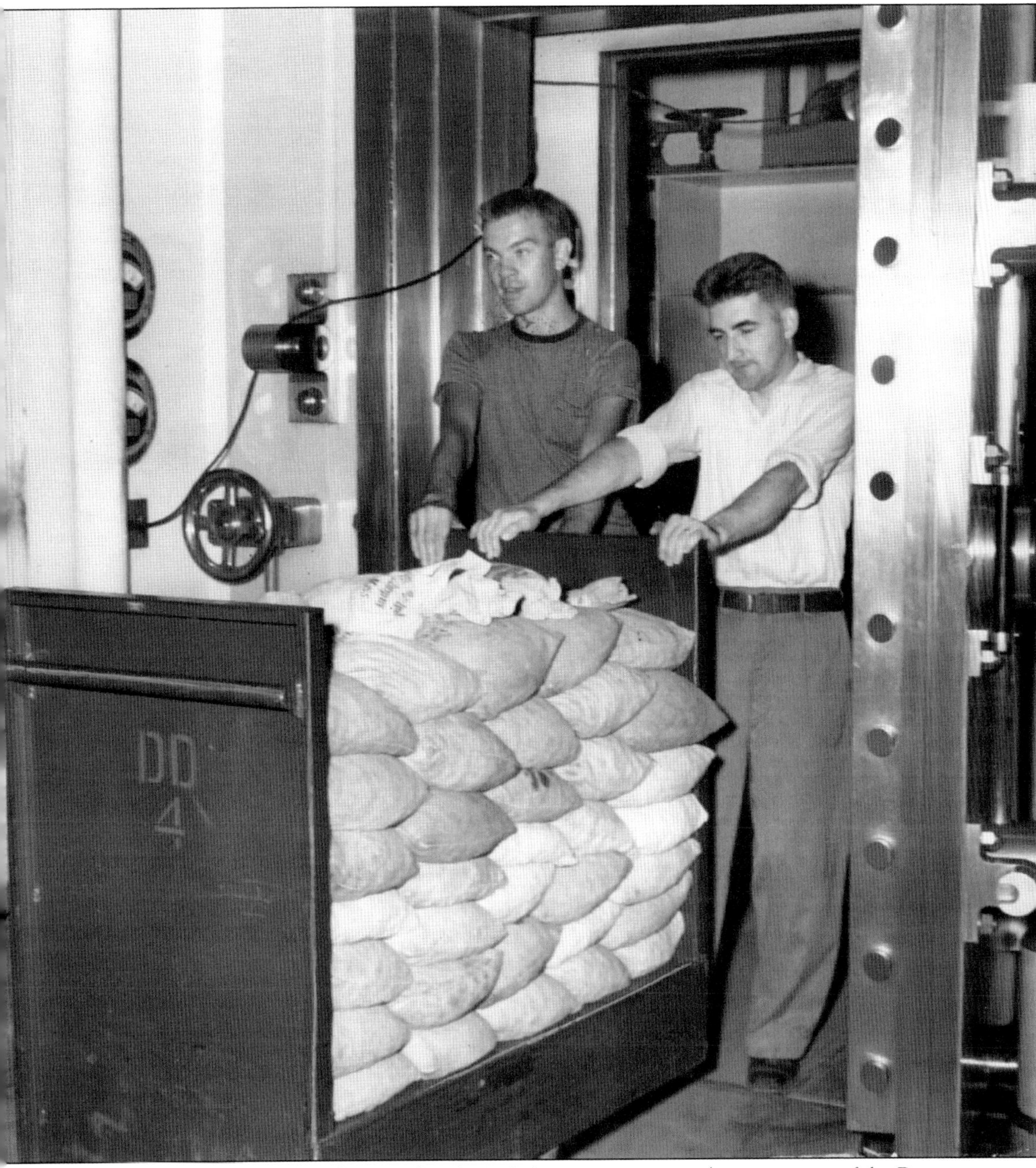

The *Boston Evening Traveler* of September 6, 1949, features a story on the one aspect of the Boson Fed that the public found endlessly fascinating: moving money. Here, Carl Meyer and Homer Richards of the Cash Department wheel 1.5 tons of nickels, valued at $14,000, out of the Pearl Street vault for distribution. This photograph was originally captioned "Money is their business."

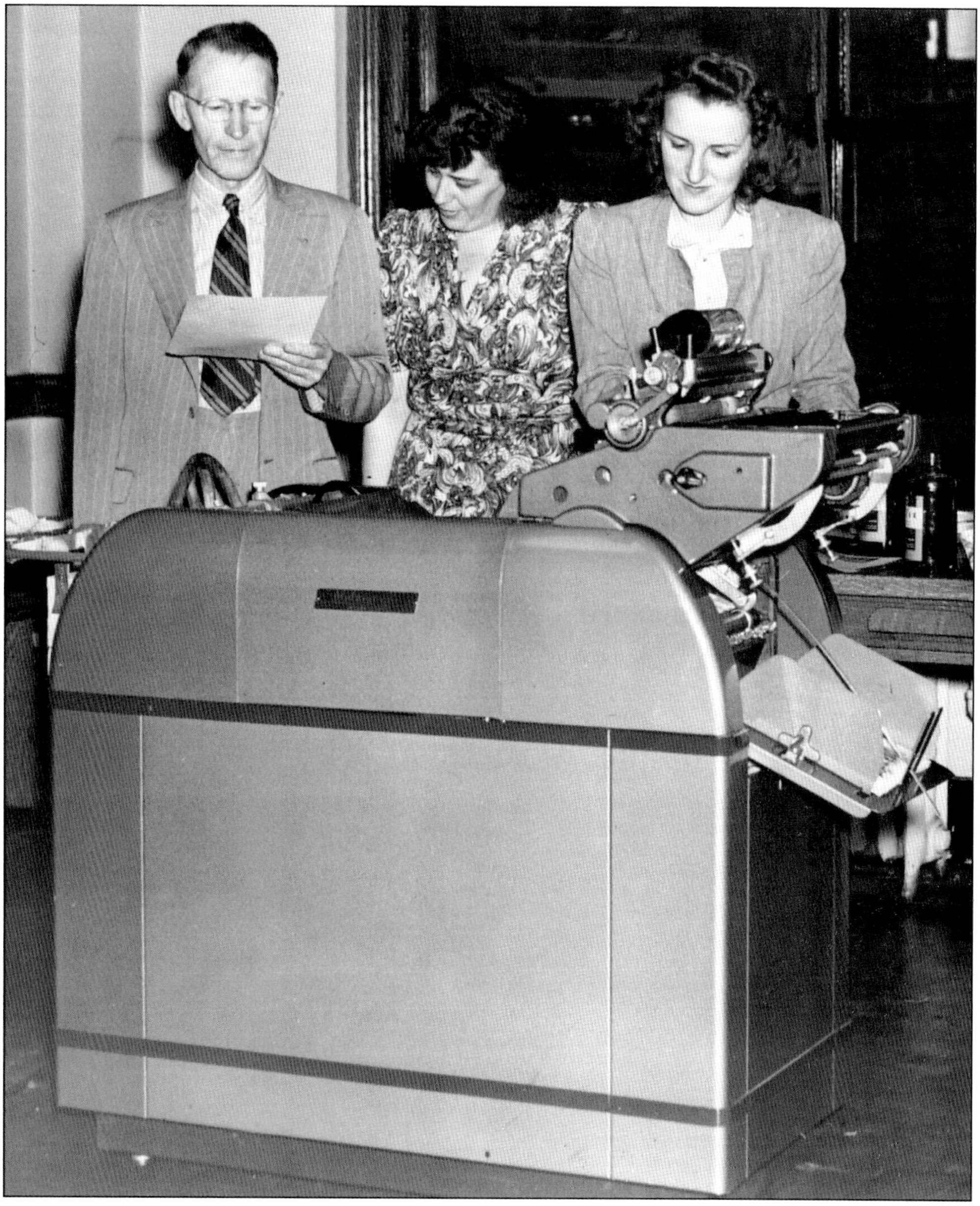

The first issue of the *Servicemen's Newsletter* to be printed on the new Multilith machine, seen here, got approval from volunteer staffers Frank White (left), Nancy Bresnahan (center), and Helen Shab in 1946. The Multilith was a relatively low-cost offset printing device "forged," as its advertisements touted, "in the white hot heat of urgency" of the late war, a time during which the heroics of mimeograph machines and their kin have generally remained unsung.

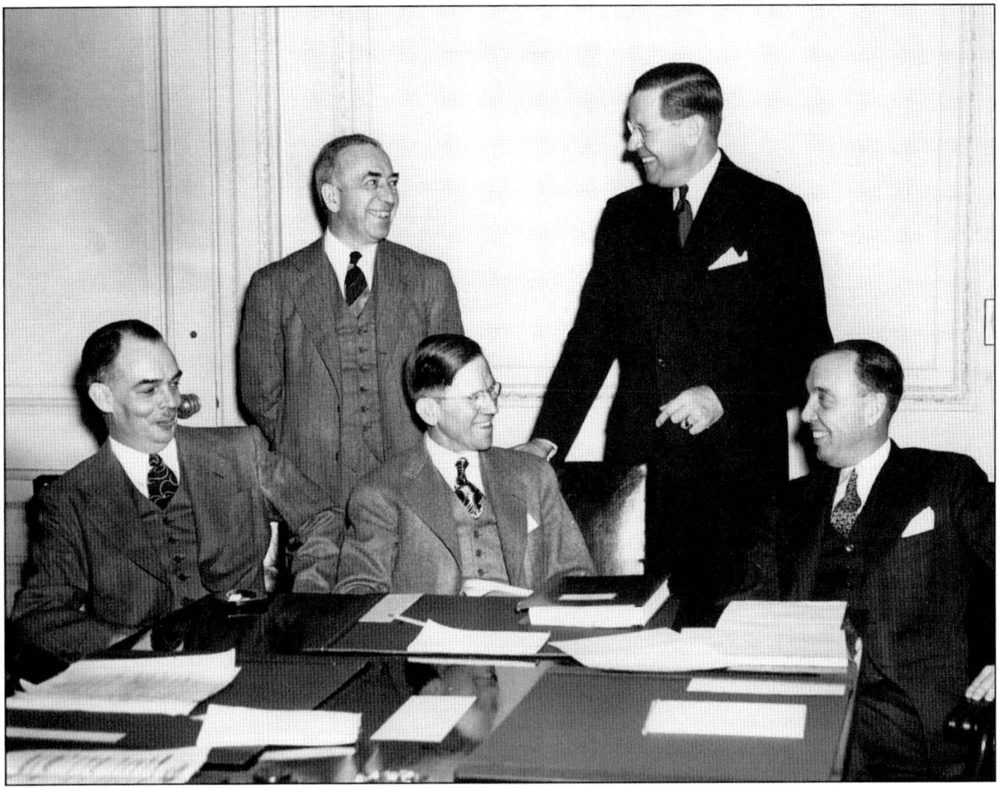

A system-wide conference of auditors was held in Washington, DC, in 1947. The agenda was set at a meeting of the standing committee at the Boston Fed in March of that year. The fact that the gentlemen above seem to be having more fun than is generally had at such affairs was attributed to David Strong (standing, left) and his propensity for telling fish stories.

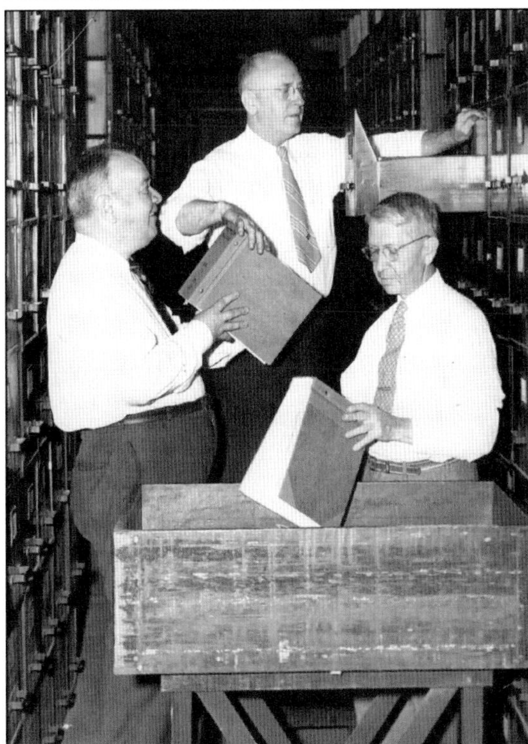

"Located in the Pearl Street end of the Bank basement is a department about which many of our personnel know very little." An introduction like this, to the old records, or "uncurrent files," department, is likely to cause palpitations in a person seeking to uncover the history of the Boston Fed. Phrases such as "corner of the basement" and reports of attempts to find "shelf room or some other space for all materials" are every bit as disheartening in reality as they sound; many of the bank's earliest records have been lost.

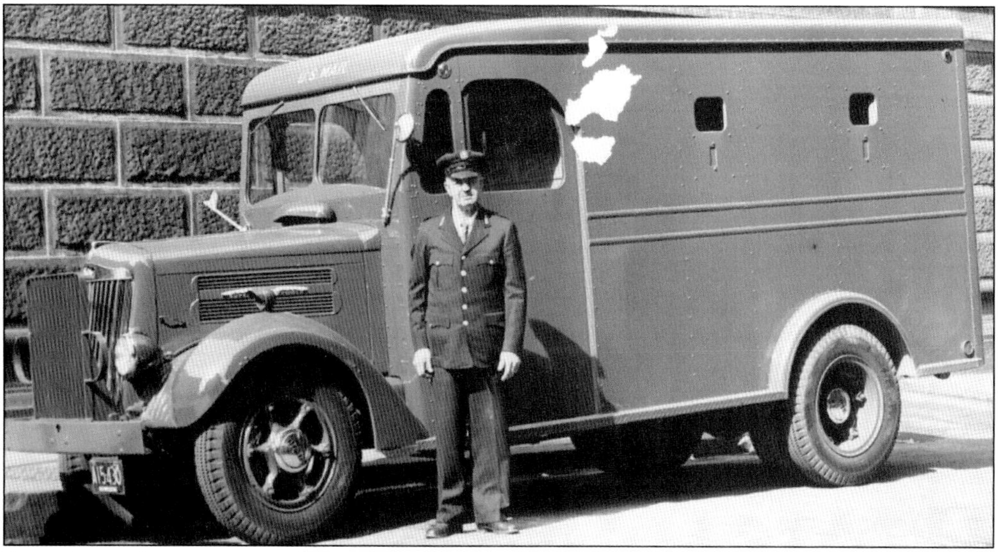

Fred Hunter, known at the Fed by the unlikely nickname "Mr. Bank Truck," joined the staff in 1918 as a chauffeur. He could truthfully report that he had never been late to work nor lost a piece of mail or currency in his tenure of over 30 years. Besides normal mail pickup and delivery, Hunter was also involved in a few large-scale special projects, including moving all the bank's money from its rented space on State Street to the new Pearl Street building, with mounted Boston police officers accompanying his every move.

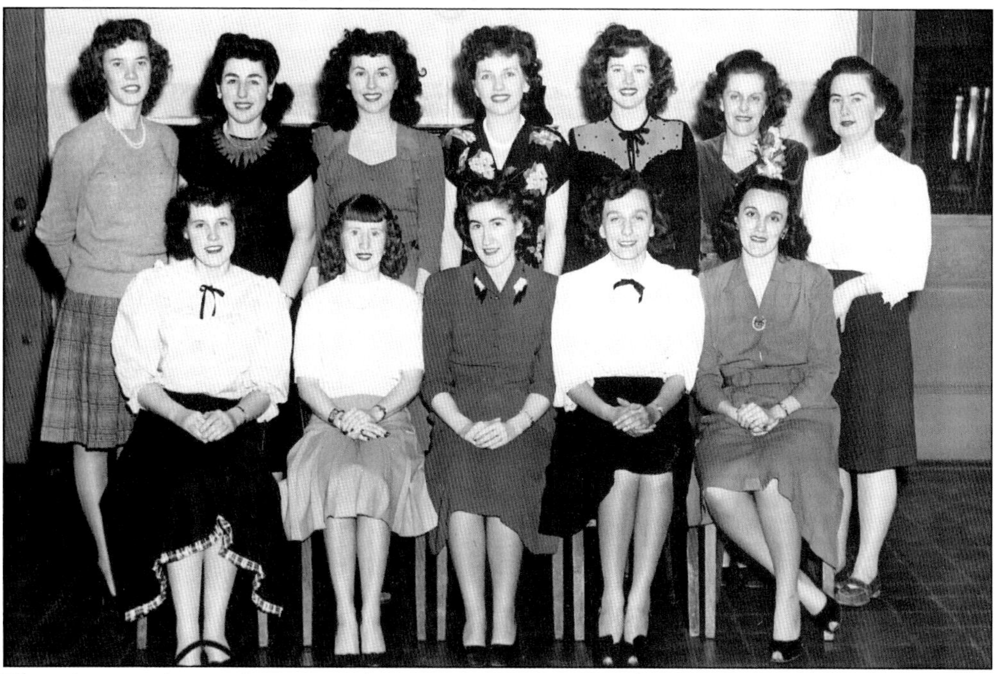

This photograph is aptly captioned "Prospective Transit Brides." The Transit Department was exclusively comprised of women, except for the managers, as was the custom. Judging by this photograph, they also seemed to be mostly young, marriageable women. No newsletter was published at any time in the 1940s that did not include a list of "Transit gals" ready to take the matrimonial plunge. For most of them, that meant leaving the Fed to set up housekeeping.

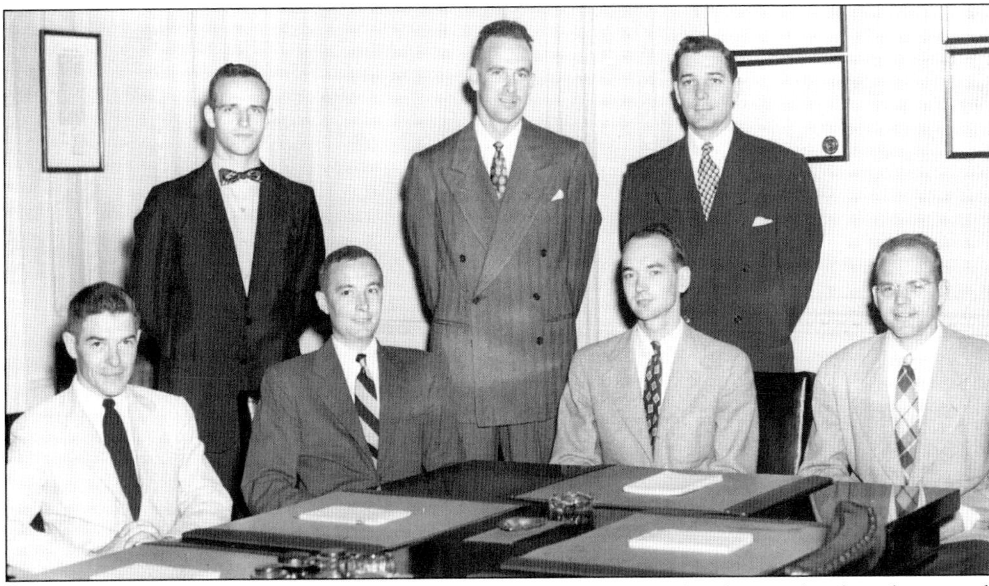

These clean-cut young men, students from Harvard Business School, pose for this photograph while getting some hands-on training at the Fed.

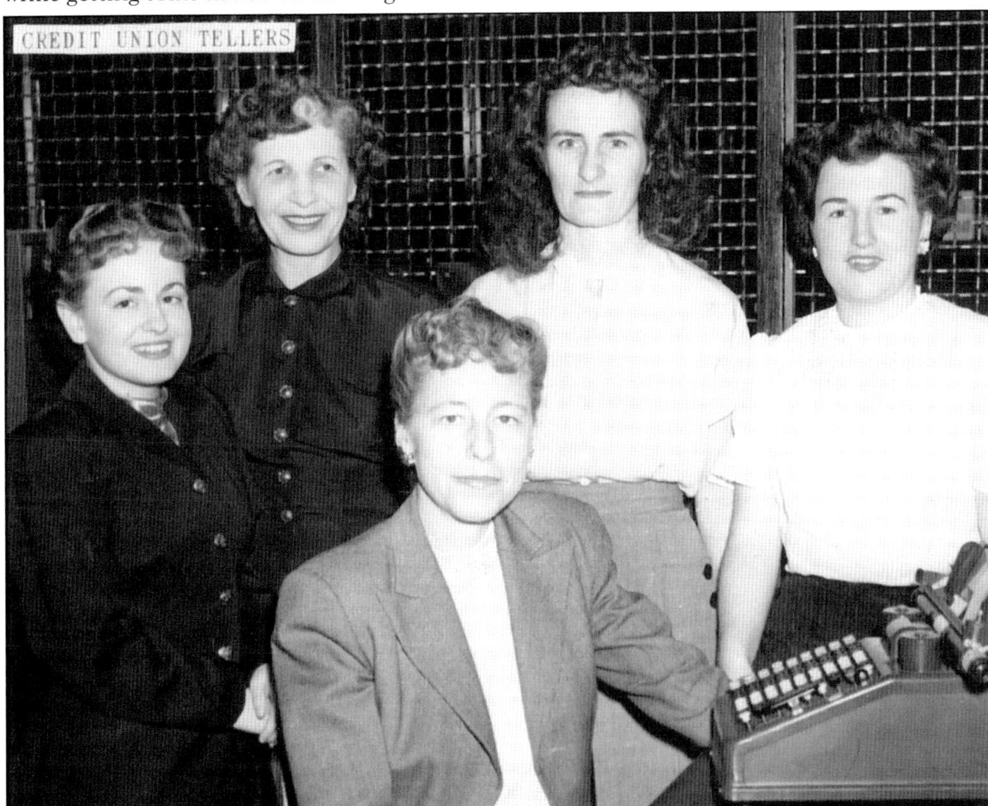

The employee credit union was established in 1949 with a stated goal of encouraging thrift. "A thrifty person is generally ready to cope with the financial problems of life," said one early member. Seen here are the original tellers.

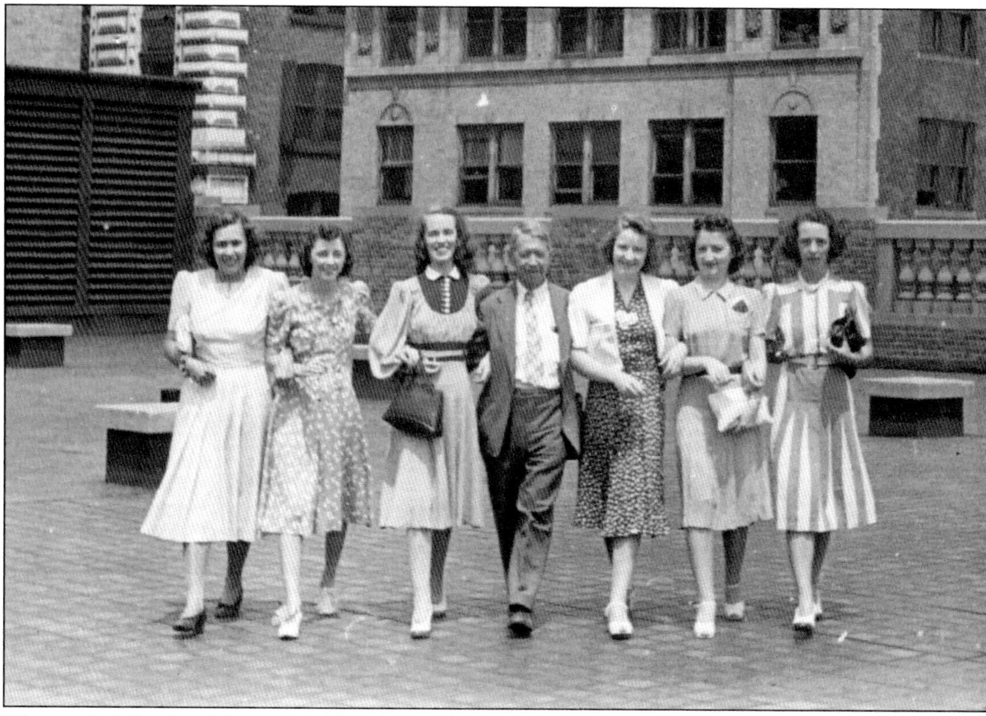

The roof of the Pearl Street building was a favorite gathering spot for employees. This attractive group appears to be in the midst of a pleasant stroll, which will land them in the middle of Oliver Street if they take many more steps.

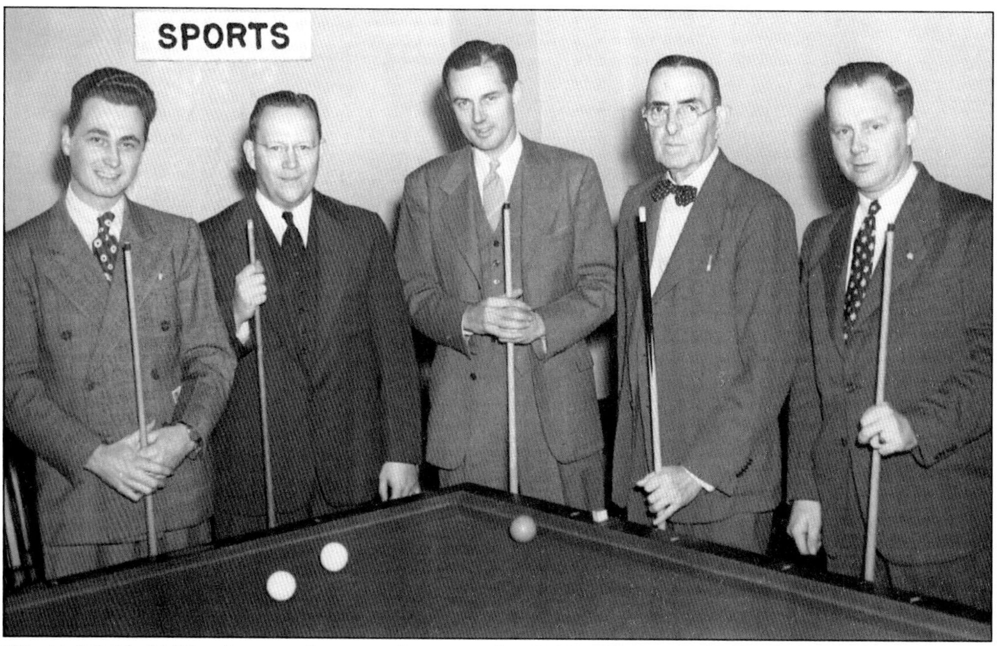

The Fed fielded billiards teams for several years in the 1940s. The team, known as the Sharpshooters, is comprised of members of the Protection Unit.

Four

POSTWAR

The nation's brief respite between wars was ended with the outbreak of hostilities in Korea in 1950 and the Cold War realities that would dominate many aspects of American life for much of the next 40 years. As is so often the case, the conflict gave a boost to the economy. This was particularly so in New England. While the traditional industries of textile and shoe manufacturing continued the downward spiral that had begun as far back as the 1920s, new, defense-oriented businesses moved to the fore of the region's economy. Electrical machinery, transportation equipment, and fabricated metal products led the way in increasing the number of manufacturing jobs to 1.5 million.

Although the Boston Fed made cautiously optimistic predictions in its annual reports, the sense that the reprieve for New England's manufacturing base was only a temporary one was never far from the minds of knowledgeable economists. Indeed, in 1955, the bank was forced to admit in its report that "it couldn't last forever, and it didn't."

While keeping its eye firmly on the fortunes of the region, the Boston Fed had its own special problems to deal with, the most pressing of which was space. The 1923 building on Pearl Street was filled nearly to the bursting point, and the bank was once again forced to rent space in other nearby buildings. The computer age was advancing, and the Fed was quick to recognize the potential of the new technology in its operations, but a state-of-the-art computer in 1950 was gigantic. For neither the first nor the last time, a building committee was organized.

The 1950s saw the Fed taking a more outward glance and increasing its visibility in the community. The Research Department, previously mostly concerned with the compiling of statistics, began to take a more proactive role in shaping policy, and educational programs were developed to engage and inform the public.

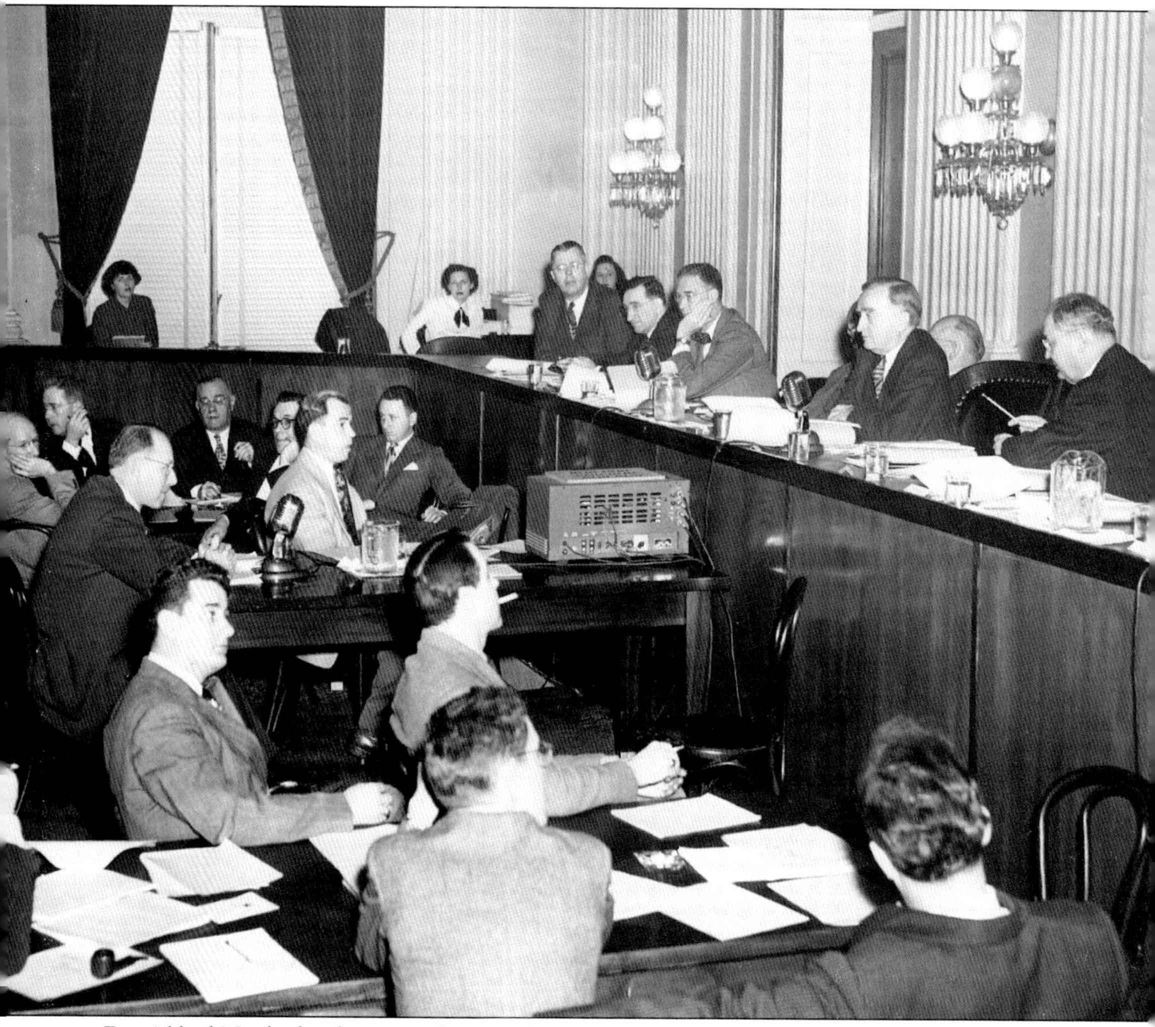

Dr. Alfred Neal, the director of research, testifies before the Congressional Joint Economic Committee in Washington, DC, in 1950. Although general topics concerning the future economy of New England were discussed, Dr. Neal's main focus was on the feasibility and desirability of establishing the steel industry here. While there was some agreement upon the latter part of the question, Dr. Neal feared that the "lack of free capital to take advantage of the project is a major stumbling block." And so it was; the steel industry never took a firm hold in New England.

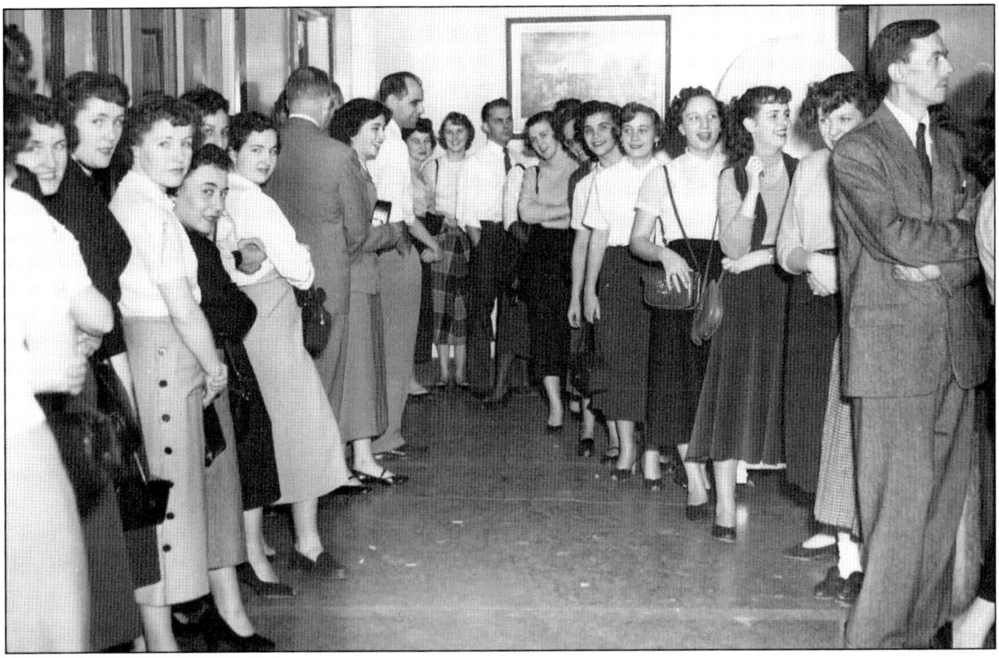

In response to intensifying Cold War fears brought about by the Korean War, civil defense authorities throughout the country staged readiness drills. In January 1952, the Boston Fed participated in a citywide air raid exercise. Although the event was met with mixed levels of solemnity, the *Society Newsletter* reported, "Members of the staff are to be congratulated on the serious and quiet manner in which they followed the instructions of the wardens."

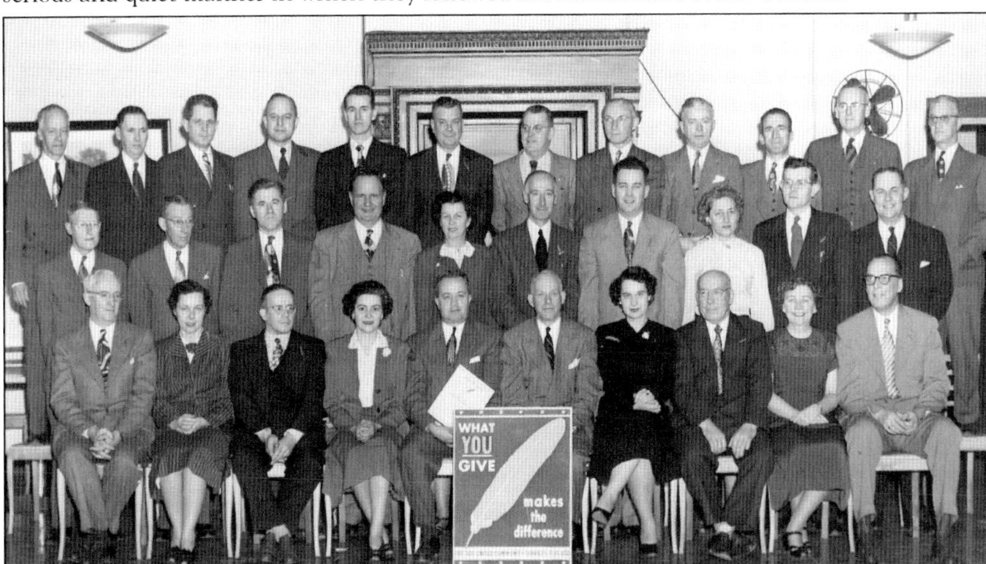

A precursor to today's United Way, the United Red Feather Campaign of Greater Boston became a regular event on the bank's calendar starting in 1952. The goal of the first year's campaign was just above $7,000 for the more than 30 Boston firms participating. Over 300 health and welfare organizations benefited from the donations. In 2011, over 120 corporate partners helped the United Way of Massachusetts Bay and Merrimack Valley collect over $43 million in support.

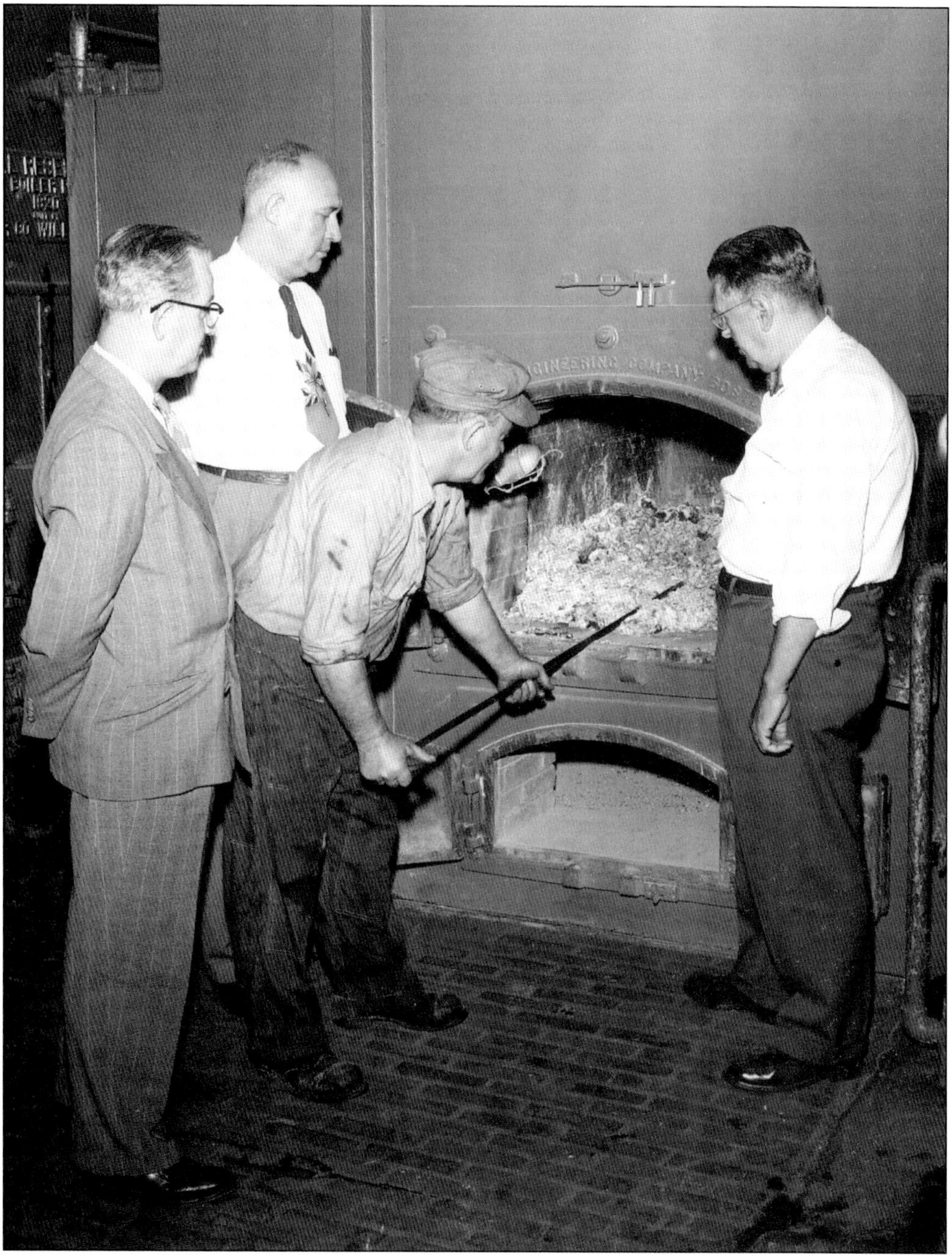

No scene connected with the bank's operation is the source of more heartache than the burning of unfit currency. (A casual observer is inclined to believe that no currency is so unfit a person couldn't make a couple of car payments with it.) The responsibility had belonged to the Treasury until 1953, when the 12 Fed districts took over in their role as fiscal agents of the US government. A special destruction unit was formed within Fiscal Agency and upwards of three million pieces of currency at a value of close to $7 million were incinerated each month in the mid-1950s.

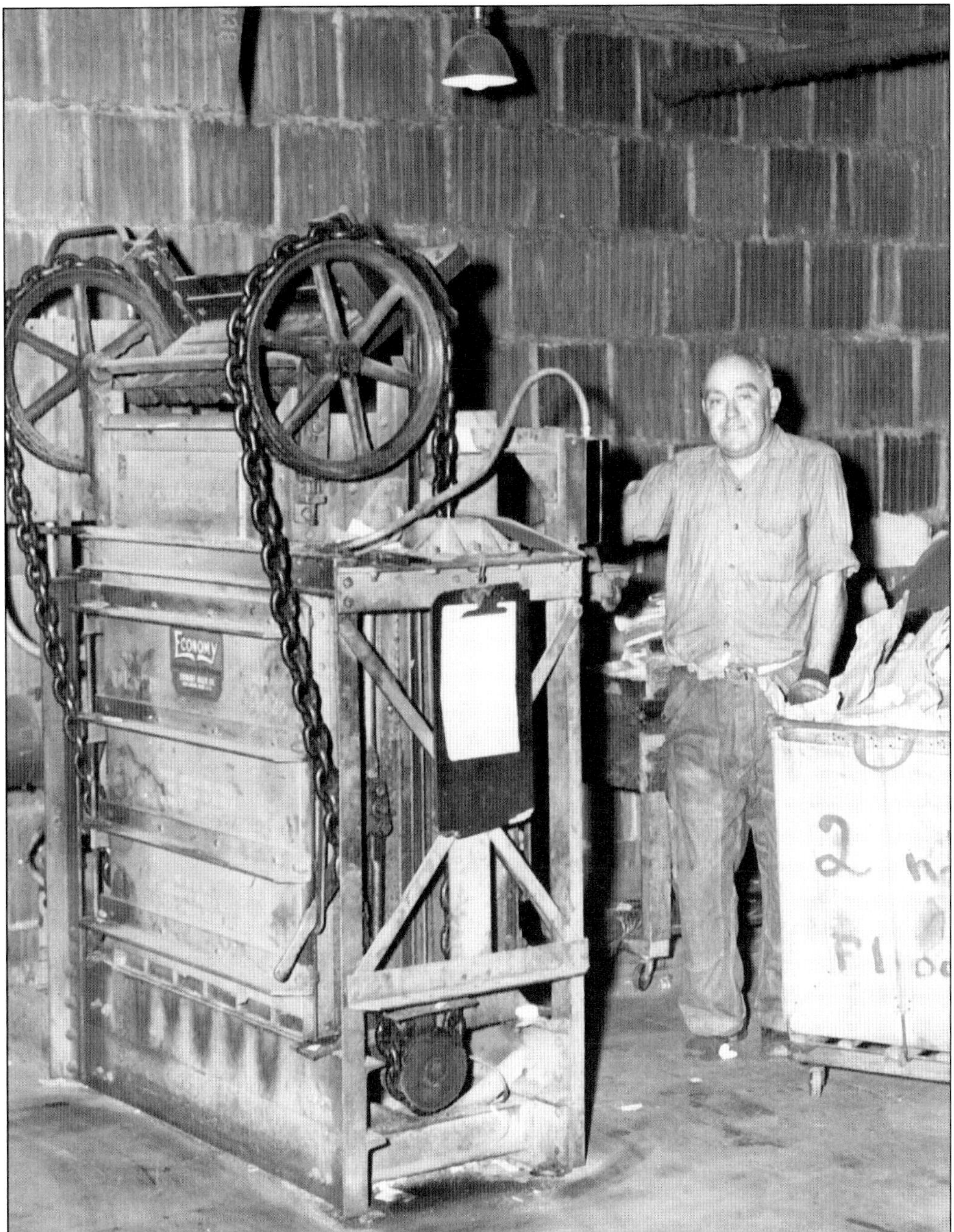

"Many of us are curious, no doubt, as to where the tremendous amount of waste paper disappears to each evening, after the majority of us have left the Bank at 5 p.m.," a *Newsletter* correspondent speculated in 1950. Likely not many were all that curious, but, in light of the bank's recent emphasis on going green, it is worth noting that upwards of two tons of wastepaper was disposed of each week, enough to warrant the bank owning and operating its own paper-baling machines in the basement, which packed the waste into convenient 400-pound bales. John Griffin, seen here, worked the 4:00 p.m.-to-midnight shift for the Maintenance Department.

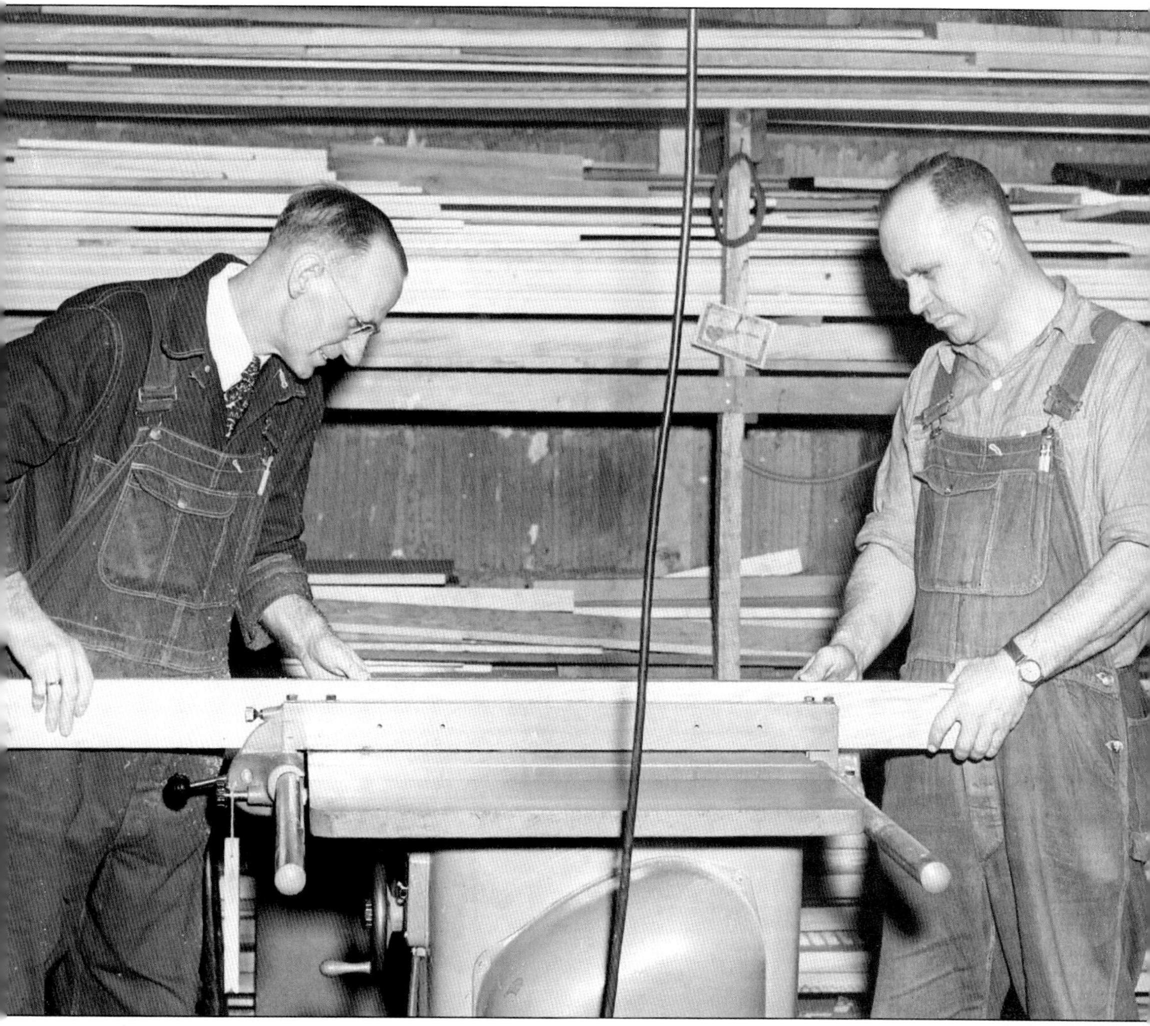

The carpentry shop at Pearl Street, although only a two-man operation, completed nearly all needed work in-house. In 1950, the shop was supplied with "a 14 inch band saw and a 10 inch circular saw, a joiner for planing and sizing lumber, and a sander which is in constant use smoothing table tops and many pieces of furniture preparatory to going to the painters. The sander is also utilized in keeping the cork floor in the officers' quarters in first class condition." Al Mercer (left) and Harry White reported that floor repairs and replacements accounted for most of their work as the Pearl Street building began showing its age.

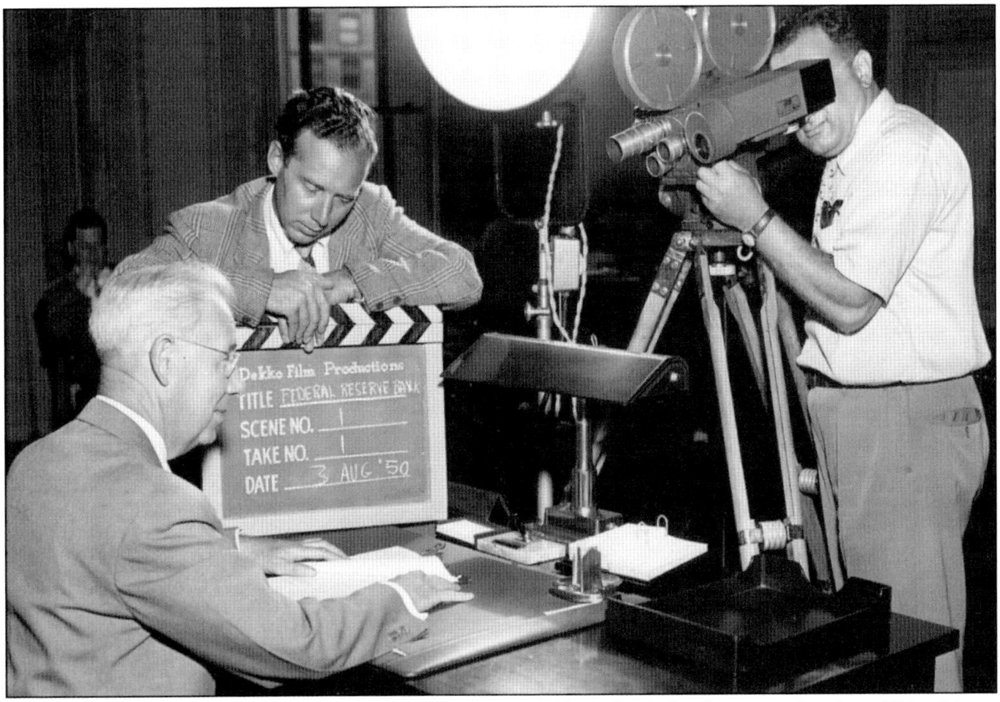

The Minneapolis Fed produced the 1950 educational film *The Federal Reserve Bank and You*. Here, Boston Fed cashier Bob Harvey (left) films additional scenes to add local flavor before the film is aired in New England. According to the *Newsletter*, Harvey gives "a brief and interesting talk on the volume of checks cleared, the amount of money issued and the number of bonds issued, received and redeemed on an average business day."

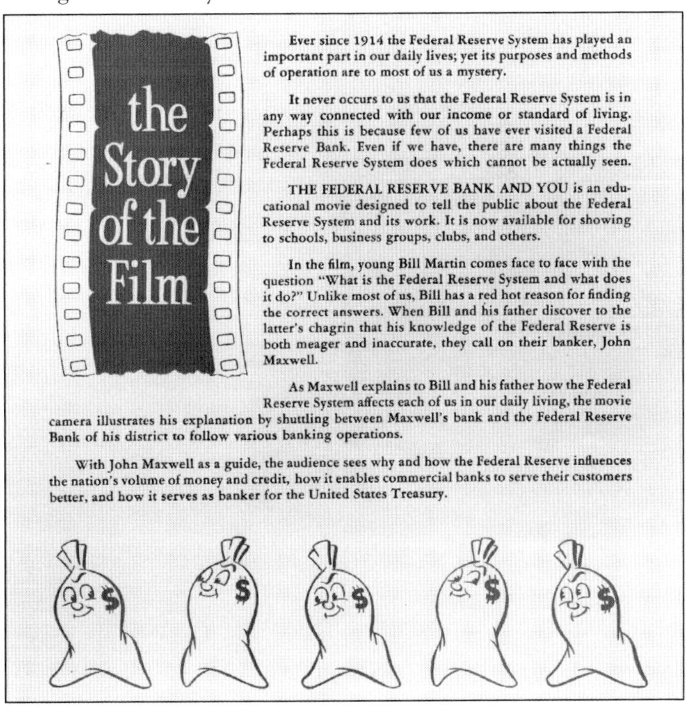

the Story of the Film

Ever since 1914 the Federal Reserve System has played an important part in our daily lives; yet its purposes and methods of operation are to most of us a mystery.

It never occurs to us that the Federal Reserve System is in any way connected with our income or standard of living. Perhaps this is because few of us have ever visited a Federal Reserve Bank. Even if we have, there are many things the Federal Reserve System does which cannot be actually seen.

THE FEDERAL RESERVE BANK AND YOU is an educational movie designed to tell the public about the Federal Reserve System and its work. It is now available for showing to schools, business groups, clubs, and others.

In the film, young Bill Martin comes face to face with the question "What is the Federal Reserve System and what does it do?" Unlike most of us, Bill has a red hot reason for finding the correct answers. When Bill and his father discover to the latter's chagrin that his knowledge of the Federal Reserve is both meager and inaccurate, they call on their banker, John Maxwell.

As Maxwell explains to Bill and his father how the Federal Reserve System affects each of us in our daily living, the movie camera illustrates his explanation by shuttling between Maxwell's bank and the Federal Reserve Bank of his district to follow various banking operations.

With John Maxwell as a guide, the audience sees why and how the Federal Reserve influences the nation's volume of money and credit, how it enables commercial banks to serve their customers better, and how it serves as banker for the United States Treasury.

The main part *of The Federal Reserve Bank and You* follows the thrilling story of "a boy and his father, their banker and a Federal Reserve Bank." The anthropomorphized moneybags are for illustrative purposes only and do not reflect any specific activity conducted by the Cash Department.

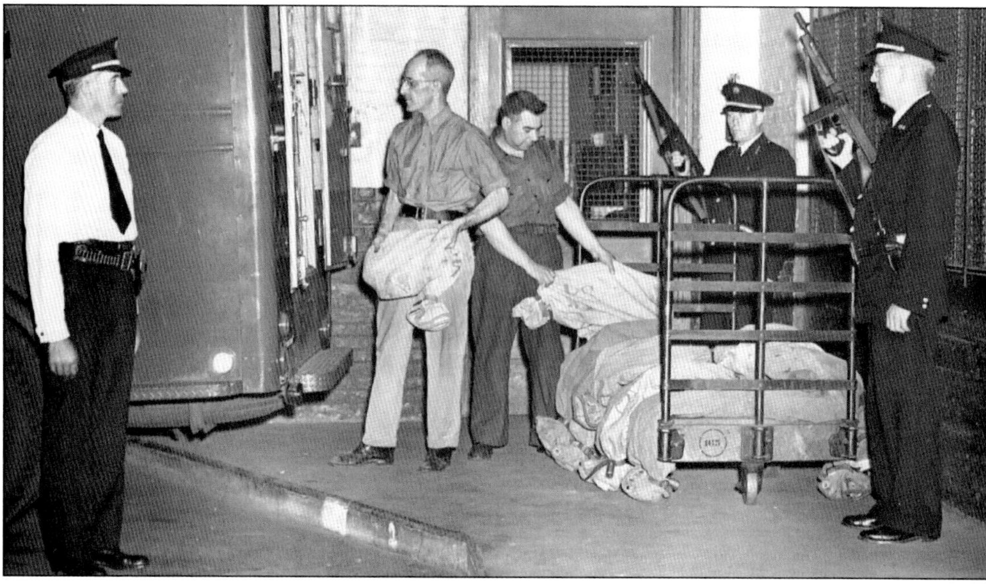

At the time of the bank's founding in 1914, an officer from the Boston Police Department was stationed on the main banking floor, at 53 State Street. Growth was so rapid that, by 1916, the Protective Department was established to better ensure the safety of the bank, its employees, and its assets. Besides supervising the loading and unloading of coins and currency, the guard team of the 1950s monitored an electronic vault control board, patrolled the entire premises, and on one occasion discovered a fire in an adjacent building.

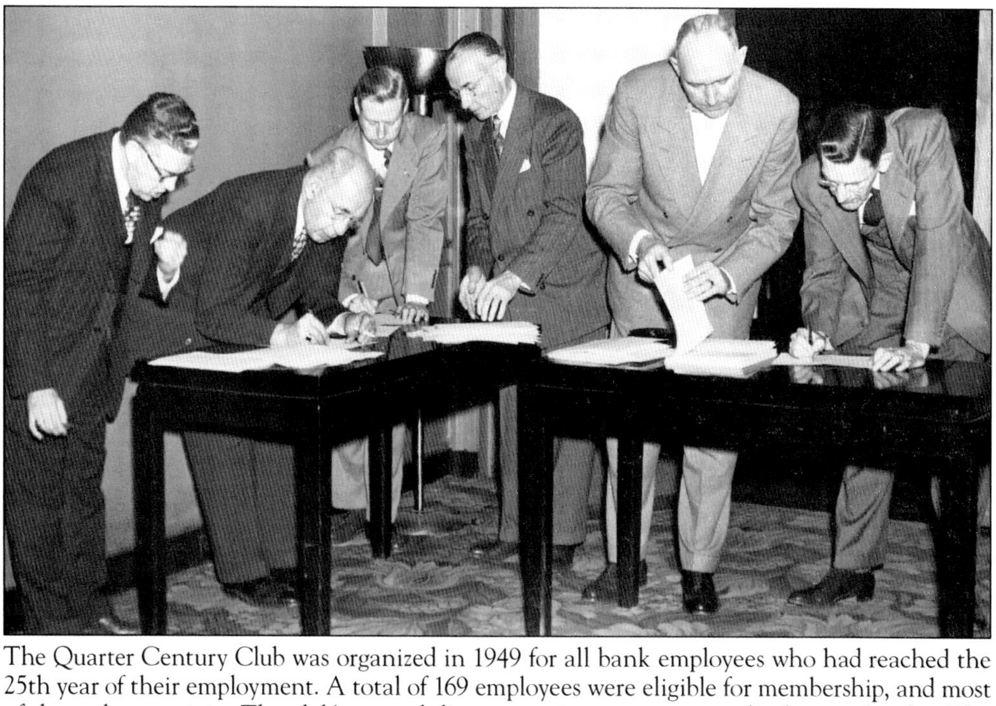

The Quarter Century Club was organized in 1949 for all bank employees who had reached the 25th year of their employment. A total of 169 employees were eligible for membership, and most of them chose to join. The club's annual dinner continues to attract a lively crowd today. The gentlemen seen here are counting the ballots for the 1952 election of officers, which took place at the banquet each year.

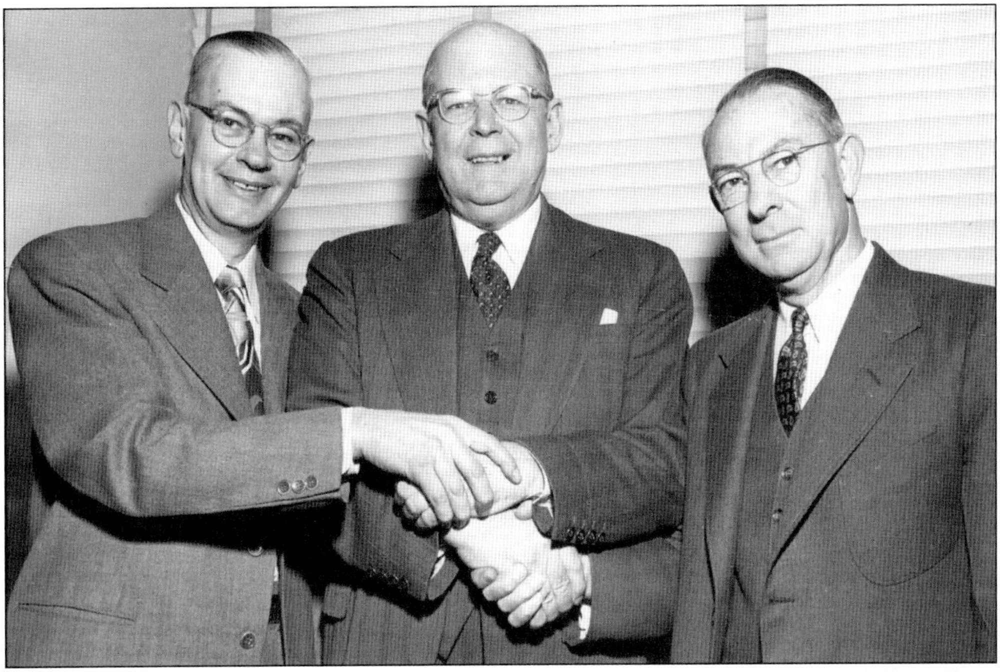

Three of the bank's original 17 employees were still on the job in 1951: Lewis Stoyle (left), William Willett (center), and Carl Pitman. This photograph was taken at the time of Willet's retirement. Willet's first position was as a paying teller; he retired as first vice president, the first person to hold that title.

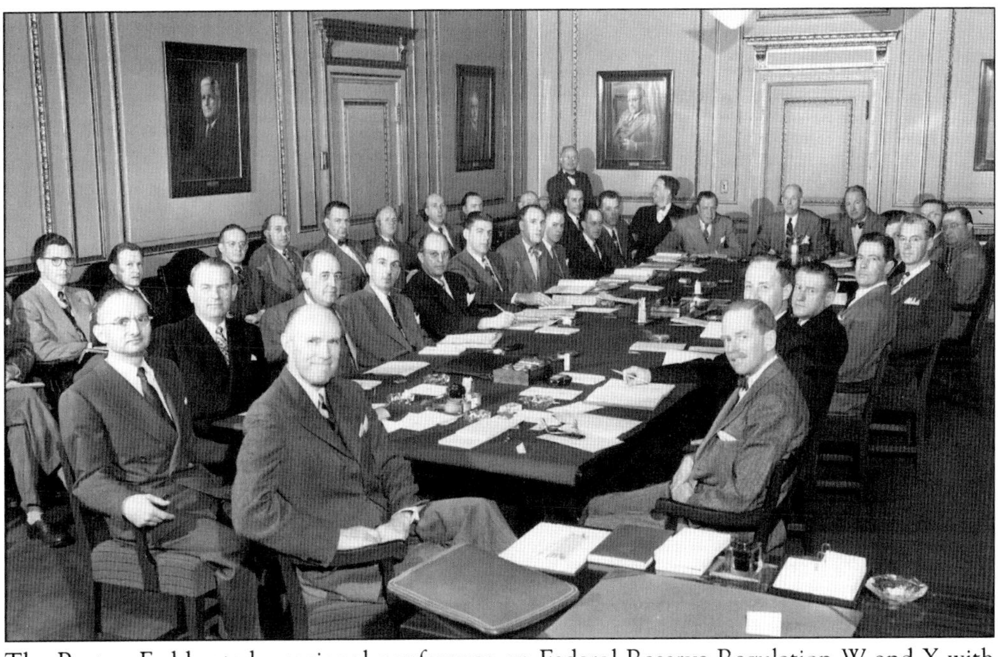

The Boston Fed hosted a regional conference on Federal Reserve Regulation W and X with representatives from the New York, Richmond, and Philadelphia Feds in attendance. These regulations were connected with consumer credit and real estate credit, which were both demonstrating some concerning tendencies in the postwar era.

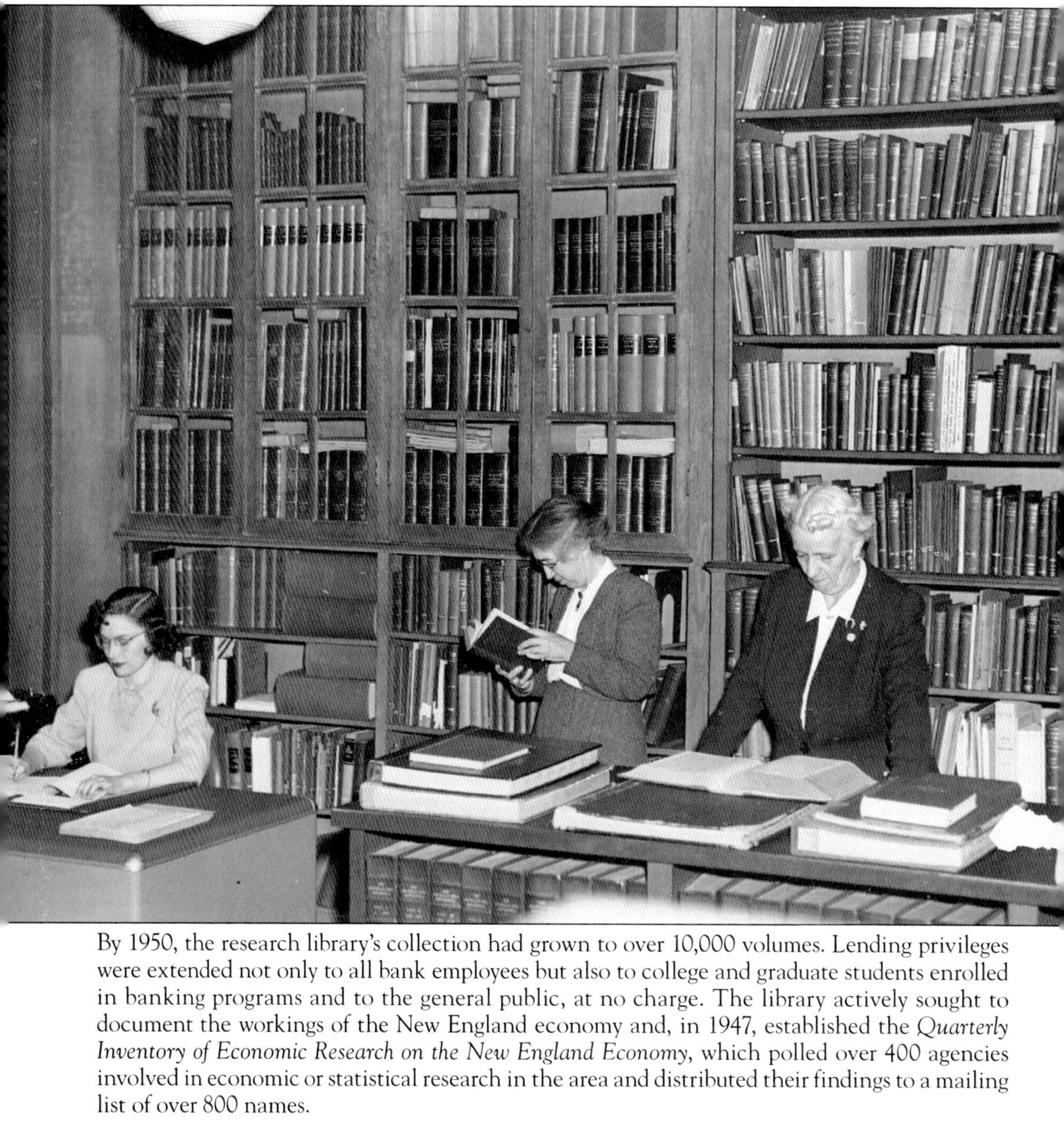

By 1950, the research library's collection had grown to over 10,000 volumes. Lending privileges were extended not only to all bank employees but also to college and graduate students enrolled in banking programs and to the general public, at no charge. The library actively sought to document the workings of the New England economy and, in 1947, established the *Quarterly Inventory of Economic Research on the New England Economy*, which polled over 400 agencies involved in economic or statistical research in the area and distributed their findings to a mailing list of over 800 names.

Beginning in 1948 and continuing into the 1960s, the "doll table" (right) was a holiday season tradition. Federal Reserve Society members turned dressmakers outfitted hundreds of dolls for distribution to local orphanages and social welfare agencies such as the New England Home for Little Wanderers. In later years, other games and toys were collected as well. Below, a few lucky recipients at the Chardon Street Home seem pleased with their gifts. Chardon Street was a temporary shelter for women and children founded in the 1860s.

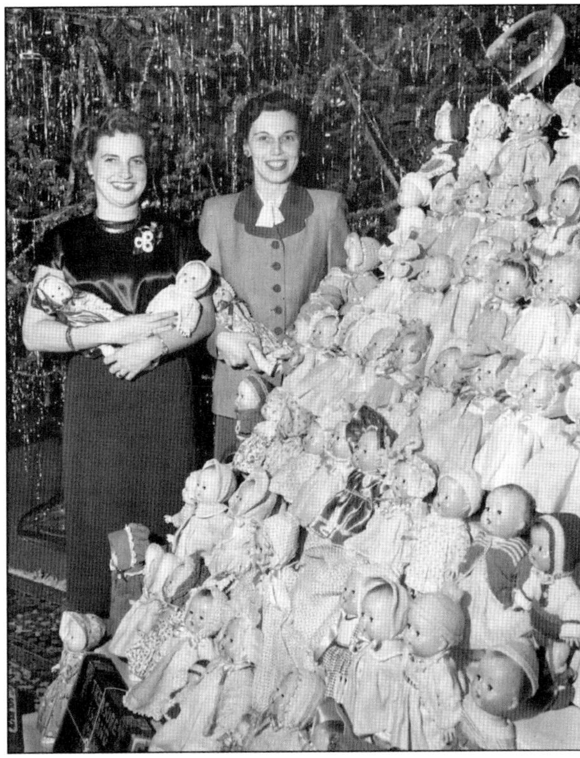

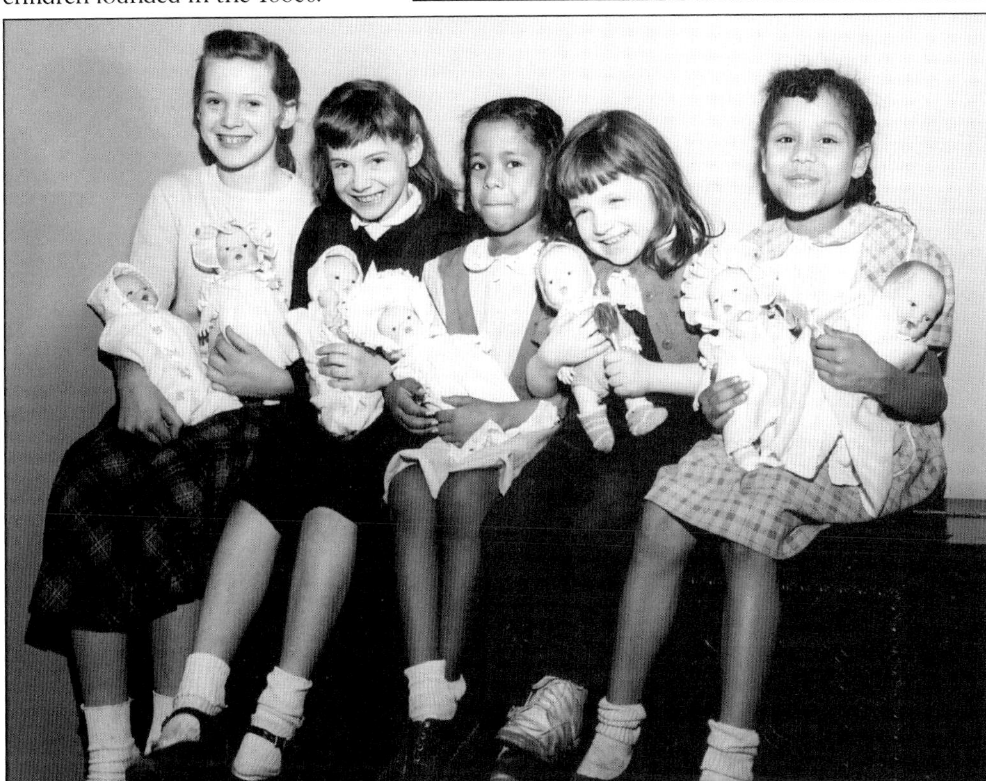

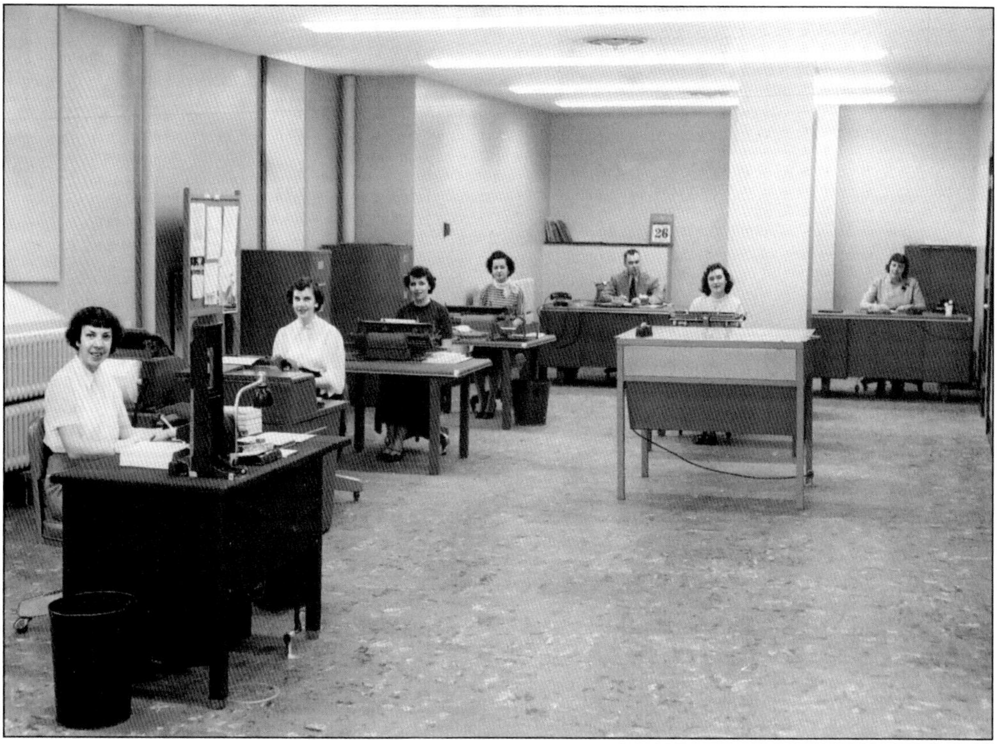

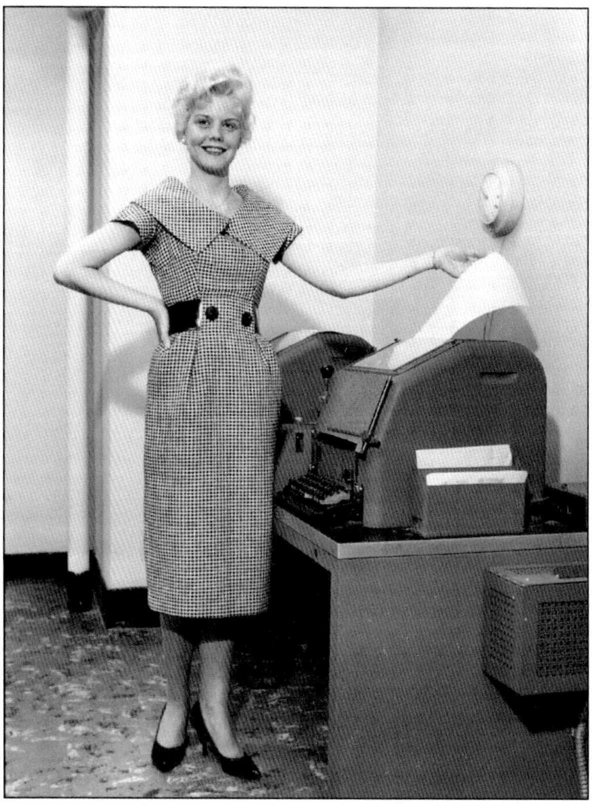

The growing number of and size of the Printing Department's machines necessitated a move to more spacious quarters on the bank's ground floor. With an array of tools both familiar and obscure, including offset, letterpress, photo-lithograph, vari-type, auto-type, addressograph, and Photostat machines, the Printing Department went through about two million sheets of paper and 750,000 envelopes in 1953, the year the photograph above was taken.

Eileen Lyons was employed in the Wire Transfer Department, although the nature of the work she is performing here is not specified. Instead, the reader is informed that she looks "fresh and alert" and has paired her "slim sheath dress" with "simple black patent pumps," in keeping with an instructive article entitled "Good Grooming: Rung 2 on the Ladder of Success," directed solely at female employees.

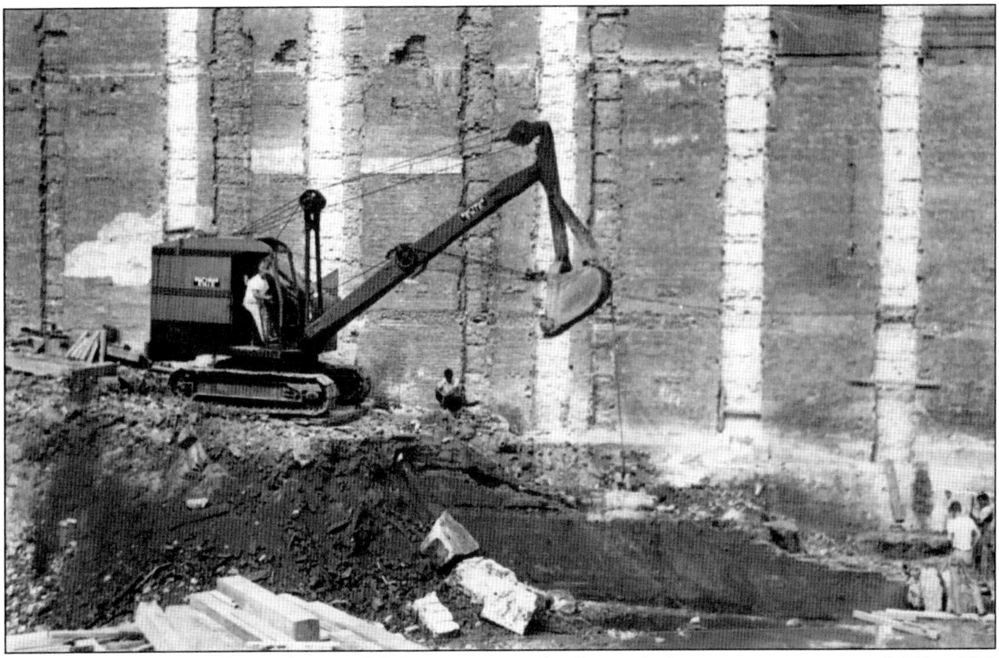

By the early 1950s, the Fed's Pearl Street quarters had simply become too cramped. The 700 employees in 1923 had grown to 1,400 by 1950, and additional space was being rented in nearby office buildings for the overflow workforce. Construction bids for an addition of approximately 55,000 square feet had been called for in January 1951, but, with the lowest bid coming in at $6 million, the directors balked. A few frills—including a second elevator bank—were cut out, the George Fuller Co. was awarded the contract for $4.1 million, and work began clearing the site in the summer of 1951.

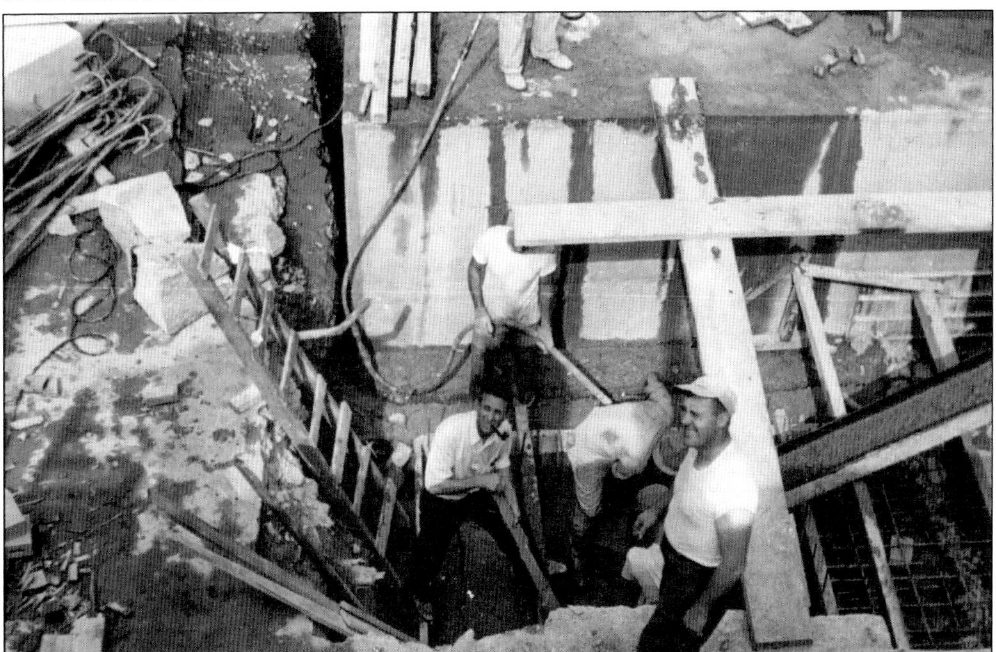

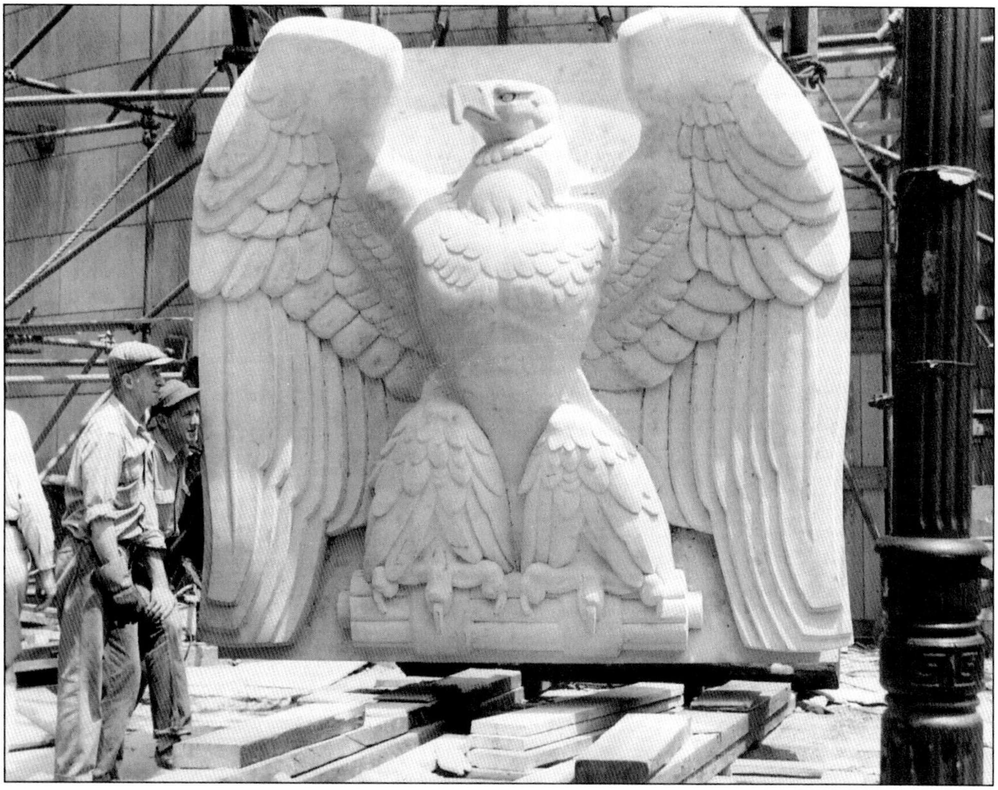

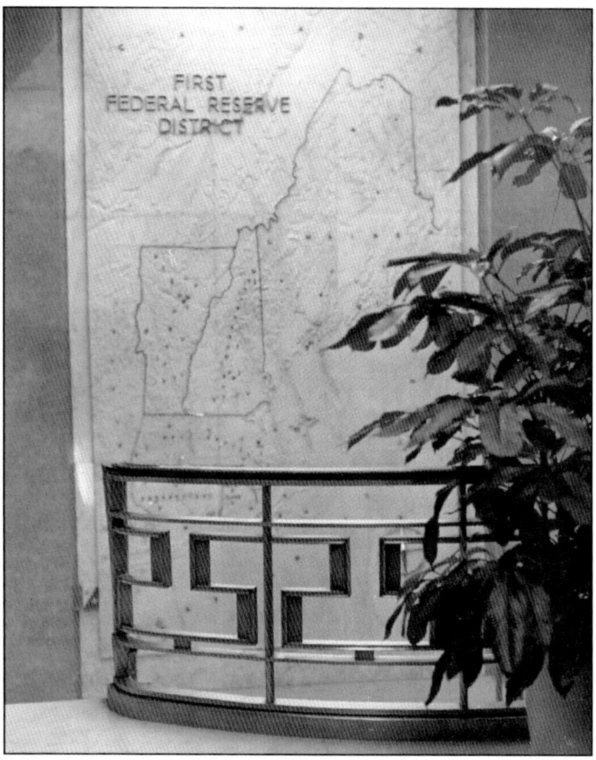

Several hundred spectators turned up to see the crowning glory of the new addition, the 18-ton limestone eagle, hoisted to its perch atop the corner of Pearl and Milk Streets on June 6, 1952. The entire process was accomplished in just 40 minutes.

The focal point of the 1953 addition's entrance was this 12-foot-by-21-foot relief map of New England, carved in Vermont marble by Connecticut artist Austin Purves. When the building was razed in 1978, the map was moved to the headquarters of the *Boston Globe*, on Morrissey Boulevard, where it remains on display today.

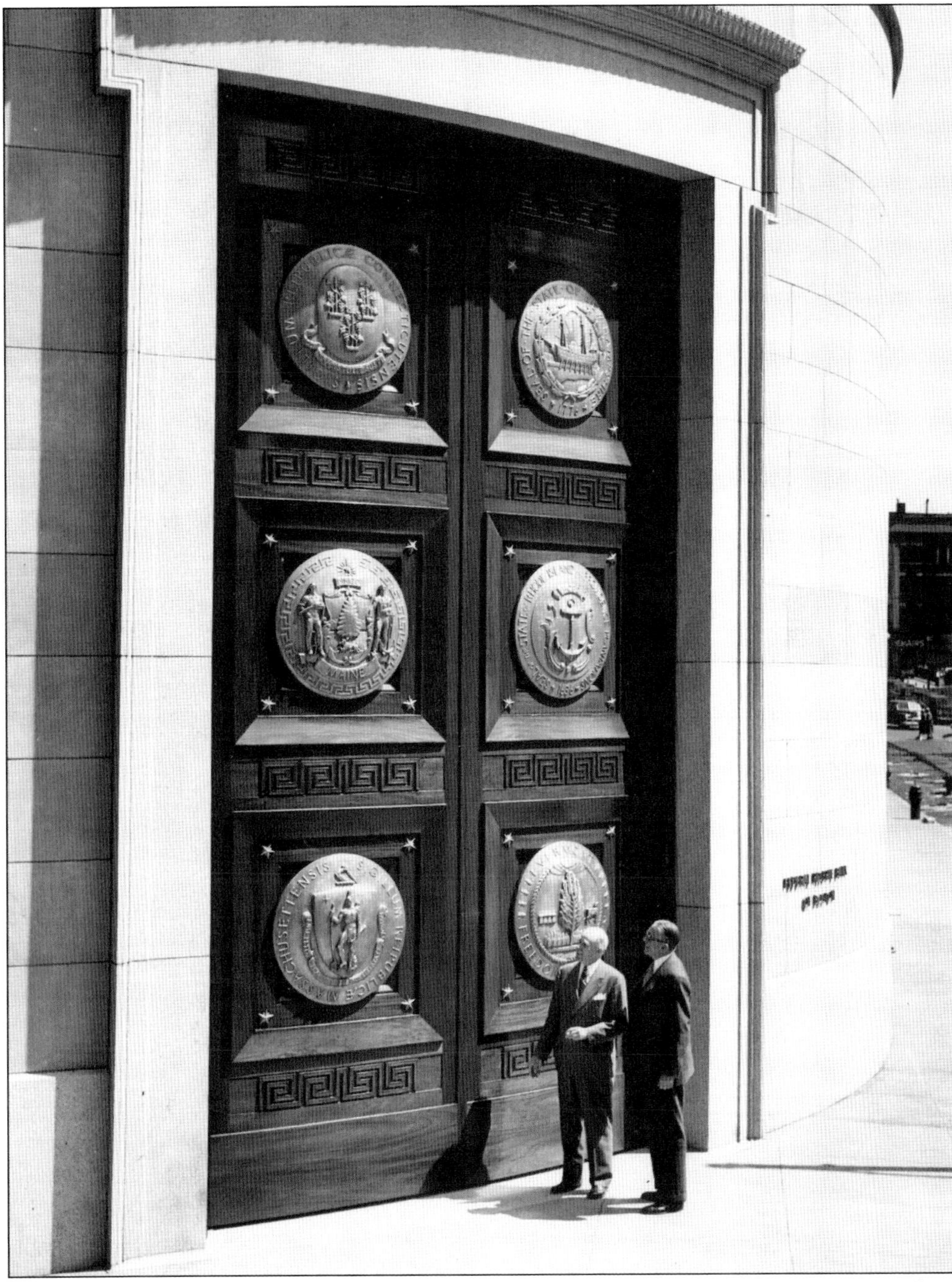

Boston Fed president Joseph Erickson and board chairman Harold D. Hodgkinson pose in front of the main entrance. The 22-foot-high mahogany doors featured six panels, each containing a bronze shield made by sculptor Donald DeLue, representing the seals of the six New England states comprising the First District. No convenient way could be found to detach Fairfield County from Connecticut's seal, so the state is erroneously represented in its entirety.

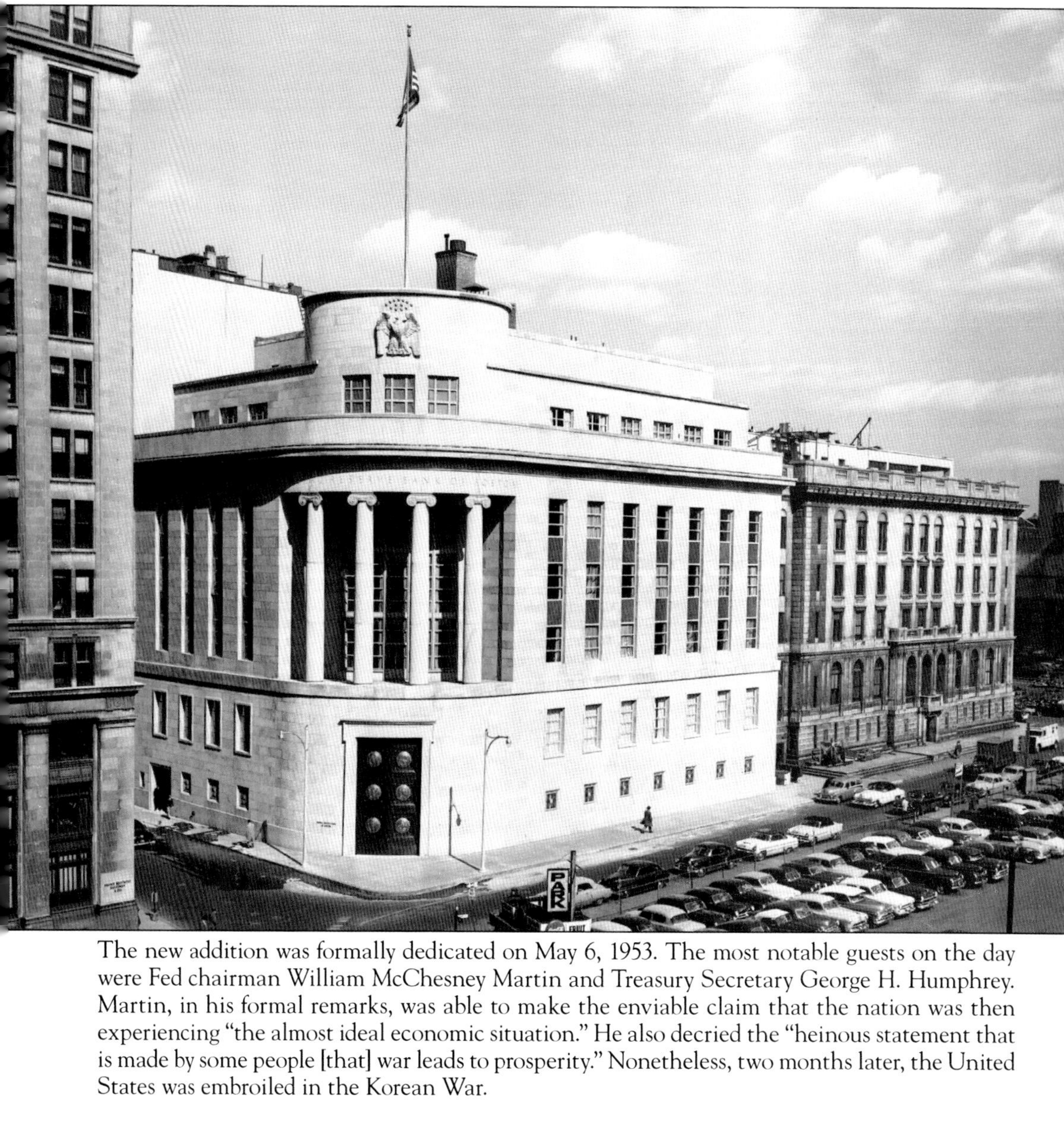

The new addition was formally dedicated on May 6, 1953. The most notable guests on the day were Fed chairman William McChesney Martin and Treasury Secretary George H. Humphrey. Martin, in his formal remarks, was able to make the enviable claim that the nation was then experiencing "the almost ideal economic situation." He also decried the "heinous statement that is made by some people [that] war leads to prosperity." Nonetheless, two months later, the United States was embroiled in the Korean War.

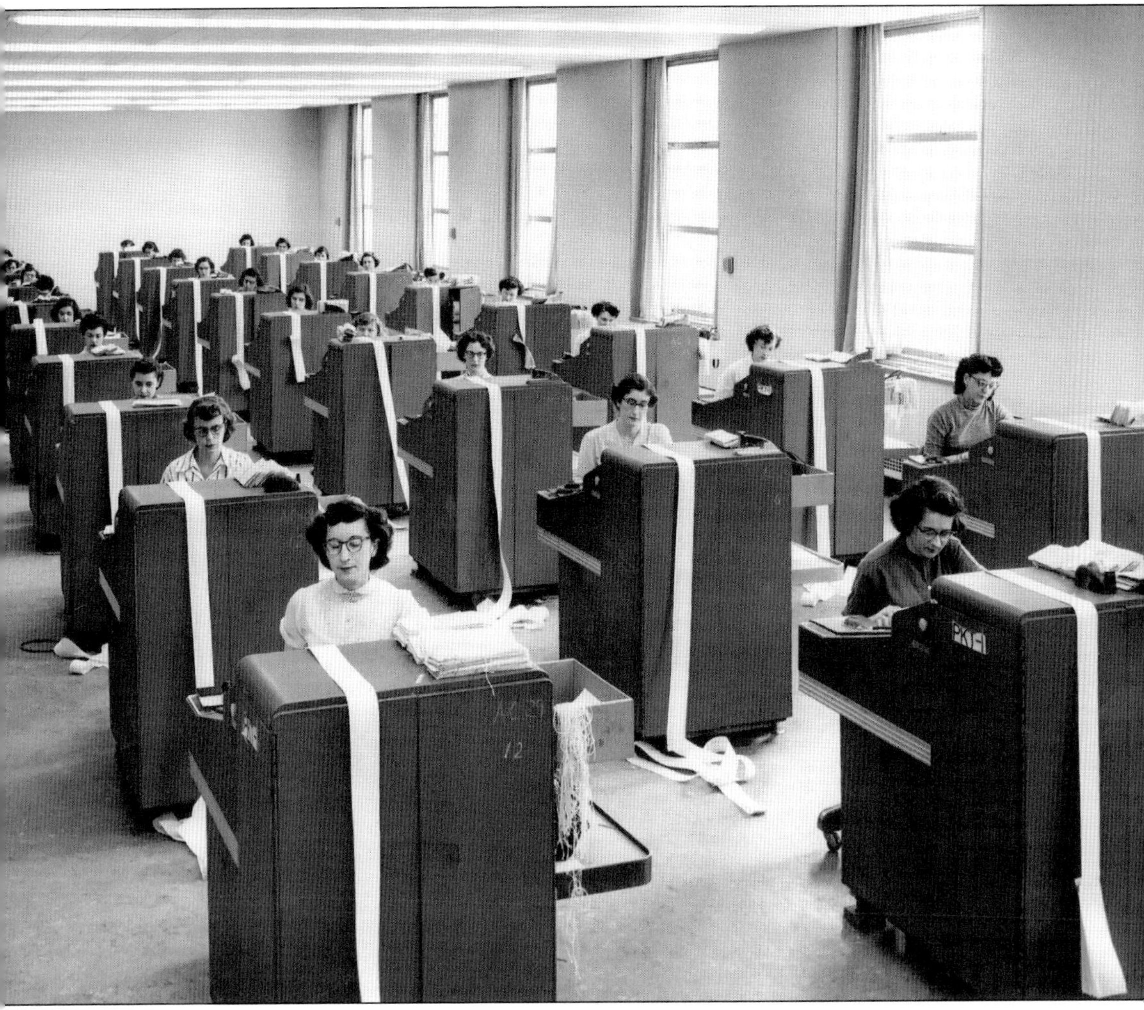

Among the upgrades featured in the bank's revamped space were 169 electronic proof machines. An average of 966,000 items per day were cleared in 1953. The banking magazine *Industry* speculated that if each day's checks were piled one on top of each other, they would make a pile as high as the John Hancock Building—not the current Hancock Tower, but the older, shorter one.

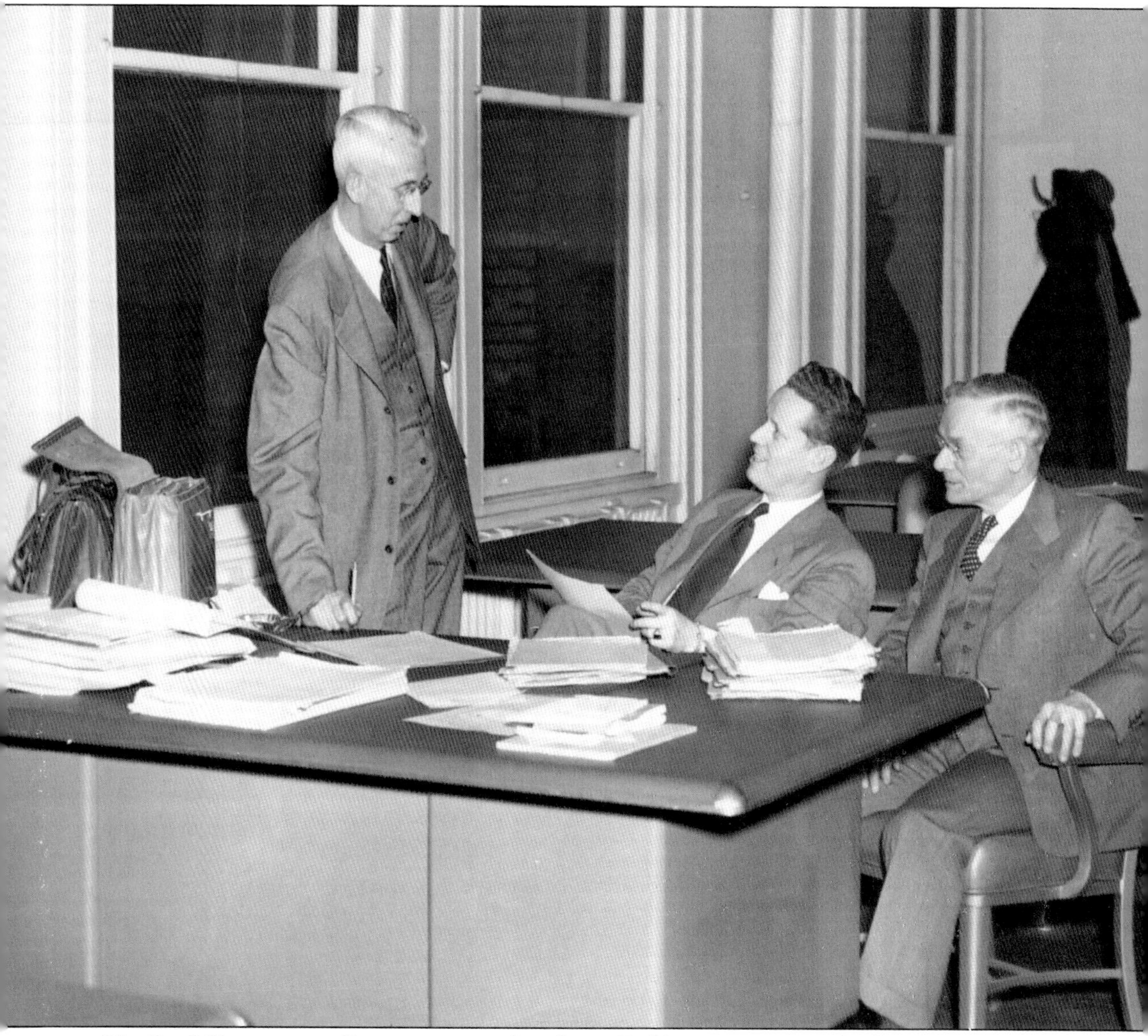

The Bank Examination Department employed a staff of 28 men in 1952. The first female examiners were not hired until 1966, when the *East Wind* breathlessly inquired, "Can a woman do a man's job?" As it turned out, yes, she could. The field force examined every member bank and trust company in the district annually. The department was also responsible for examining bank holding companies, investigating applications for new national bank charters, and processing applications for the exercise of trust powers by national banks. It is no wonder the *Newsletter* reported that the examiners were not well known to the rest of the bank staff; it is likely they were not all that well known to their families.

Wire Transfer employee Gloria Kennedy is cheerier than most folks getting a chest X-ray. The bank sponsored free examinations in 1952, when the dangers of radiation were held in such light regard that shoe stores often had X-ray machines on-site to give the impression of a "scientific fit." Chest X-rays, however, were used to detect the much more serious condition of tuberculosis, then still a deadly disease.

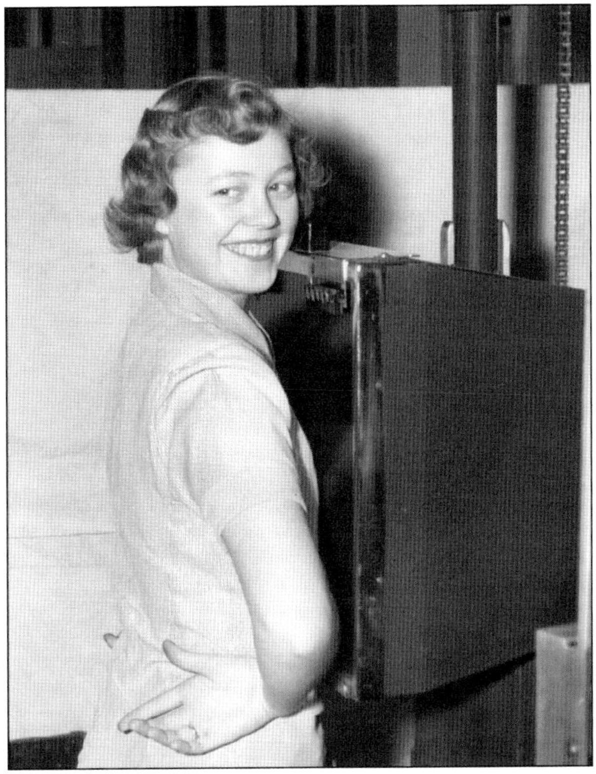

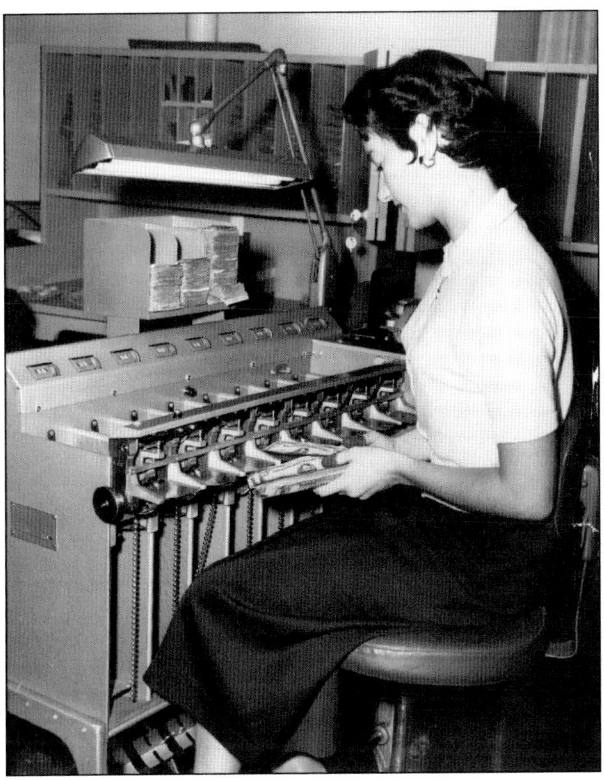

The currency-sorting machine in use in 1957 still required hand feeding and relied on the judgment of experienced staff to sort the fit currency from the unfit and the counterfeit. Apparently, there is no reading audience that does not enjoy looking at money; this photograph accompanied an article in a monthly publication called *Food Marketing in New England.*

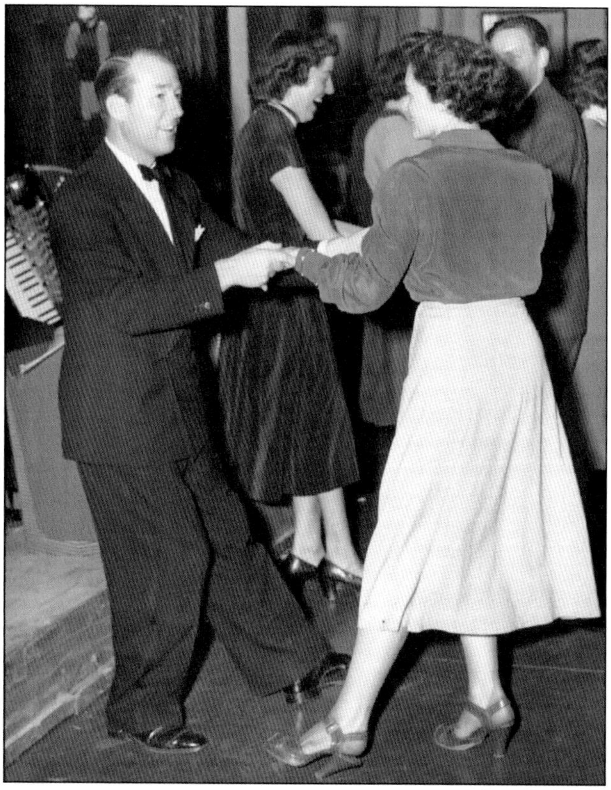

Always stylish, always debonair, Boston Fed employees cut a smart figure at this society Halloween party around 1955.

The Boston Fed celebrated its 40th anniversary in 1954. While this cake pictured is festive enough for all normal purposes, it was reported that the 50th-anniversary cake reproduced the Pearl Street building and the addition.

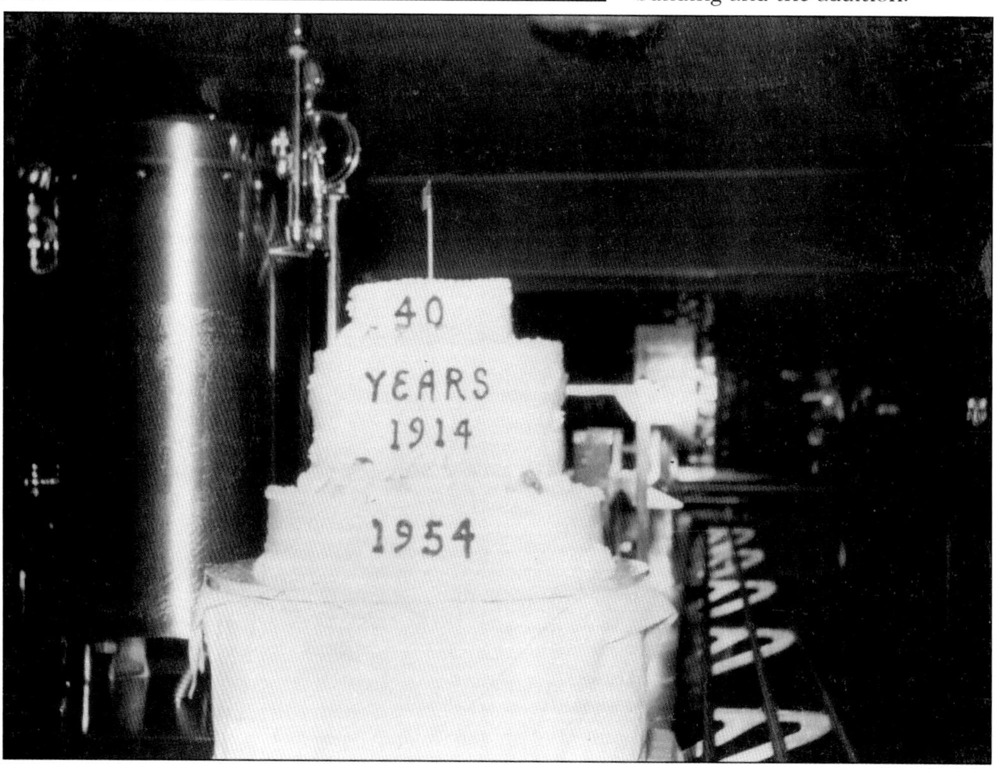

Five

EMERGING TECHNOLOGIES

The civil rights movement and the expanded uses of technologies were the twin themes running through the story of the bank, and the country as a whole, in the 1960s. Computers were still new enough and astonishing enough that every advance in their abilities was reported in breathless terms that can appear amusing in an age when planned obsolescence is a given. The bank's prized acquisition was the Burroughs 3500, installed by Data Services in 1967, which forced the entire Bank Examination Department out of the main building and into rented space on Oliver Street a mere 14 years after the opening of the addition that was expected to solve the bank's space problems for a generation. It seemed a minor inconvenience in the face of a machine that, the *East Wind* crowed, "strikes such a commanding pose." It also reported that it was "the eighth one off the production line."

While the Fed cannot claim a leading role in the cause of Civil Rights, by the 1960s, the face of the workforce had slowly begun to change. It would take some time for diversity to take hold as something to be actively pursued, but the most egregiously insensitive practices of the past had been safely consigned to oblivion. The last pinup girl had been chosen and the last minstrel show had been performed.

As the Federal Reserve System marked its 50th anniversary in 1964, the Boston Fed observed it with a series of conferences designed to foster better understanding between the bank and its members, particularly those outside Boston, who occasionally had cause to feel slighted by the Boston-centric nature of pretty much everything in New England.

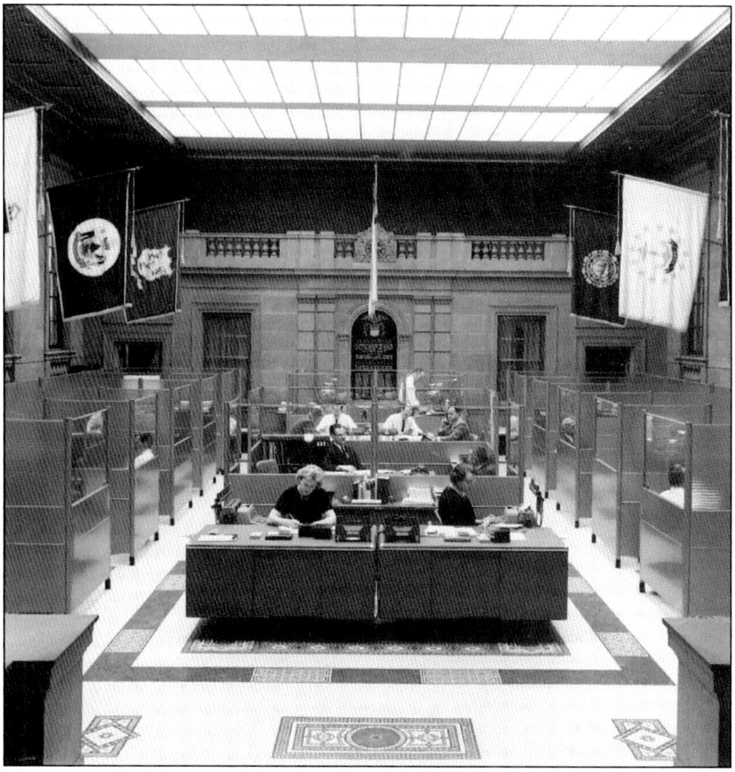

The immediate impetus for establishing the Planning Department in 1950 was the bank's need to expand its physical space. By 1960, the staff had grown to a team of 10 analysts and two stenographers. The department played a key role designing and expanding workspaces for maximum efficiency but found itself rather uncomfortably shoehorned into the old Members' Court at Pearl Street. Only seven years after the addition was completed, space was already at a premium again.

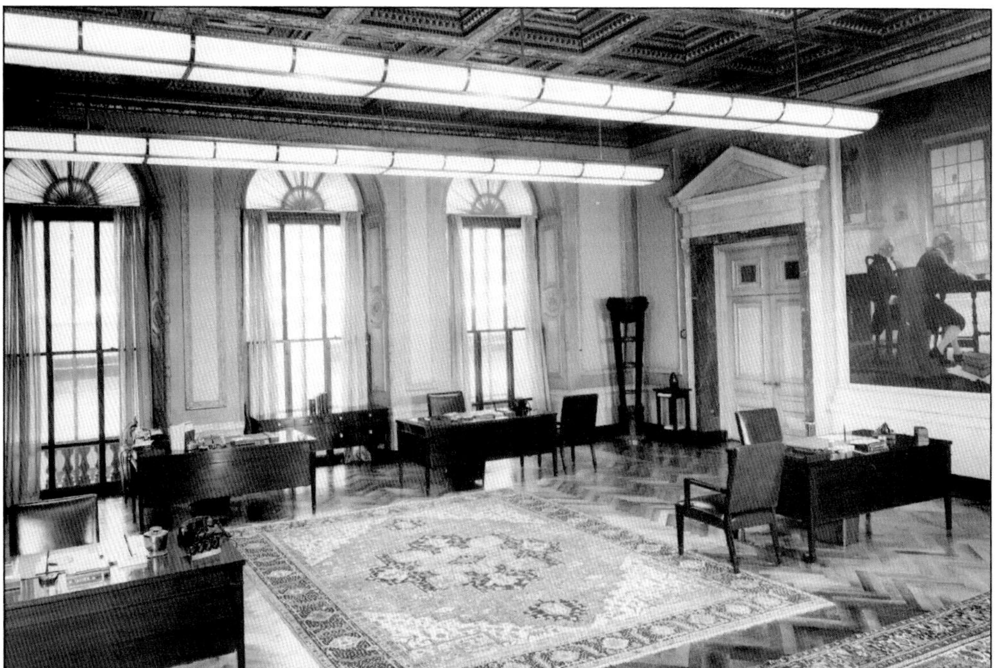

Just as the Members' Court had been, the junior officers' room, with its magnificent Wyeth murals, was also converted to extra office space in the early 1960s. The fluorescent light fixtures are the crowning insult to the formerly grand room.

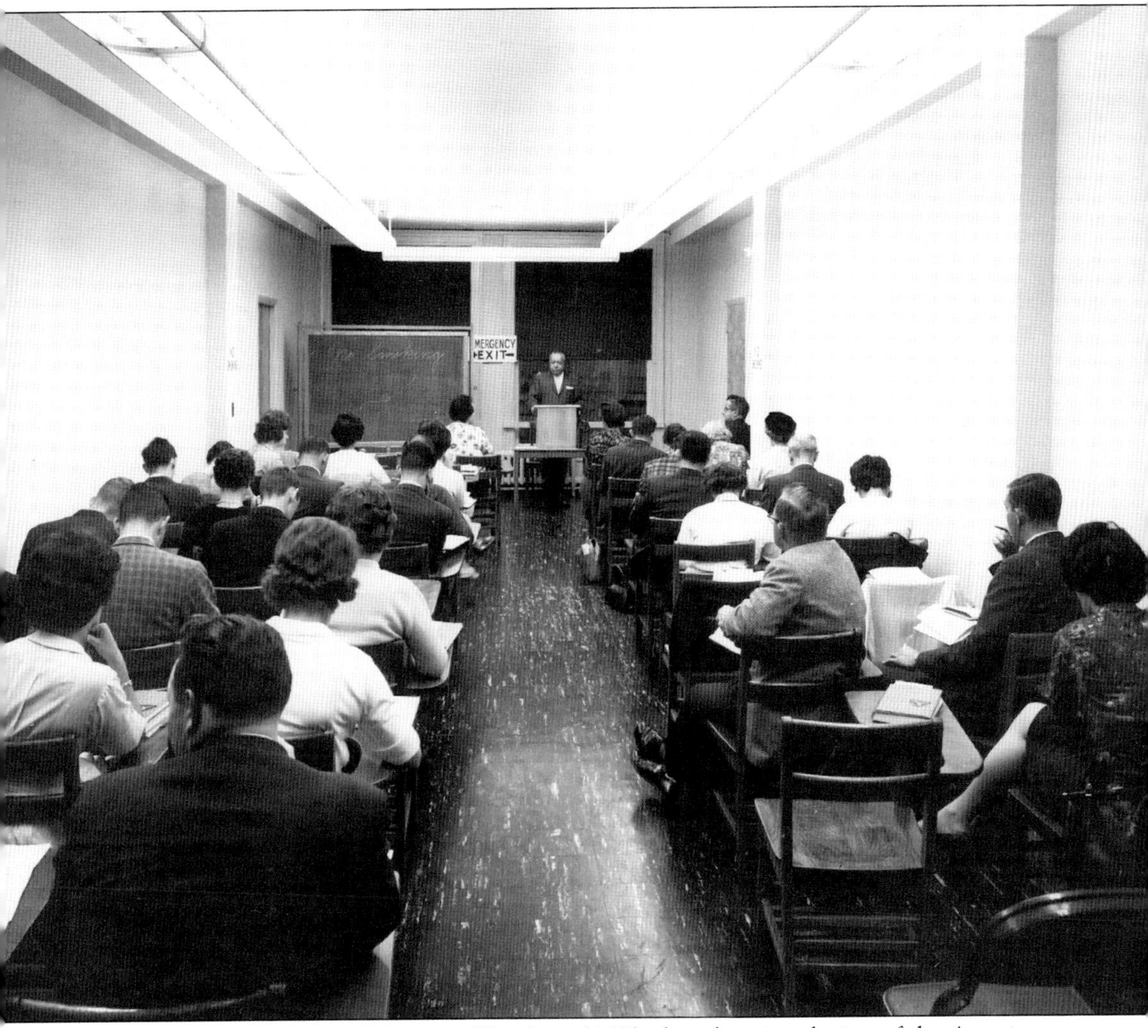

Courses from the American Institute of Banking (AIB), the educational wing of the American Bankers Association, had long been sponsored by the Fed for employees wishing to further themselves in the profession. In 1963, membership was a mere $3 per year, "painlessly deducted from your salary," and tuition and text fees were refunded to every student who successfully completed his or her courses. "Women as well as men" were encouraged to take advantage of the opportunity; indeed, Boston Fed women were among the first in the state to complete certification. The AIB opened these new classrooms in 1963 on Chauncy Street, which, for unclear reasons, the *East Wind* described as "spacious and comfortable."

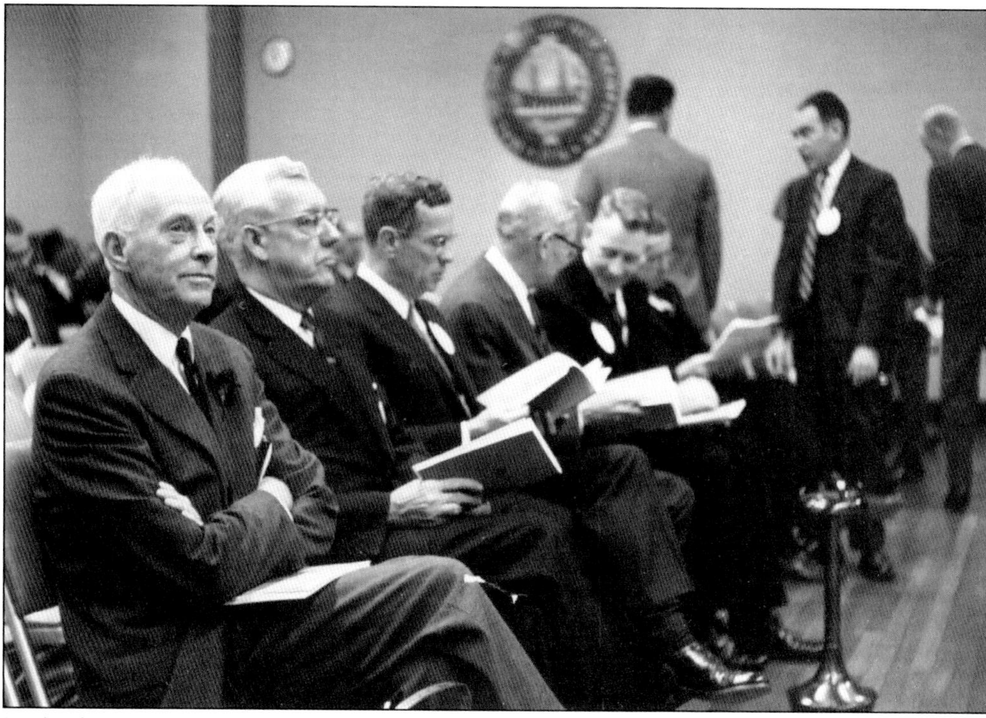

In the face of proposed legislation that would affect the Fed's independence, the stockholders' meeting in 1964 produced this resolution: "That the Federal Reserve System as presently constituted should be preserved and strengthened to assure, as was originally intended by Congress, its independence and freedom from political pressures and other consideration; and that the Federal Reserve System should continue to exercise its independence in regulating credit and the money supply in order to assure the integrity of the dollar and sound economic growth."

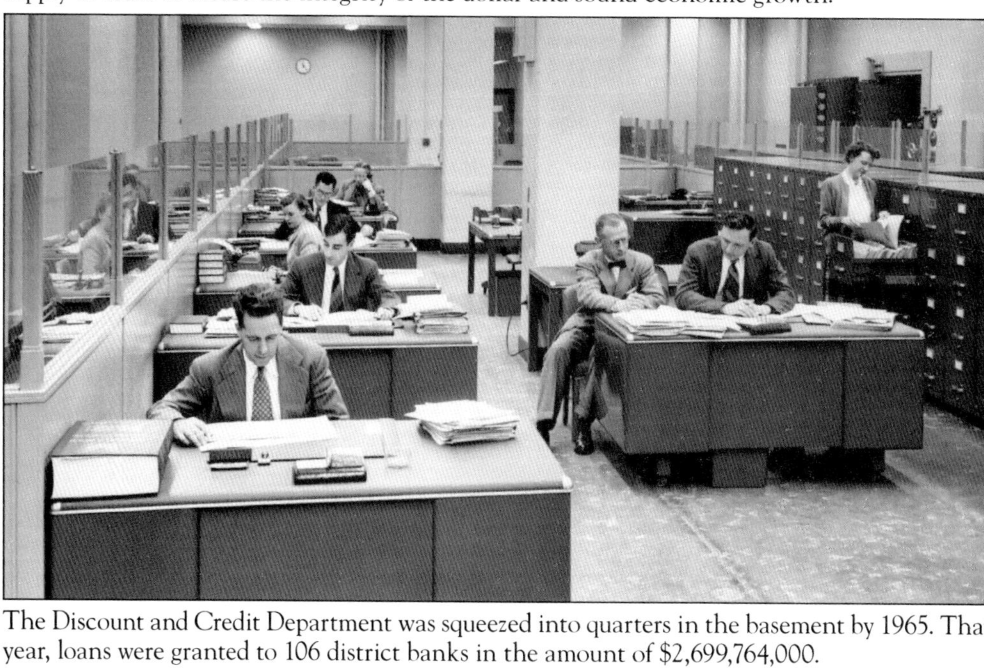

The Discount and Credit Department was squeezed into quarters in the basement by 1965. That year, loans were granted to 106 district banks in the amount of $2,699,764,000.

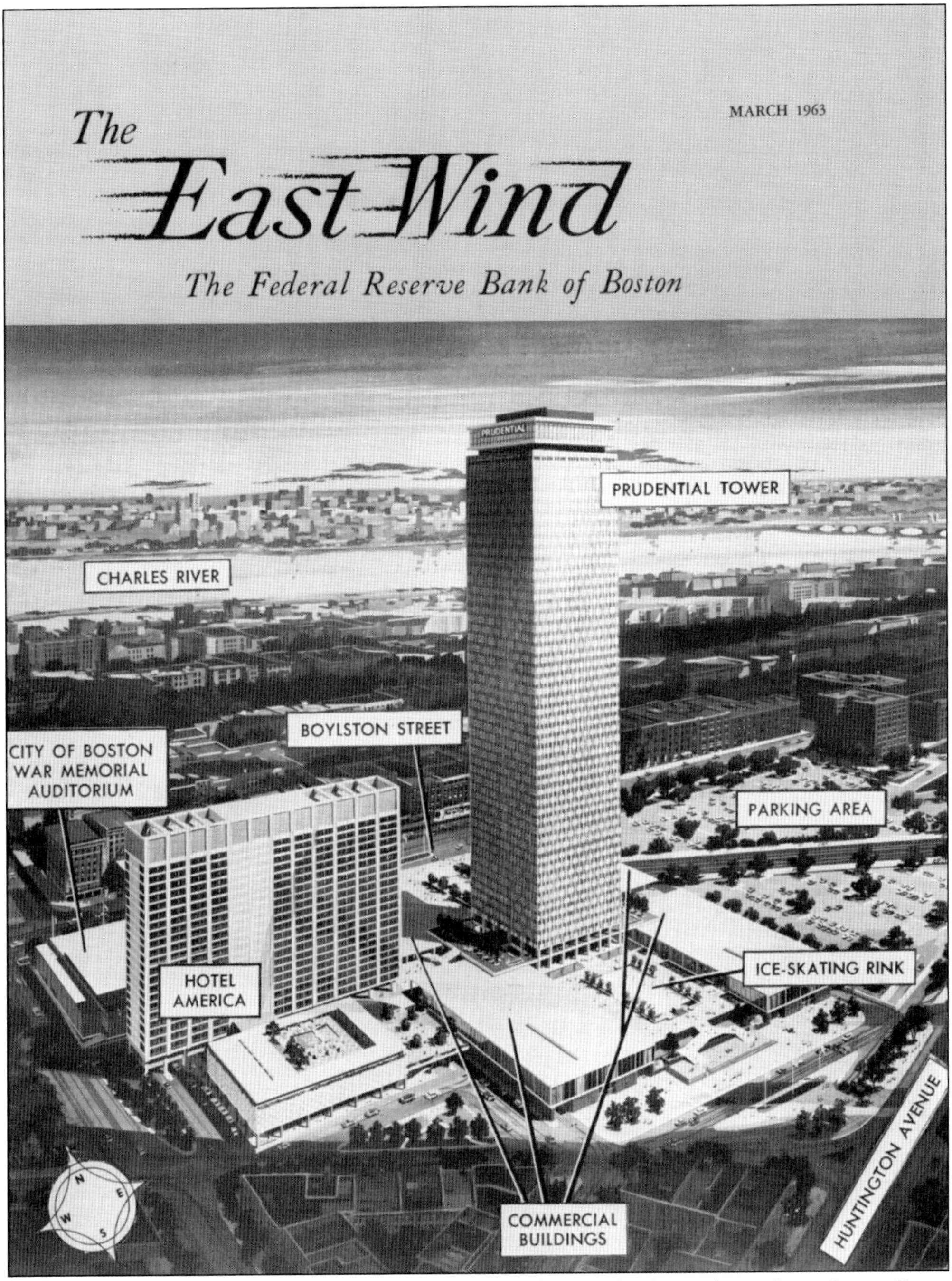

In the 1960s, the bank joined civic and business leaders in the hope that a "new Boston" was on its way. It was, but it took longer to arrive than an optimistic person might have expected. The Prudential Insurance Company's new 750-foot tower on Boylston Street was a centerpiece of the revival. In 1963, after a series of delays, construction began. The *East Wind* reported that the tower's site was "the last open area near the heart of the metropolitan city district that was suitable for a large investment center." A few years later, the Boston Fed did its part to enlarge that metropolitan center.

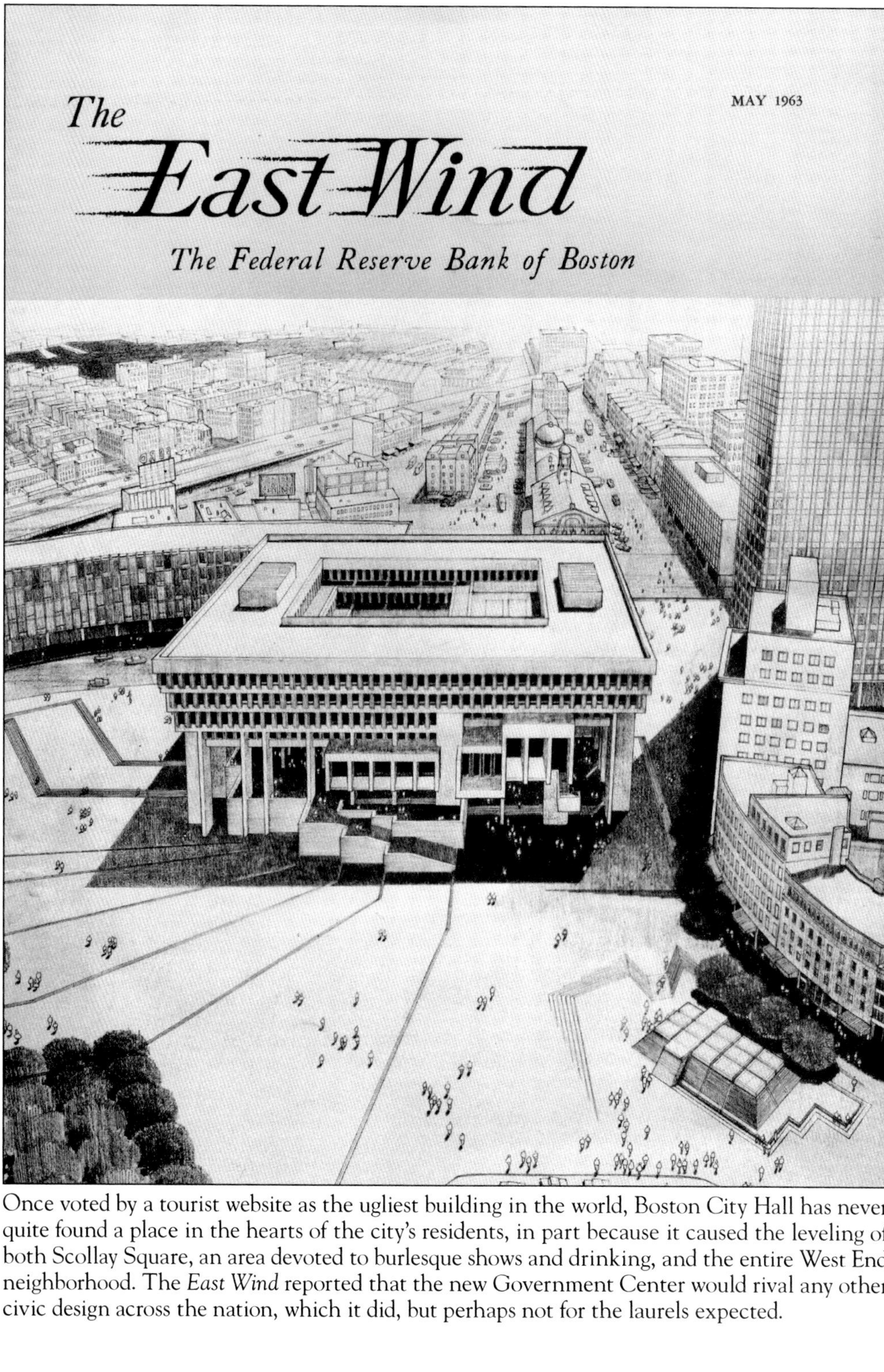

Once voted by a tourist website as the ugliest building in the world, Boston City Hall has never quite found a place in the hearts of the city's residents, in part because it caused the leveling of both Scollay Square, an area devoted to burlesque shows and drinking, and the entire West End neighborhood. The *East Wind* reported that the new Government Center would rival any other civic design across the nation, which it did, but perhaps not for the laurels expected.

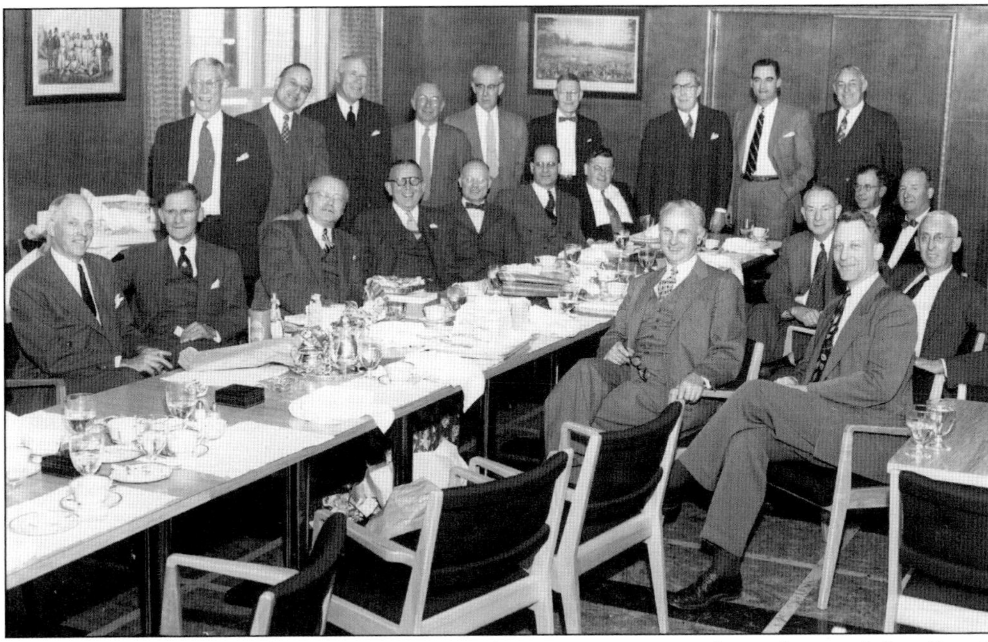

The addition included a new executive dining room, seen here during John Fogg's retirement party.

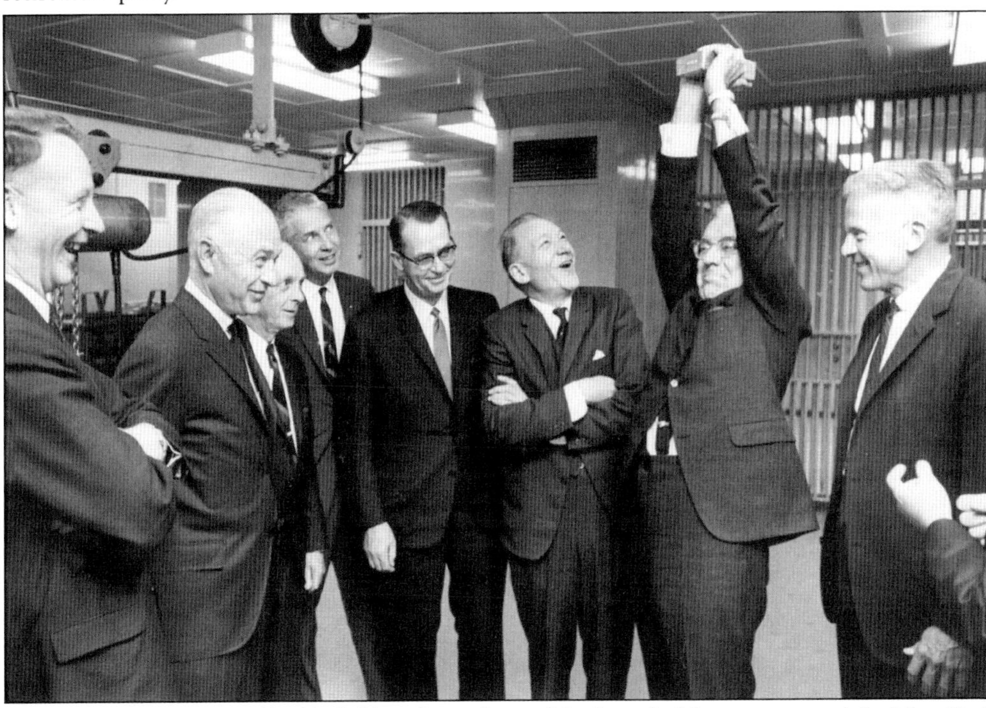

Bank president George Ellis (far left) and members of the board of directors toured the New York Fed in May 1967 because of Ellis's idea that they would benefit from a broader knowledge of the Federal Reserve System. They were particularly interested in the foreign exchange and open market operations, which were exclusive to New York. Like most visitors, however, they found the gold vault the highlight of the trip.

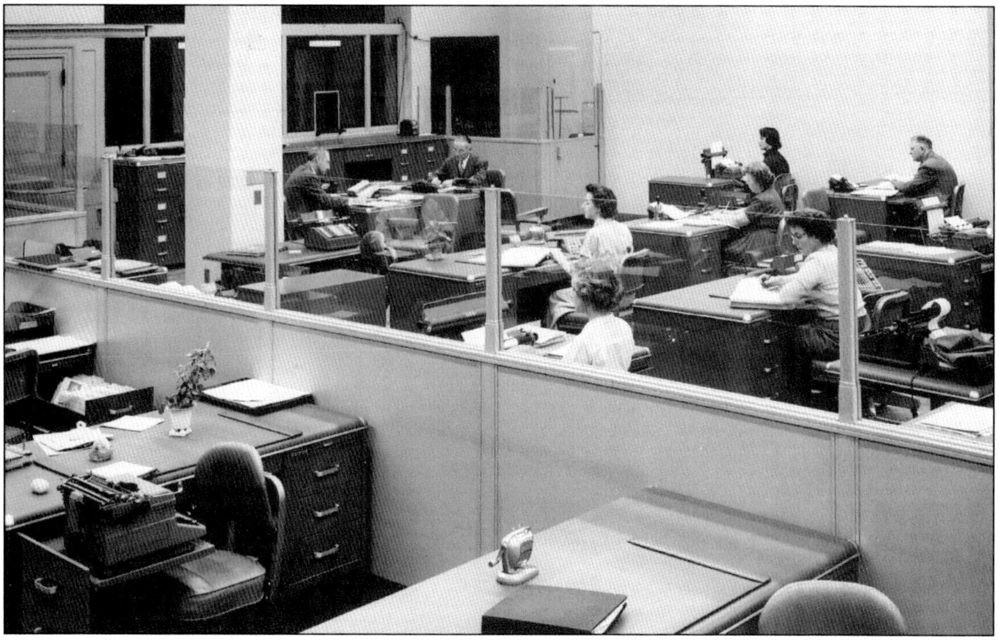

To make room for computers, the Bank Examination Department was moved to 18 Oliver Street, where Printing had temporarily been during World War II.

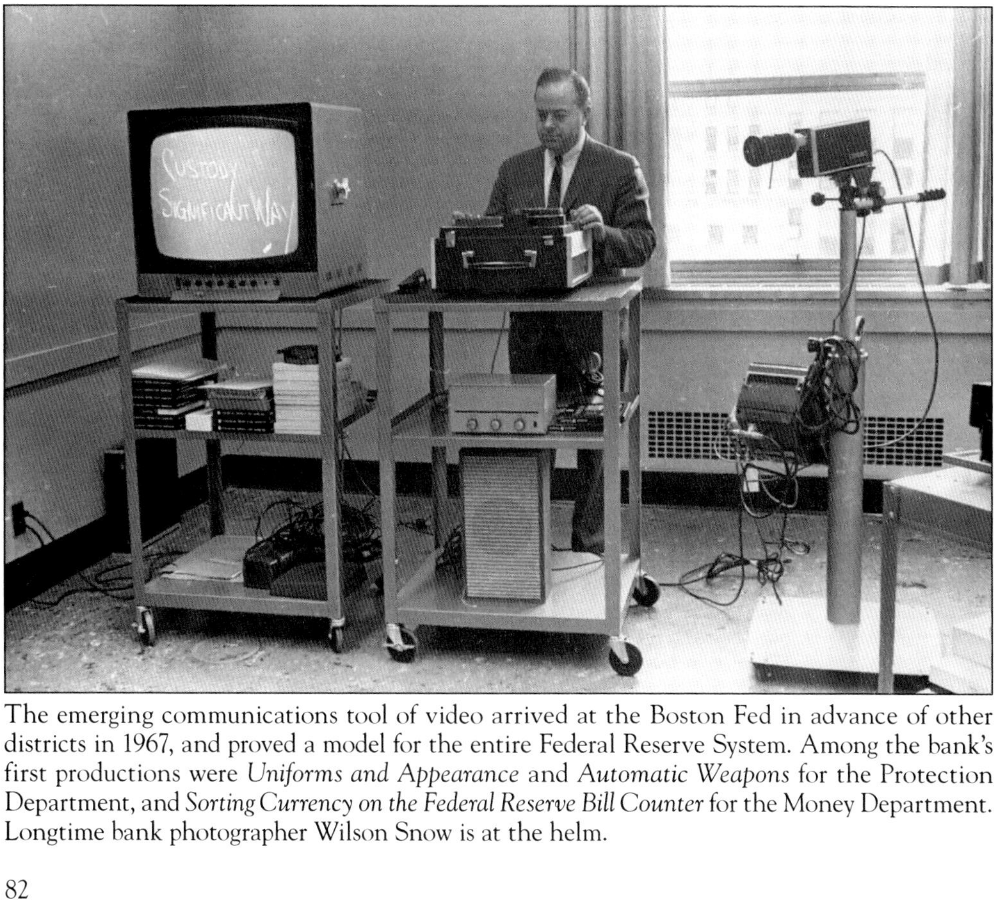

The emerging communications tool of video arrived at the Boston Fed in advance of other districts in 1967, and proved a model for the entire Federal Reserve System. Among the bank's first productions were *Uniforms and Appearance* and *Automatic Weapons* for the Protection Department, and *Sorting Currency on the Federal Reserve Bill Counter* for the Money Department. Longtime bank photographer Wilson Snow is at the helm.

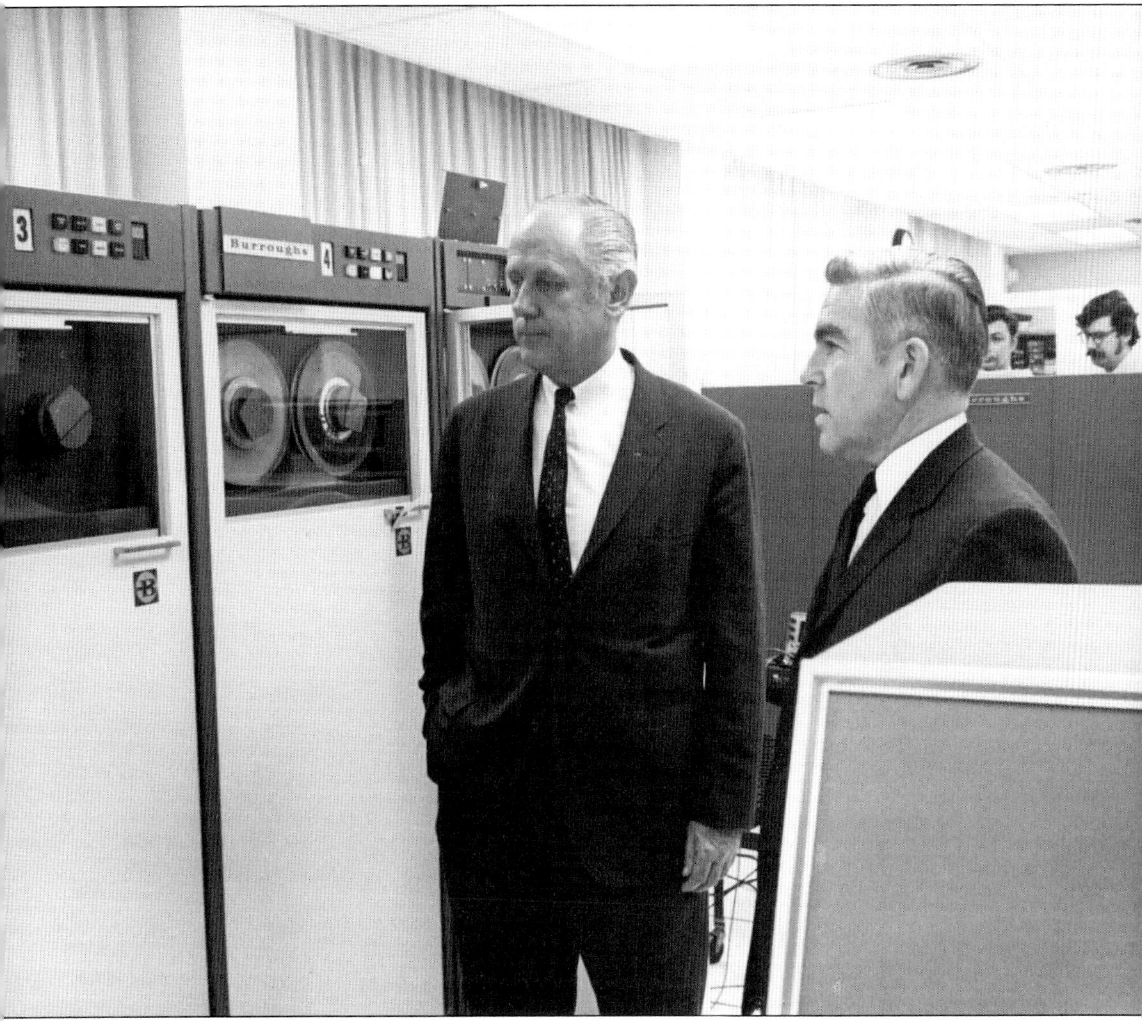

According to the *East Wind*, "the Federal Reserve Bank of Boston exemplified its forward thinking and registered a new first on January 1, 1967, with the formation of a Data Services Department." The most pressing task facing the new group was planning and selecting a new system that could process the combined work of the Data Processing 1401 and the Research 1620 then in use. The Burroughs 3500 was chosen, and installation took place almost exactly a year later, in January 1968. The B 3500 apparently inspired fierce loyalty among those who worked most closely with it, being described by one as "a gay socializer, but also a stern task master . . . However those who know him best receive the kindest treatment."

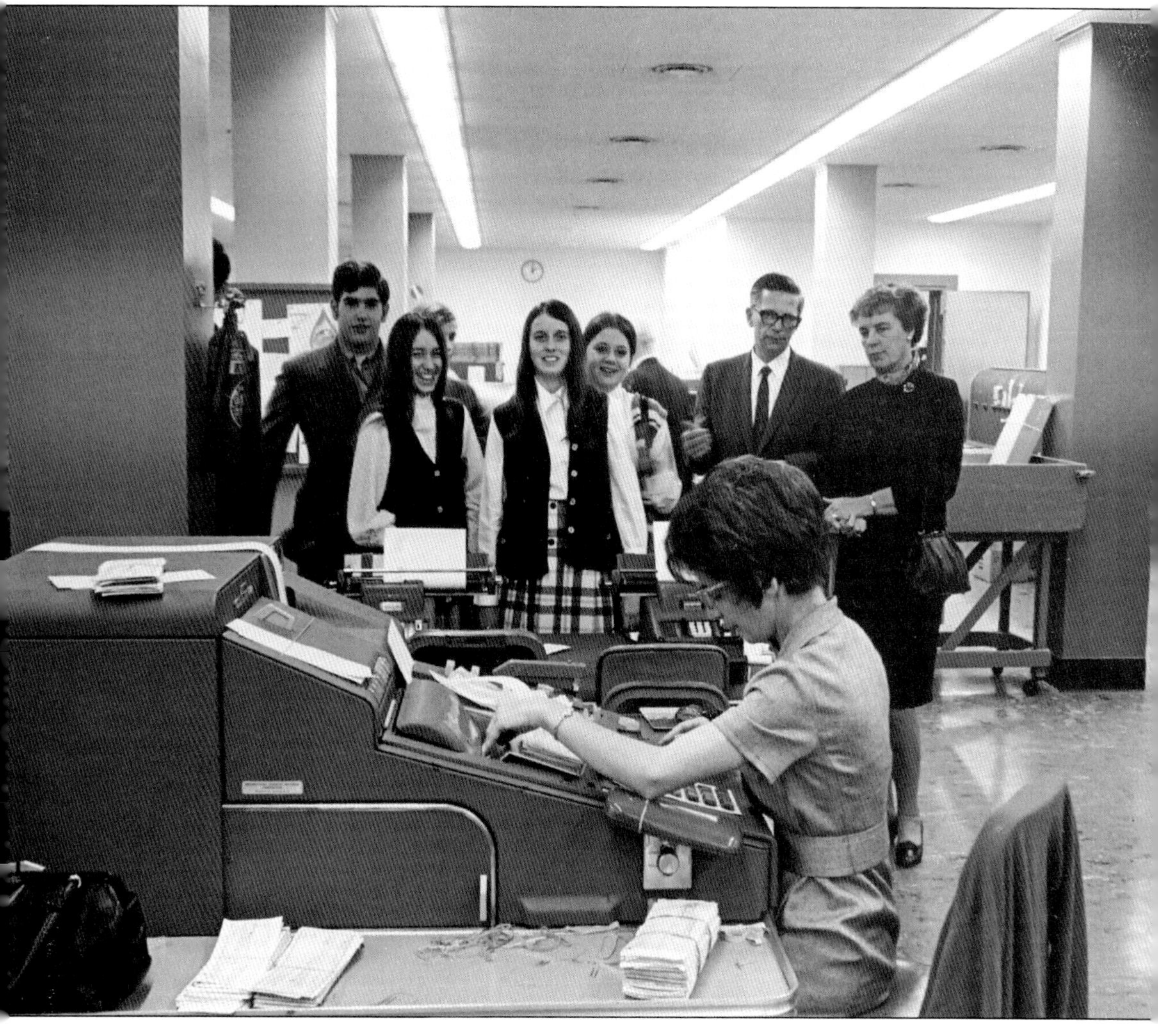

Although the bank had offered educational tours before, efforts were stepped up in the late 1960s to the extent that visitation rose by 50 percent annually for four years running. This 1969 group gets a close look at check operations, but visitors in the 1940s got an even closer look. According to the *Society Newsletter*, "The greatest thrill of all for both young and old seems to be to hold, without effort, a million dollars in ten thousand dollar bills, just 100 of them to be exact."

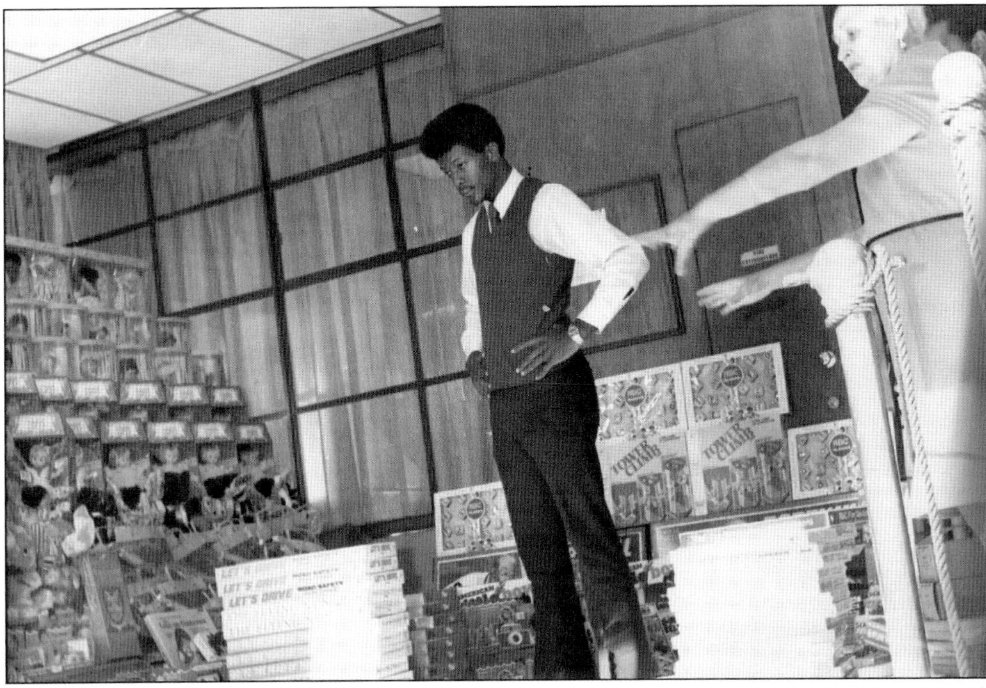

By the late 1960s, Fed employees were still generously donating toys at holiday time, but homemade doll clothes were replaced by more commercial products, possibly because fewer young women were learning to sew.

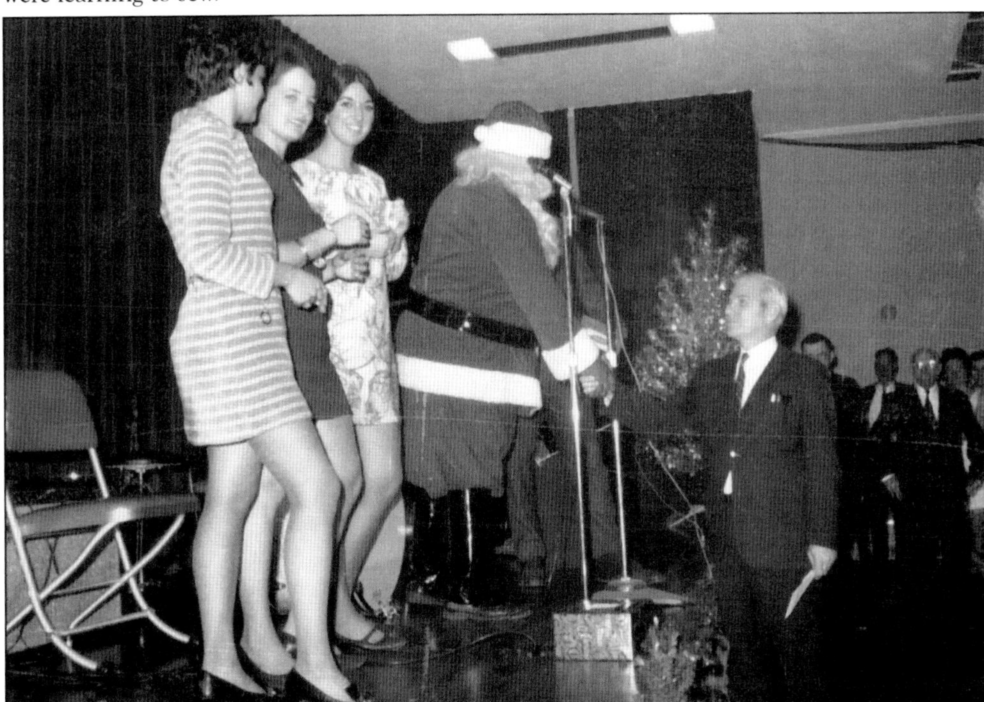

At the bank's Christmas party in 1969, door prizes included a cassette tape recorder, a transistor radio, an instamatic camera, and an AM-FM clock radio.

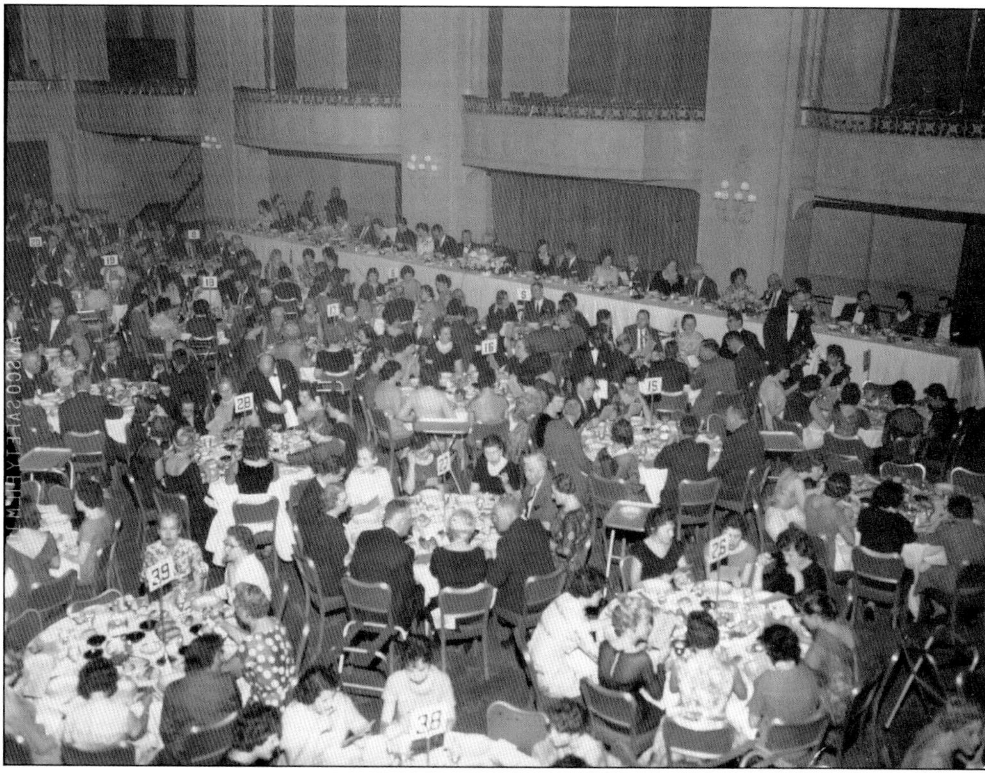

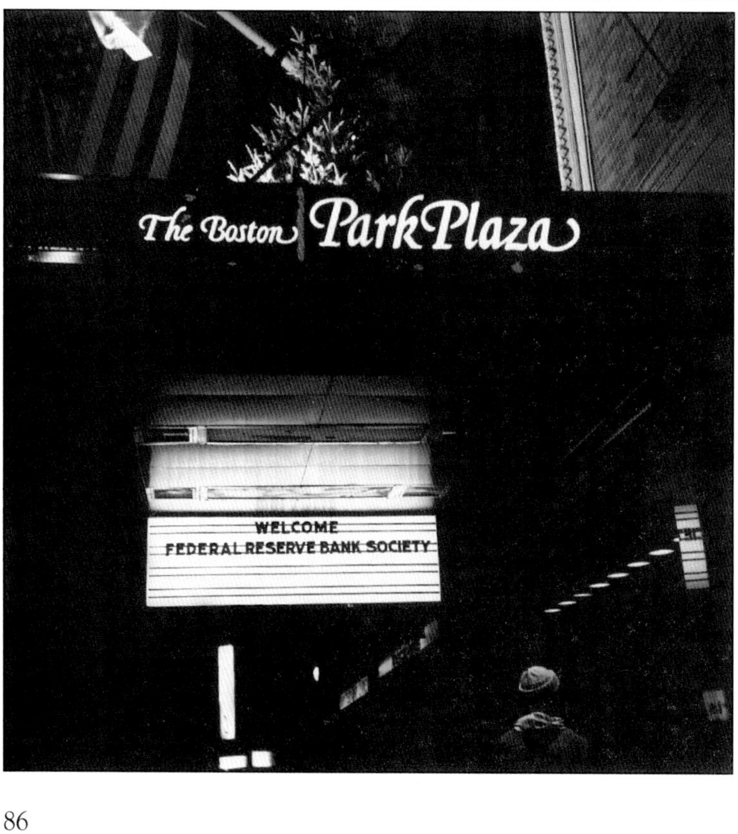

The Federal Reserve Society's annual banquet continued to draw crowds of highly fashionable Fed employees. The 1960 event (above) was held at the Hotel Statler, which later became the Boston Park Plaza.

Six

A New Fed for a New Boston

The 1970s opened with the bank facing a familiar problem: an operation that had vastly outgrown its physical space. Few people with a good memory will look back upon the decade as one of the high points in Boston's history: The school busing controversy had polarized residents, tough economic times had hit New England harder than other areas of the country, the urban renewal projects of the 1950s and 1960s had failed to renew much of anything, and the city seemed on a path of slow decline.

No single institution can claim credit for halting the slide, but the Boston Fed contributed its share with the construction of its new headquarters on the fringe of the Financial District at Fort Point Channel. Frank Morris had assumed the Boston Fed presidency in 1968 and had steadily and discreetly—or as discreetly as is possible in a city that likes to talk—put together the largest private purchase of real estate in downtown Boston's history: a six-acre site bounded by Atlantic and Dorchester Avenues and Summer and Congress Streets. By the time the first public announcement of the bank's plans was made, it was already a fait accompli.

The new building was the most obvious of the changes going on at the Fed, but not the only one. As the workforce slowly but steadily became more diverse, so too did the board of directors, as the first minority and female directors took their places. New legislation and regulations such as the Home Mortgage Disclosure Act, the Community Reinvestment Act, and the Humphrey-Hawkins Act shaped the way the entire Federal Reserve System worked in fundamental ways and expanded its responsibilities.

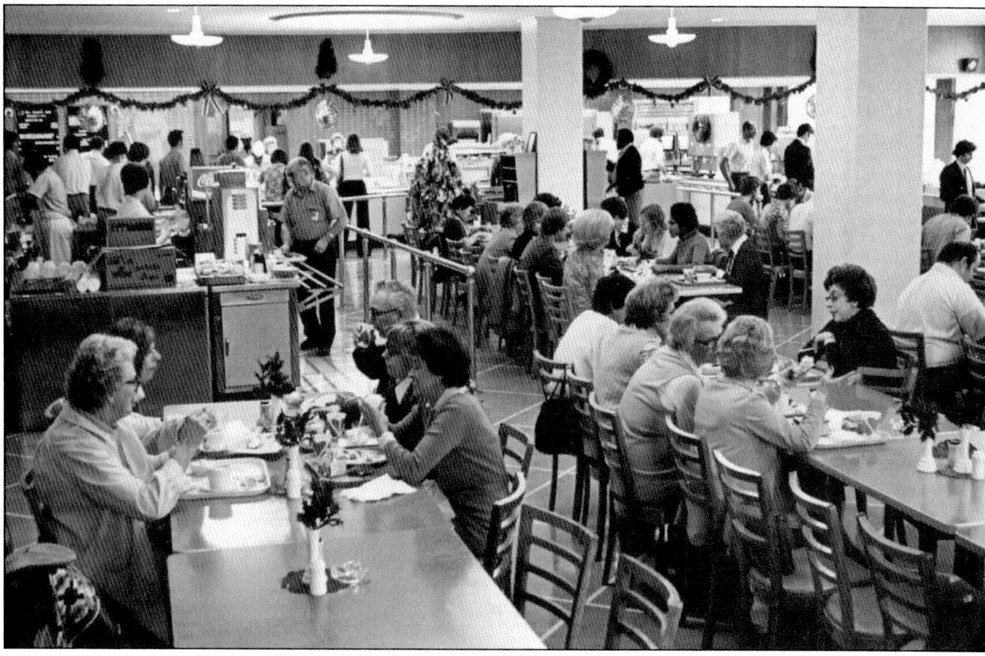

The cafeteria at Pearl Street was showing its age by the 1970s. It was still doing a brisk business, but, most likely, no one was singing its praises at quite the level of their counterparts in 1923, who were delighted by the concept of an "all-electric" kitchen.

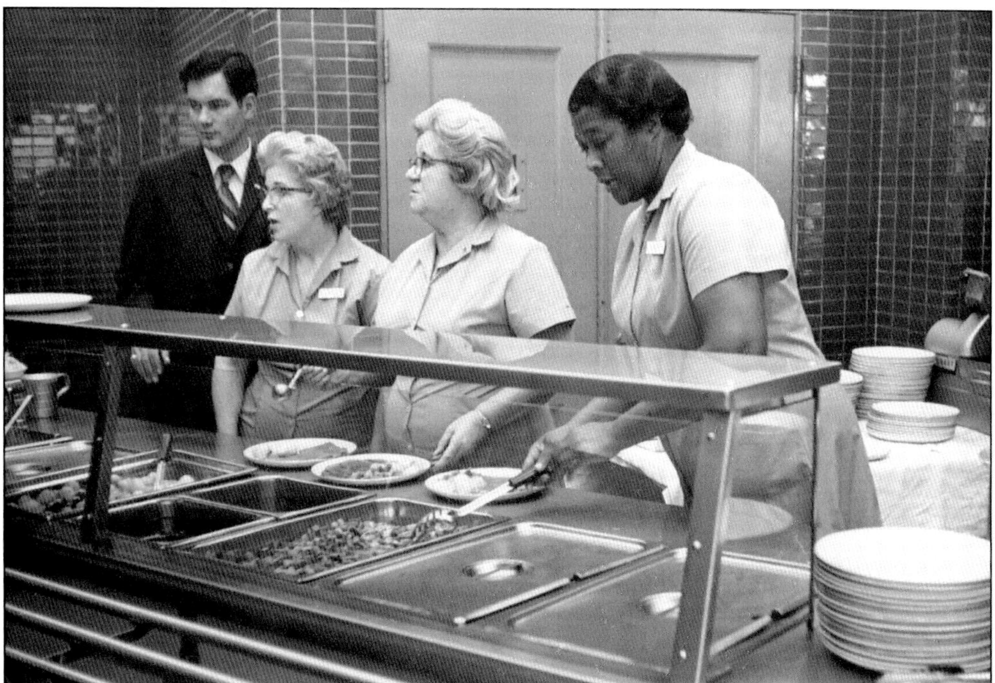

Cafeteria staff prepare for the annual stockholders' meeting in 1971. In reporting the event, the *East Wind* felt compelled to inform its readers that "stockholders are people, too!" Surely there cannot have been much confusion on that point.

The six-acre site where the new Fed would rise up was not necessarily the most prepossessing parcel in the city. A proposed plan to reinvigorate South Station, across Summer Street, into a "modern transportation hub" was going nowhere fast; warehouses—some occupied, some not—were the main tenants of the area; and the Central Artery/Interstate 93, one of the most maligned stretches of road in America, was mere yards from the proposed front door. (Courtesy of Aerial Photographs of New England.)

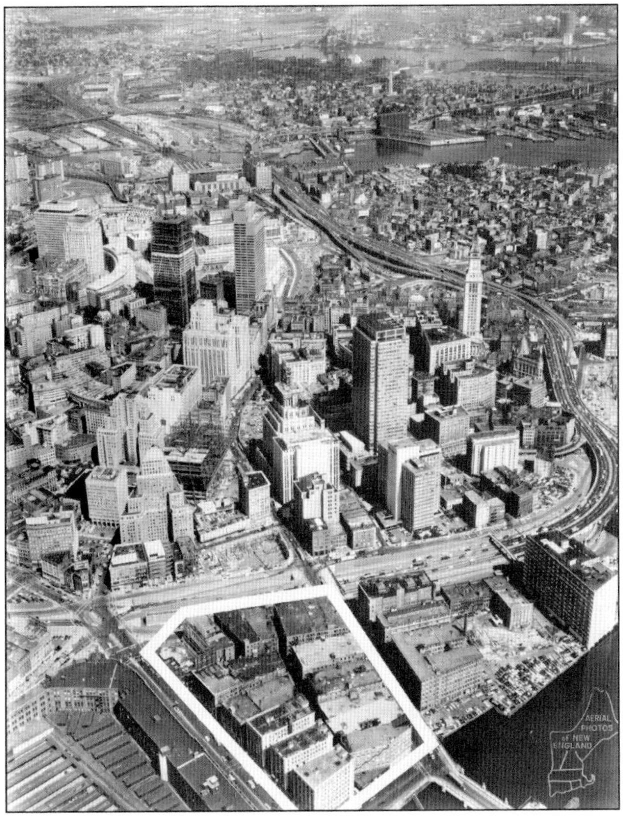

"New Fed Project on Schedule" proclaimed a headline in the *East Wind* in April 1970. To the surprise of no one, it did not stay that way.

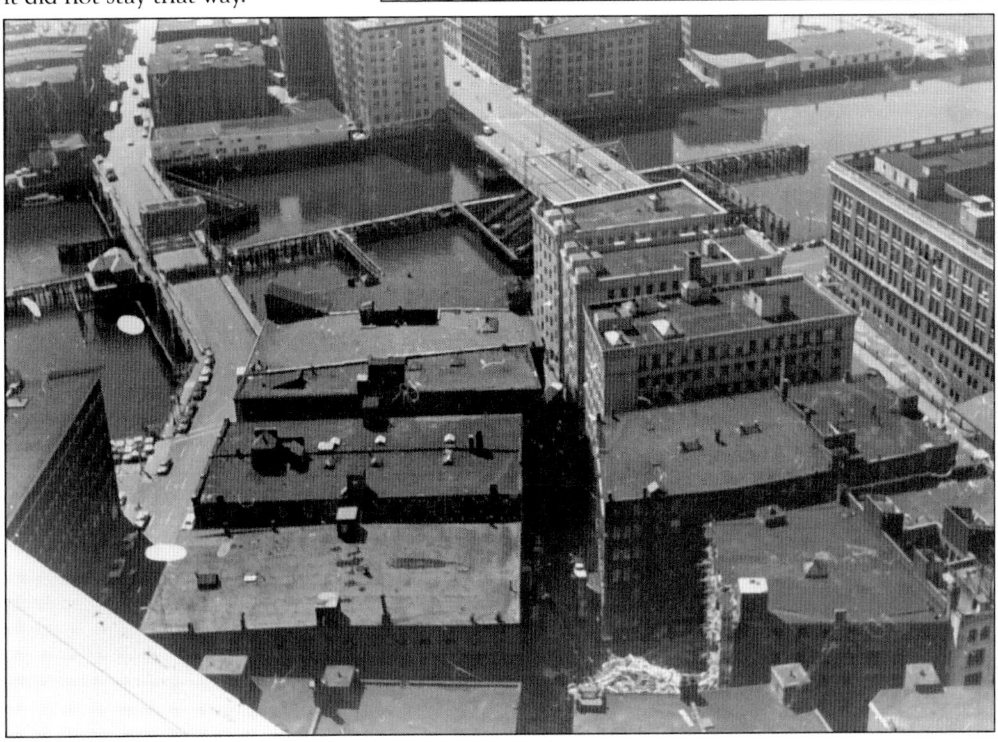

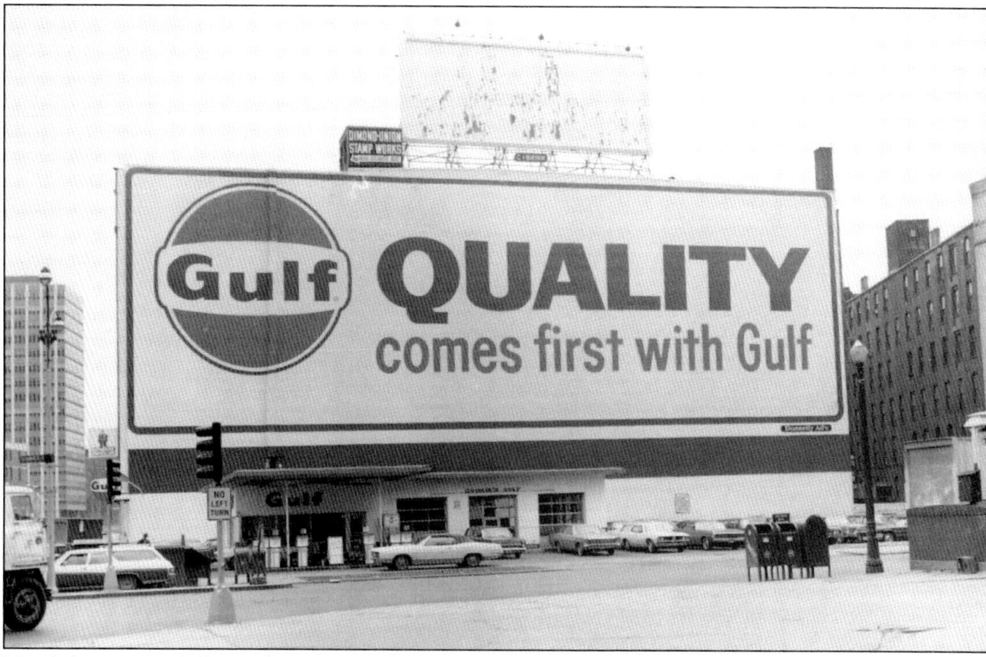

If it did not exactly have the same cachet as Kenmore Square's Citgo sign, the huge Gulf Oil sign at the corner of Atlantic Avenue and Summer Street was still a well-known Boston landmark. It was set to be the first to fall when demolition began. It stood in the exact spot now occupied by Federal Reserve Plaza.

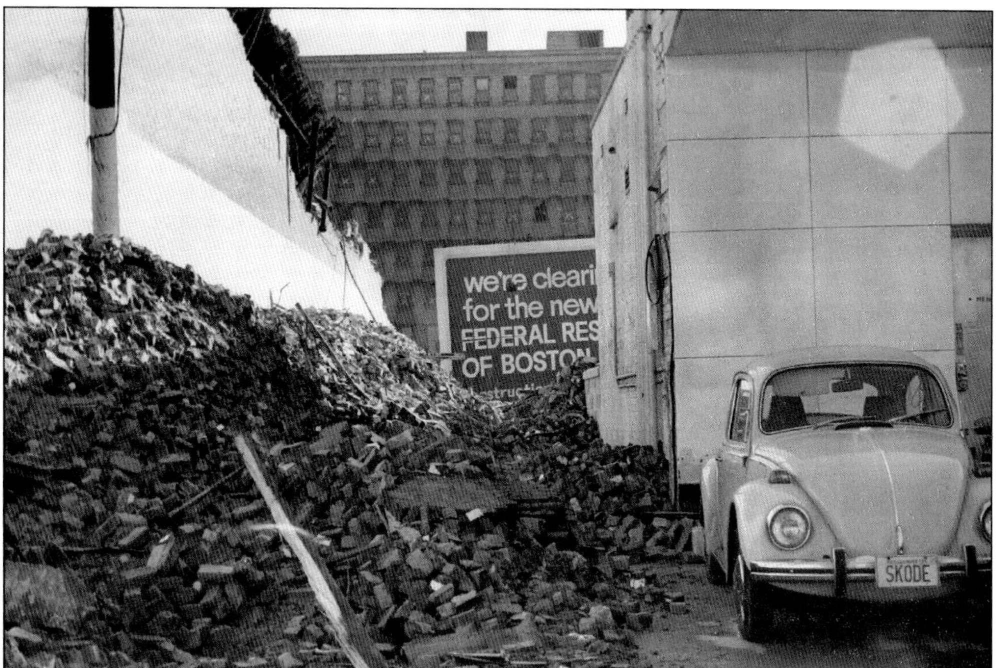

Demolition began in June 1971 at a ceremony attended by local government officials and a sizeable crowd of interested onlookers. The public affair was mainly ceremonial, as Cleveland Wrecking Company had already begun demolition work on the interior.

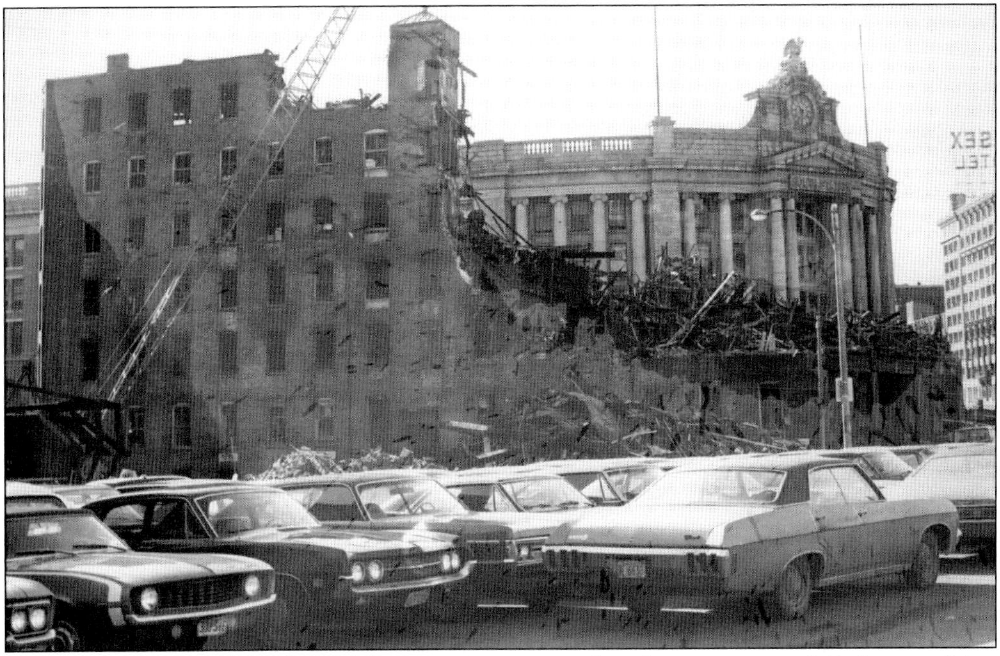

South Station appeared to be standing in a war zone as demolition progressed. Perhaps nothing is more astonishing, however, than the presence of parking spaces on Atlantic Avenue.

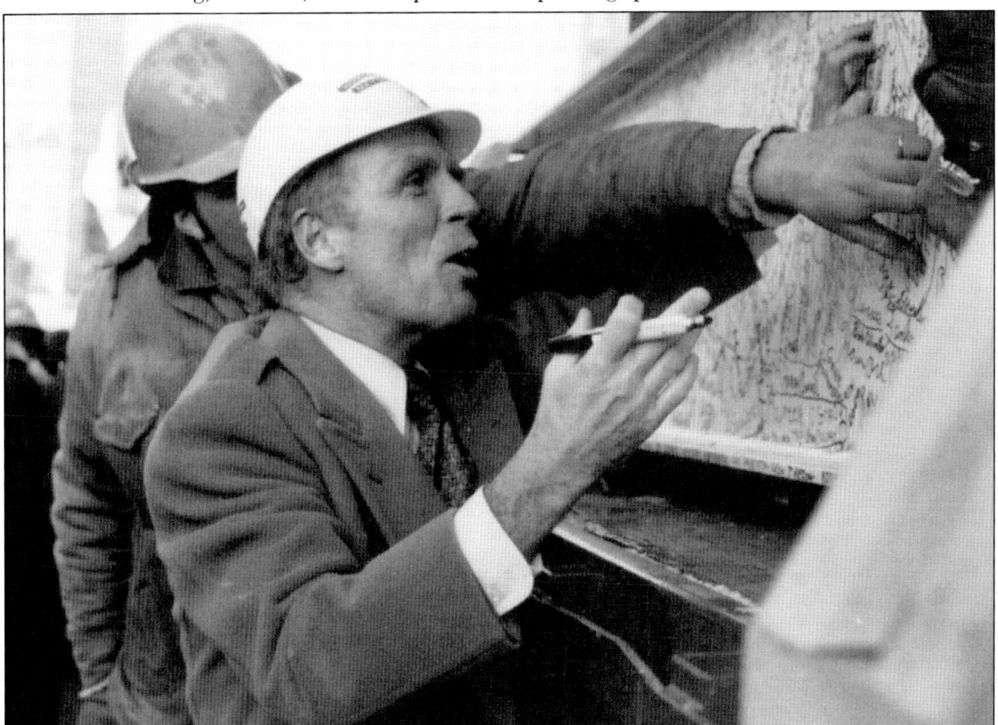

The topping-off ceremony—the placement of the highest point on the building—was another occasion for a public ceremony. Invited dignitaries included Boston mayor Kevin White, who signed one of the steel interior beams, as did the entire bank staff and construction crew.

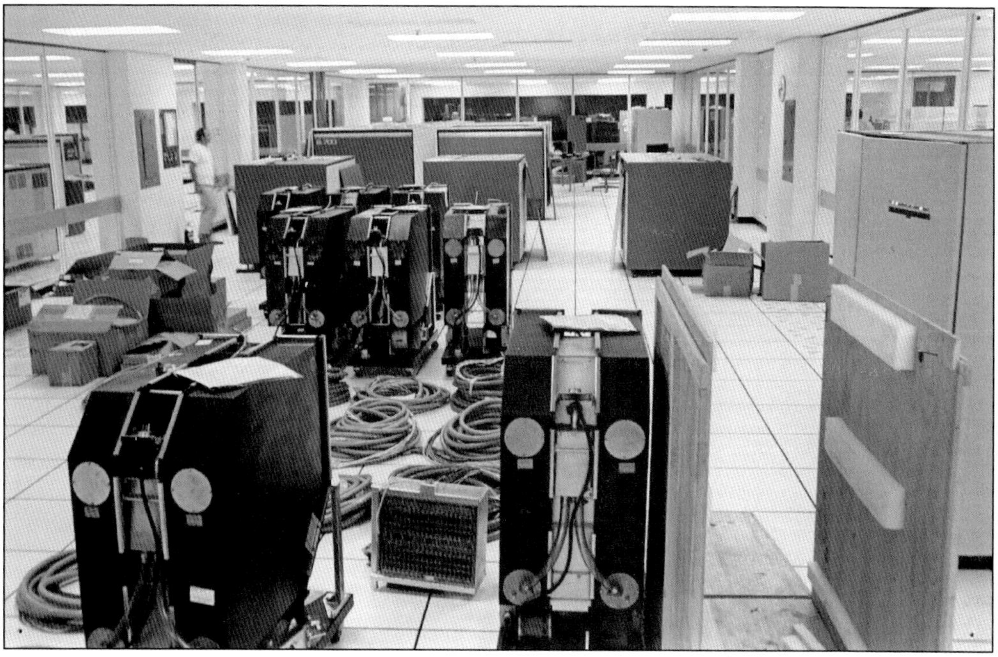

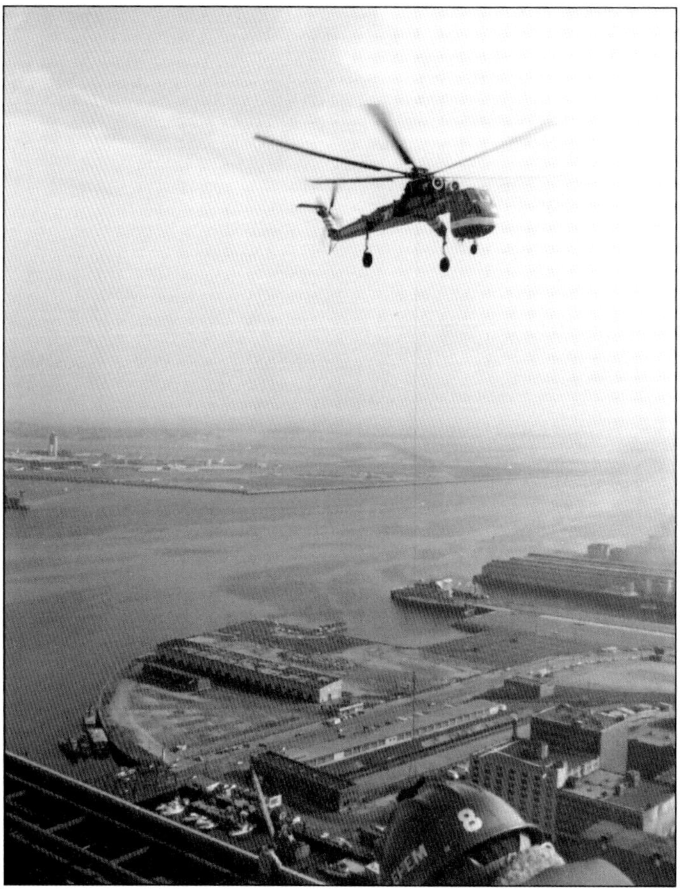

The lack of space for computer operations was one of the driving forces behind the new building. By May 1976, the second and third floors of the secure wing were complete and computer installation was underway.

This sky crane helicopter, one of only eight then in use in the country, made 21 lifts to hoist window-washing and cleaning apparatus into place on the tower roof. The mammoth machine had 35-foot-long rotor blades and the capability to lift up to 20,000 pounds.

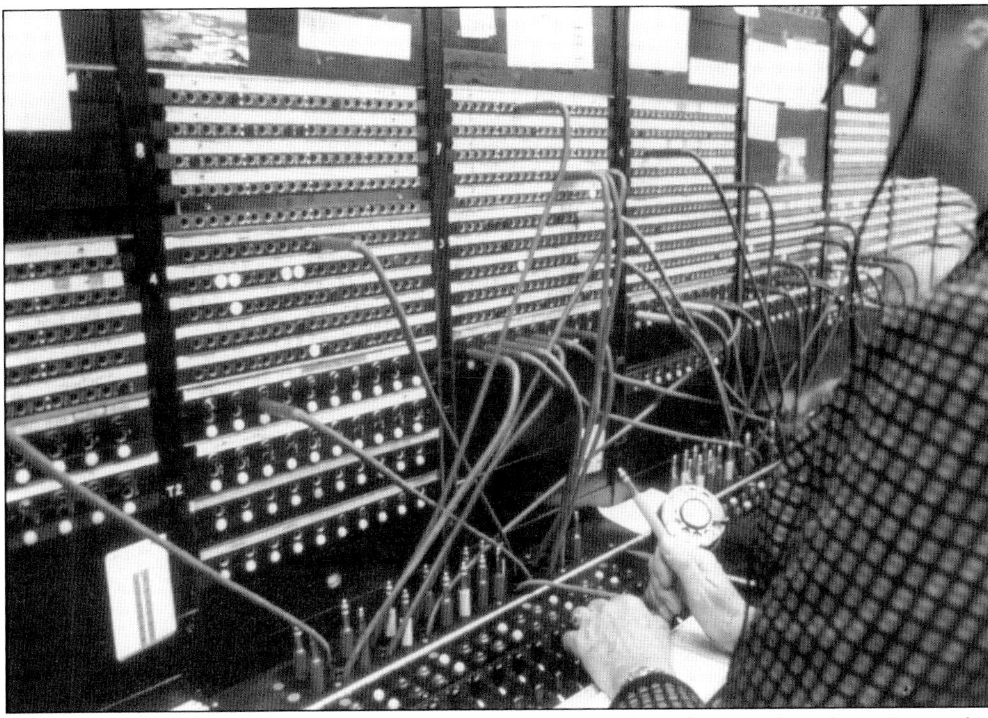

Progress on the construction was updated regularly on employee bulletin boards. In September 1975, the focus was on telephone systems: "Today—all calls coming into the Bank have to go through the switchboard operators who are required to transfer all your calls."

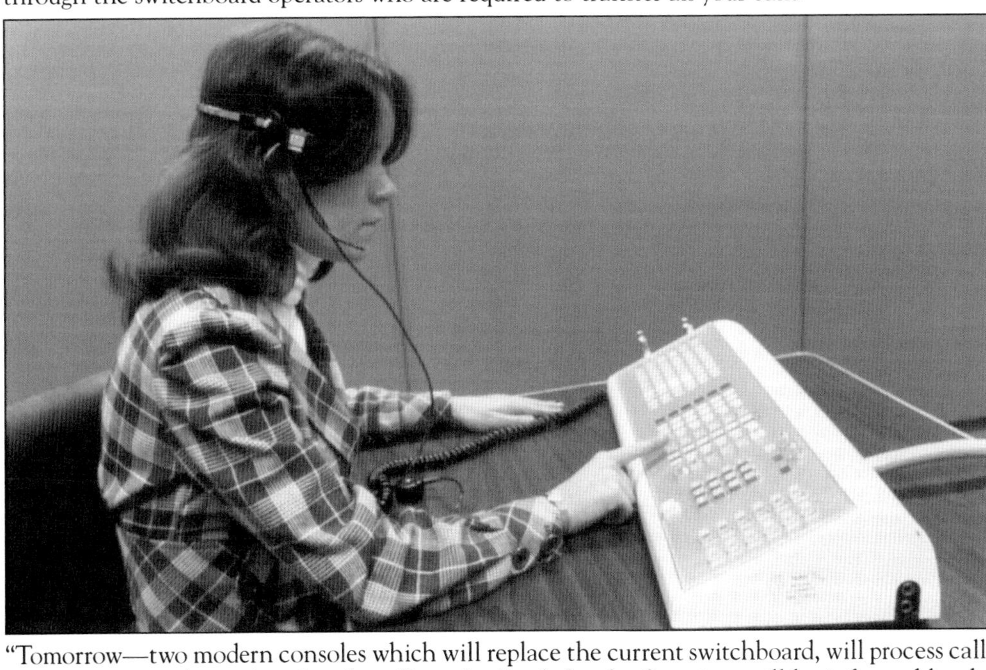

"Tomorrow—two modern consoles which will replace the current switchboard, will process calls to the main Bank number. People calling the Bank for the first time will be informed by the console operator of your CENTREX number so that the caller may dial direct the next time he wishes to reach you."

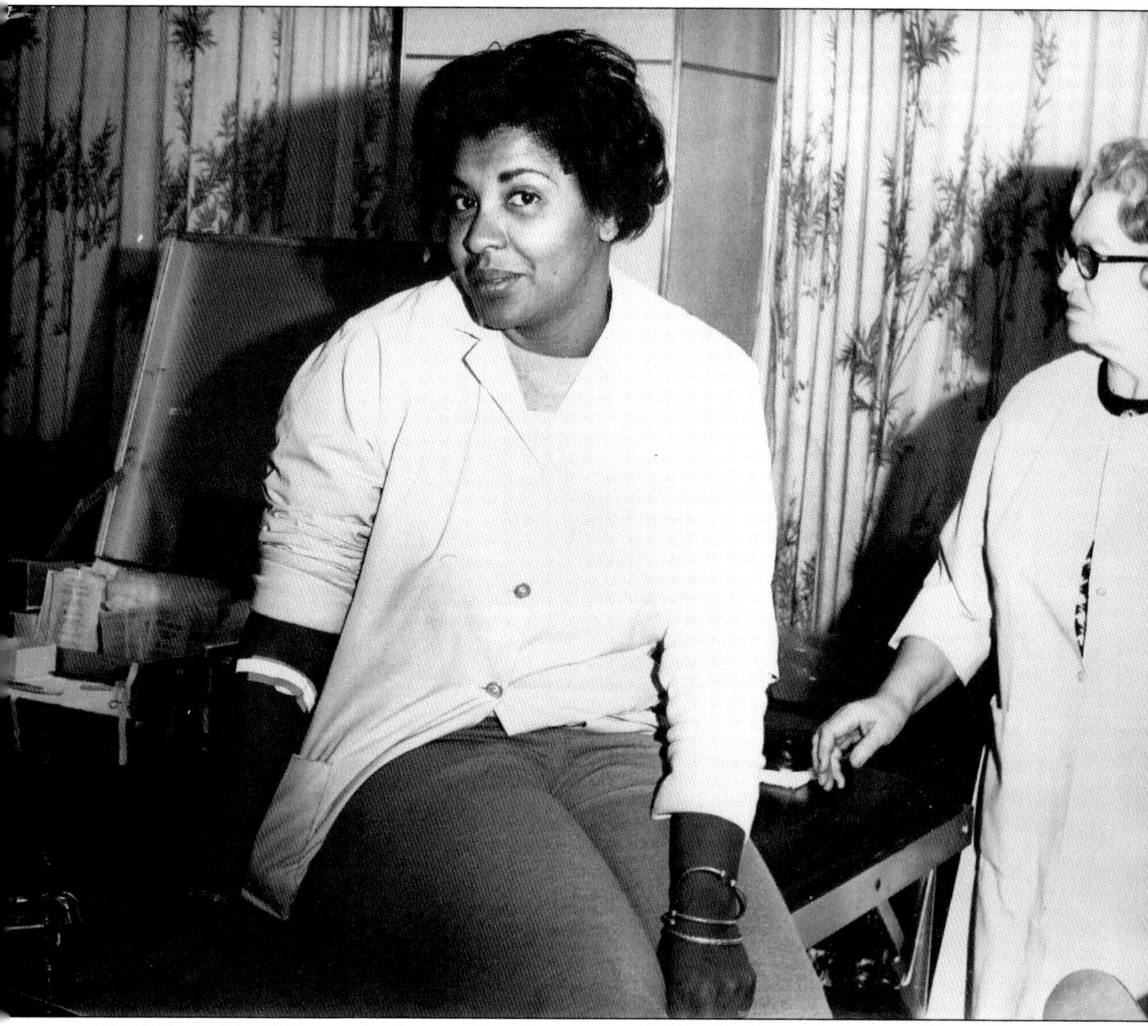

Red Cross blood drives also have a long history at the bank, where they were first instituted in the 1950s and continue to be held regularly today. Over 30 employees volunteered for the event in 1971, when this photograph was taken.

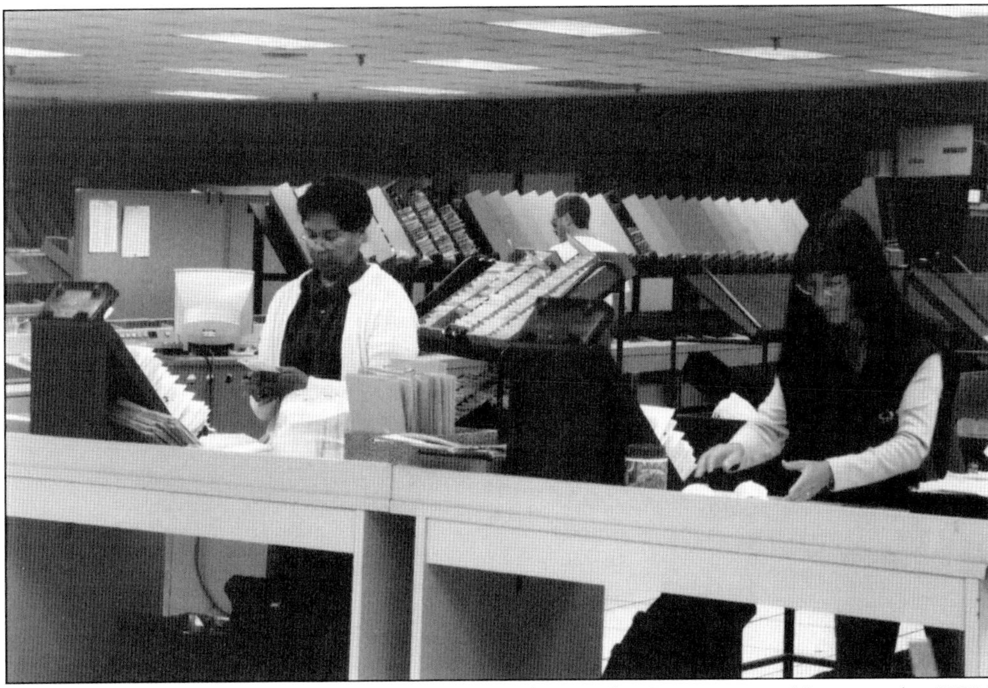

Two regional check-processing centers, one in Windsor Locks, Connecticut, (above, in the 1990s) and one in Lewiston, Maine, were opened in the early 1970s to manage the high volume of checks needing clearance in the New England region. By the late 1990s–early 2000s, electronic payments had overtaken paper checks to such a degree that the centers were closed—Lewiston in 1997 and Windsor Locks in 2009—and check processing for the entire system was moved to the Cleveland Fed.

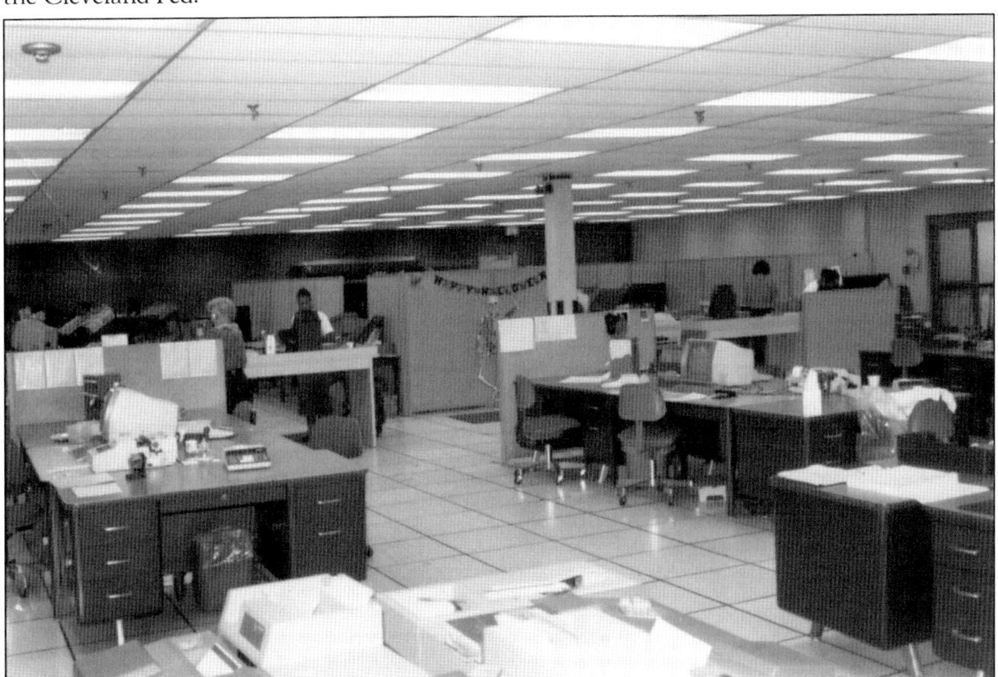

the LEDGER

Economic Education Newsletter

Banking Nickel by Nickel

Imaginative teachers emerge in every generation. Consider Alphonso Tarr, a teacher at Lynn English High School, Lynn, MA. His innovative programs would meet the highest standards of educators today, but he was teaching two generations ago.

In 1914, with the sponsorship of the Commercial Department, a student-run savings bank opened at Lynn English High School. Its purpose was to provide bookkeeping practice for juniors and seniors in the Commercial Course. Committed to the belief that high school prepares its students to survive in the adult world, Alphonso Tarr saw broader possibilities for the bank. He transformed the pilot project into a central activity for teaching self-sufficiency to the entire student body.

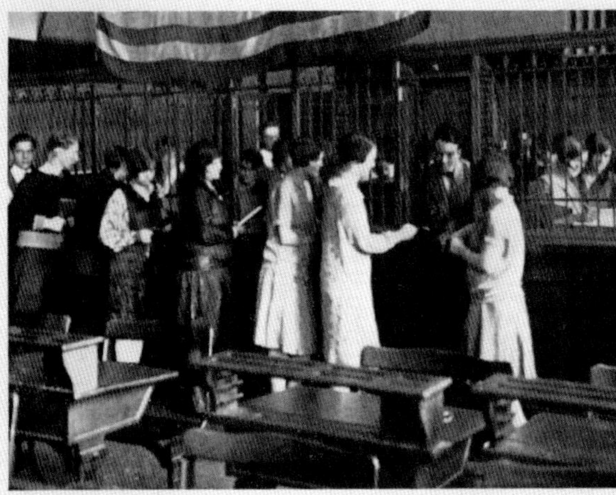

At the Teller's Cage 1928 Courtesy, Lynn Public Library; *The Red and Gray*

Under Tarr's direction, the Lynn English High School Savings Bank grew from its initial 221 depositors in 1914 to 1774 depositors at its height in 1927. Total deposits swelled from $1250 to over $17,000. Such growth is dramatic in light of the comparatively low student wages and allowances of the era. Birthday and Christmas money always helped fill the coffer, but the bulk of bank funds came from conscientious saving of small sums.

By its fourth year of operation, Lynn English's Bank was a large, well-organized institution. Students deposited their money at the teller's cage, located in the rear of the Bookkeeping Room, before and after school, or during the 15-minute period in the school day allotted for bank business. Deposits were transferred daily to Lynn Institution for Savings (now First East Savings Bank). As deposits grew, affiliation with Lynn Institution for Savings minimized the potential security problems of keeping large amounts of cash on school property.

At the project's peak, over 300 students were balancing bank books, writing financial reports, or collecting funds in each homeroom when the teller's cage was overburdened.

Alphonso Tarr was, in some ways, a behaviorist. To him, saving lump sums, no matter how large, was unimportant compared to developing the habit of saving patiently and predictably. He believed saving should become a ritual as natural as "parting one's hair a certain way." Although the bank accepted Christmas and birthday windfalls, students were encouraged to save as little as 5¢ at a time, week after week.

Continued on page 3

Federal Reserve Bank of Boston Vol.4, No.4 · Nov. 1977

In the 1970s, the bank made a concerted effort to increase its efforts in the area of economic education. The *Ledger*, a newsletter compilation of economic education news and resources, was published by the bank and the Public Information Center beginning in 1974 and then periodically through the mid-1980s.

In the summer of 1978, two three-day workshops were held for middle school and high school teachers from throughout New England. Each session covered three major areas: money, banking, and the Federal Reserve; consumer issues; and economic education.

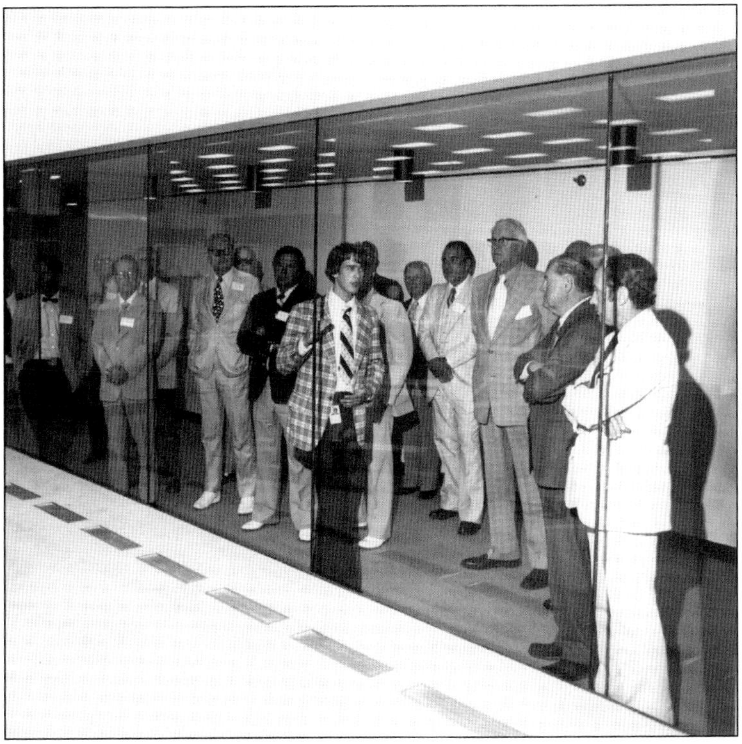

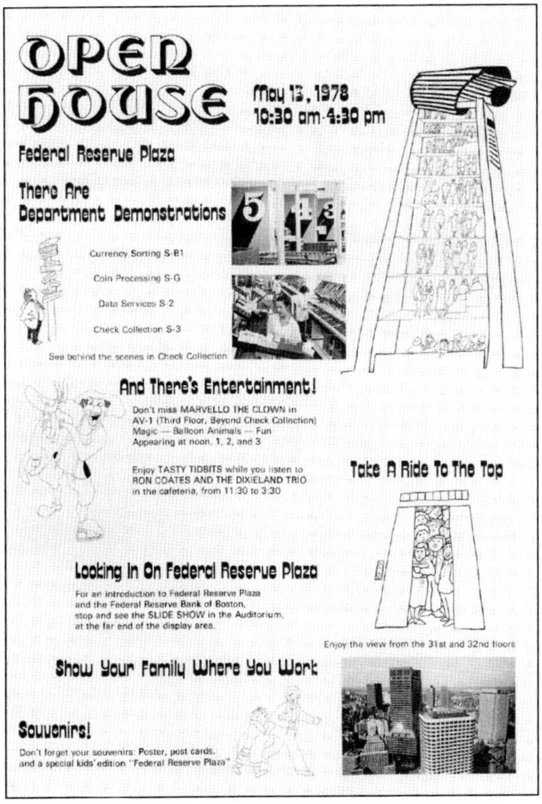

A gala open house was planned for employees, family, and guests on February 11, 1978. Readers of a certain age will recognize the date as perfectly coinciding with the legendary Blizzard of '78. Fearless and doughty though Fed employees may be, most respected the governor's request that they stay off the highways. Staff who found themselves stranded at the bank worked around-the-clock to keep all essential services up and running. The celebration was moved to the more weather-friendly month of May.

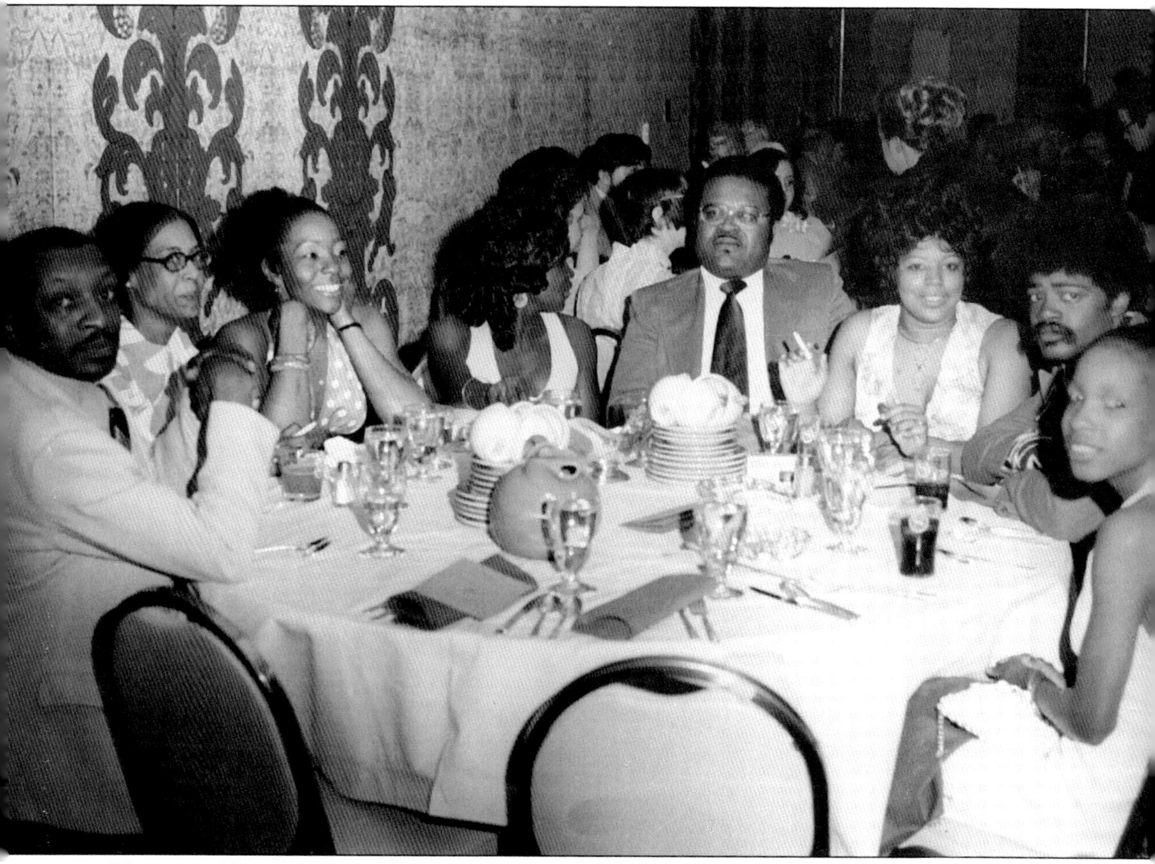

The annual banquet moved seamlessly into the disco era in the 1970s, as evidenced by this group of well-dressed employees.

Seven

Expanding Technologies

The 1980s saw the Fed's role expanding on several fronts, mostly as a result of the passage of the Monetary Control Act (MCA) of 1980. The legislation brought significant changes to the Federal Reserve System by requiring all depository institutions to hold reserves at the Fed, whether they were members or not, and that the Fed begin pricing its services and making the discount window available to all depository institutions.

The expanded role impacted nearly every aspect of the bank's operations. The Accounting and Research Departments, and the Statistics Division in particular, saw a vast increase in the number of institutions now reporting submitting weekly reports on conditions and reserves. Over 800 institutions were now, whereas only 170 members had previously done so. With the Fed now pricing its services, they needed to be made an attractive value. Bank Services was charged with marketing something that had previously been provided at no cost, a requirement that called for careful examination of those services to maximize efficiency and value for the consumer. The Loan and Credit Department was perhaps the most widely impacted at the bank, as the number of institutions now able to use the services of the discount window increased dramatically.

Elsewhere, the bank took a leadership role in developing check imaging technology and standards; developing Fedwire, the first standardized depository institution network; and continuing to supply operational support to the Automated Clearing House (ACH), which had begun in the 1970s. On the technology front, Data Systems engineered the switch from the old Burroughs computer to an IBM environment as part of a system-wide effort to standardize computer applications.

The 1980s were generally a time of economic growth in New England, fueled in a large part by the growth of the high-technology sector, but cracks were showing by the end of the decade—cracks that disproportionately impacted the region compared to the nation as a whole.

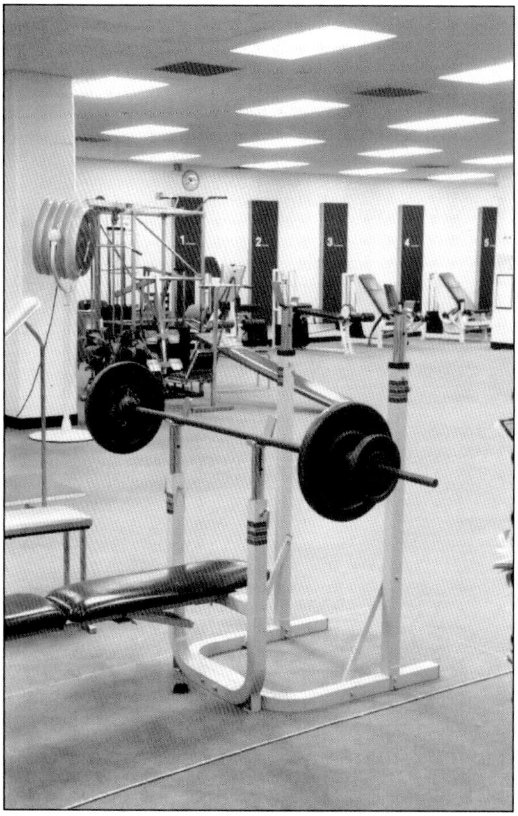

A fitness center that was open 24 hours a day and seven days a week for employees and tenants made its debut in April 1980. The facilities included stationary bikes, treadmills, dumbbells, wall-mounted pulleys, and a punching bag, among other equipment. The center has been regularly updated over the years and now includes group exercise classes and nutritional counseling as well.

The Federal Reserve Society remained active, sponsoring summer outings in addition to the annual banquets. About 500 people attended the 1980 event (pictured), which took place at Camp Bournedale in Plymouth. A softball game between officers and staff ended in a 14-10 officers' victory. In other softball news, Coin 1 beat out the Protection Department for the Bank League championship.

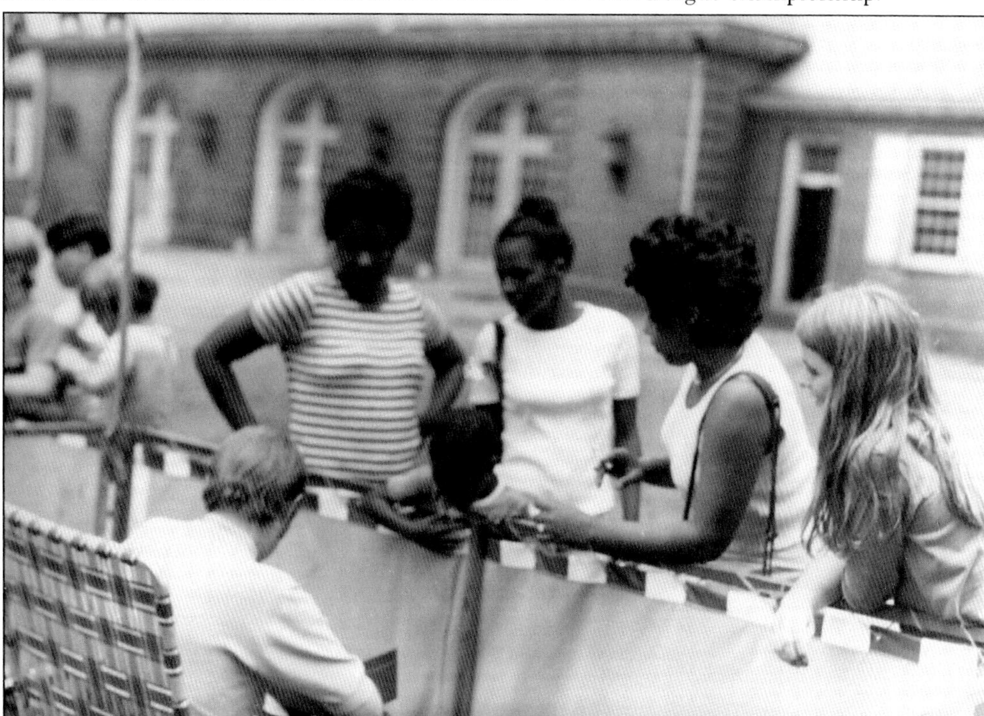

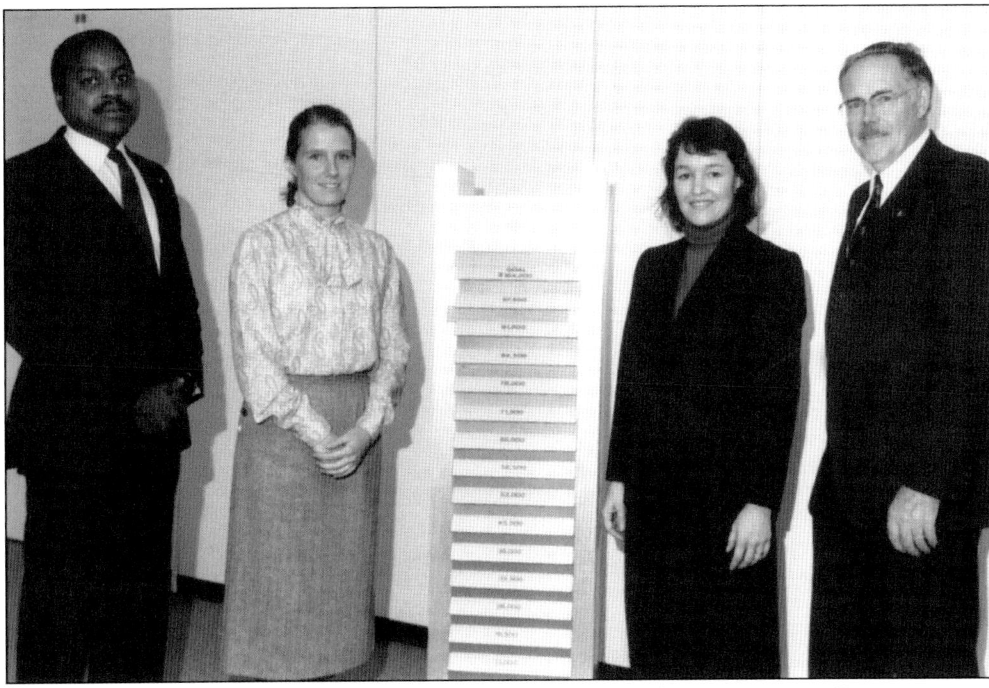

A model of the bank made a handy barometer for 1982's United Way campaign. Donations were through the roof, as the contributions exceeded the goal of $85,000. In each year of participation, the goal has been met or exceeded.

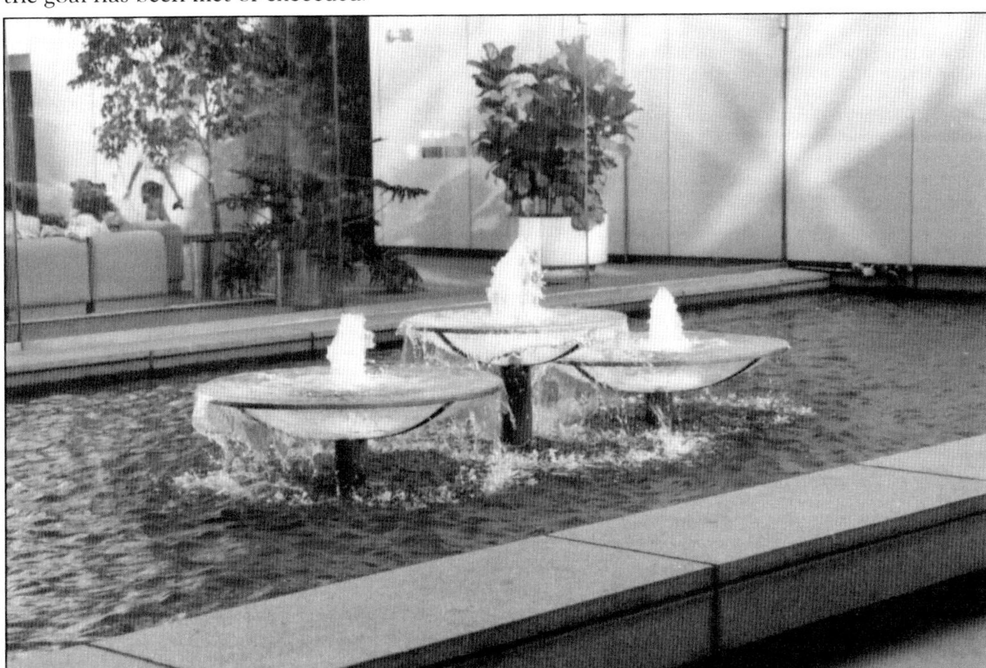

The inner courtyard once featured this dramatic reflecting pool, which was viewable from the lobby. In 1988, the Frank Sellner–designed fountain was added, which received an award from the Boston Society of Landscape Architects. Security concerns eventually forced its dismantling.

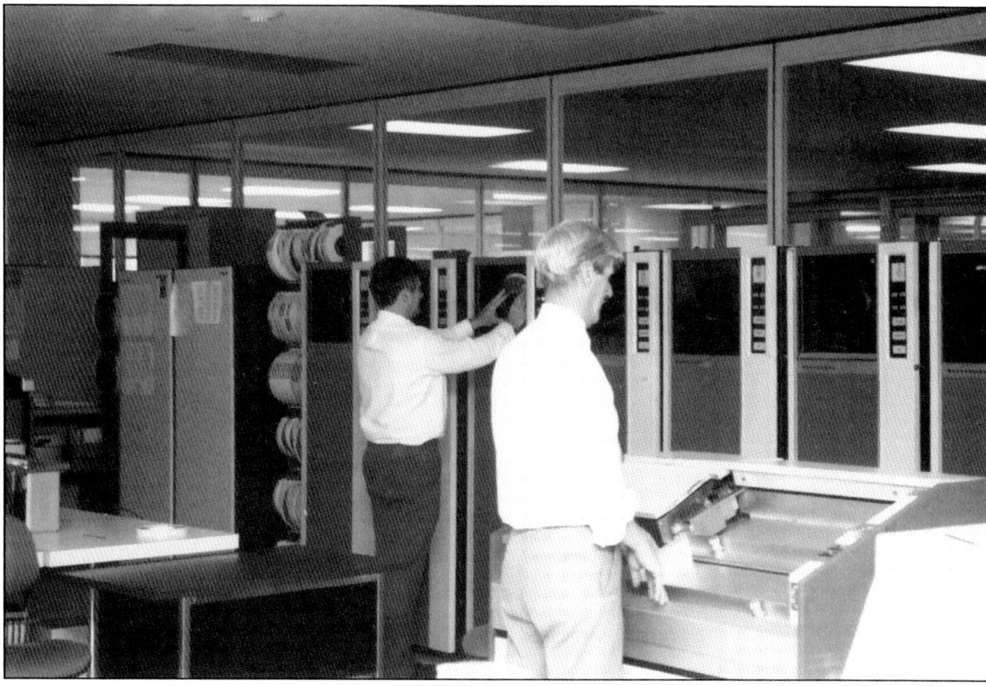

After an eight-year phase-in of large scale IBM systems was completed, data systems bid a fond farewell to the last of the bank's Burroughs computers, the B4800, in 1989. The superiority of IBM's networking abilities was the key selling point. Jerry Giacai, Tom Savage, and Al McKinnon see to the Burroughs's final phaseout.

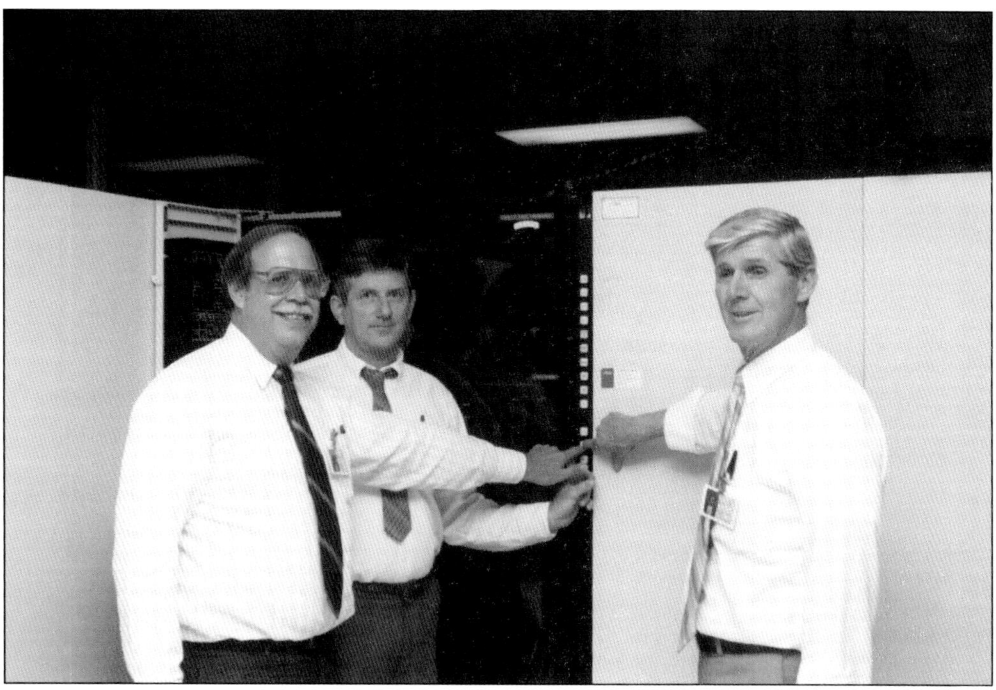

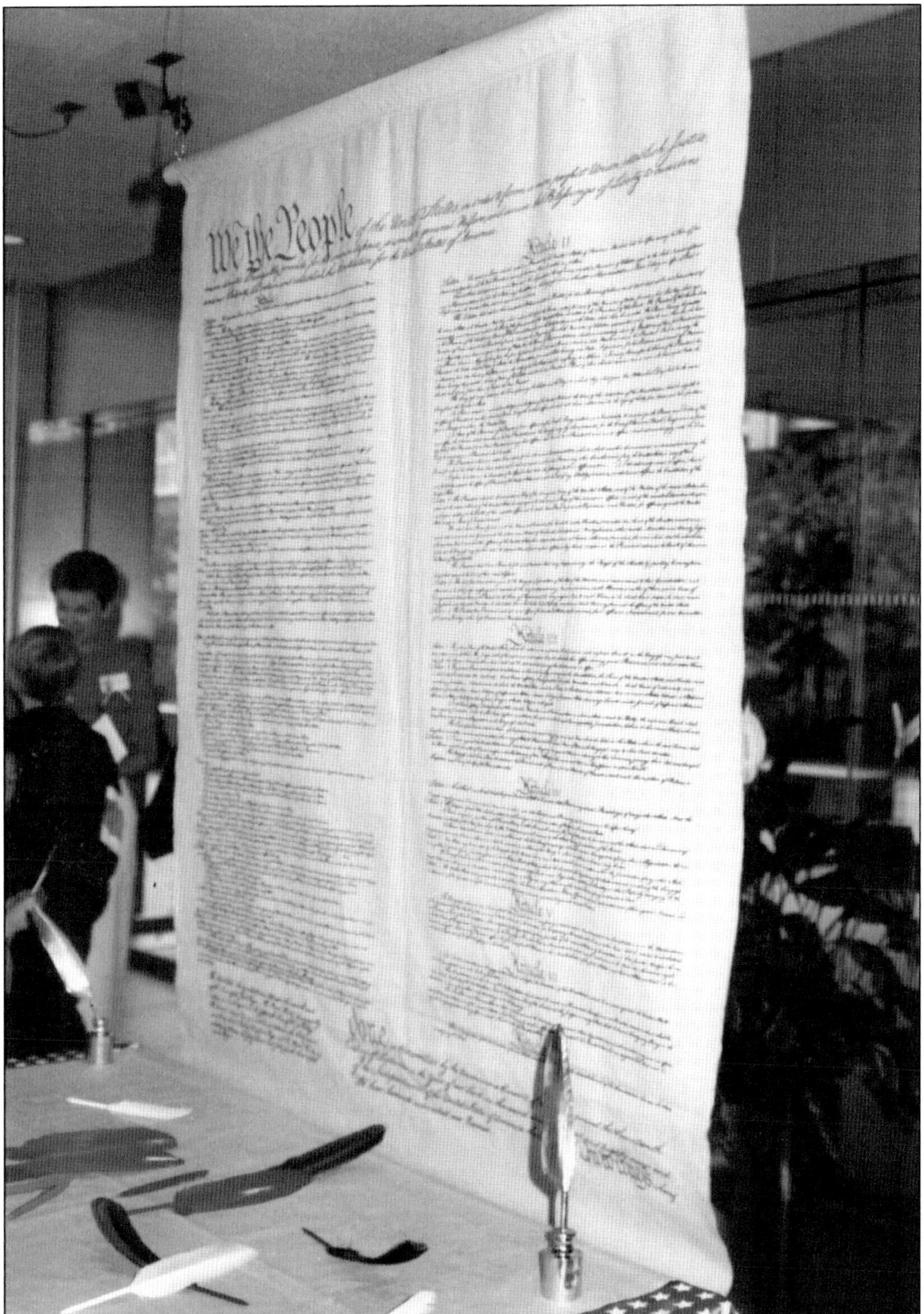

The US Constitution had its bicentennial in 1987, and the bank celebrated with harbor tours, a "We the People" road race, and a champagne toast, none of which had much bearing on the event being celebrated but were apparently enjoyed by some 1,800 employees and guests. Closer to the actual theme was the six-foot-tall canvas replica of the document that guests could embellish with their own signatures.

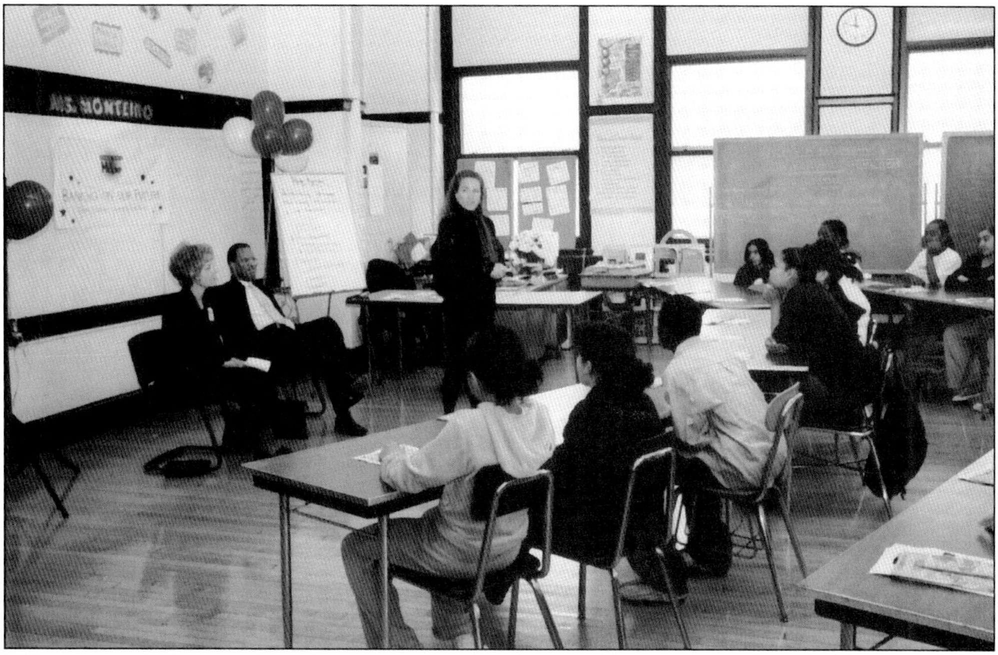

The Community Affairs Department formed a partnership with School Volunteers for Boston to initiate a mentoring program with Dearborn Middle School in Roxbury. Students received one-on-one educational and motivational support from a group of 23 Fed volunteers.

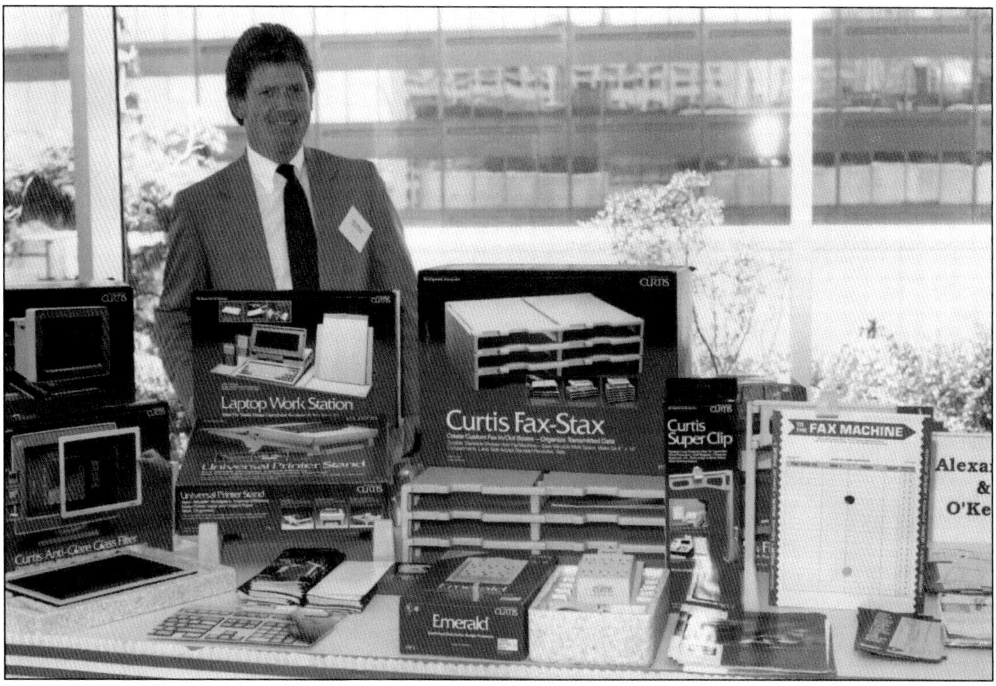

General Services first hosted the New Products Fair in 1987, and it was an annual event for several years. Vendors who contracted with the bank's primary office supplier demonstrated products both high-tech and low-tech. In 1989, IBM's new fax machine competed for attention with an erasable highlighter; only one of these was destined for great things.

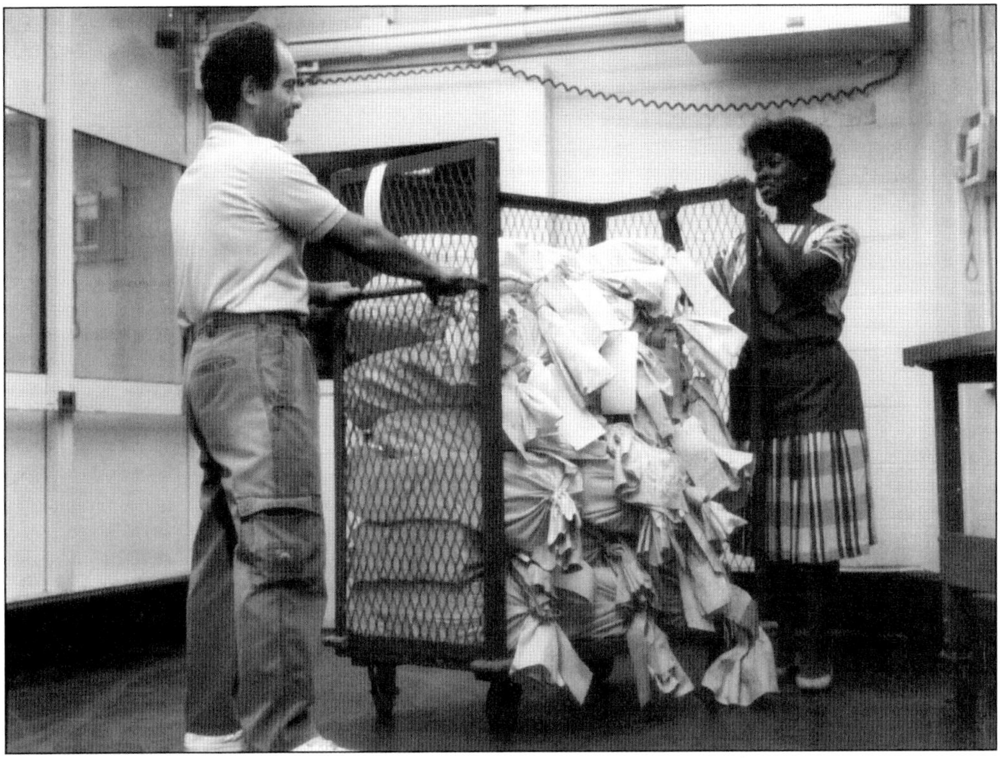

Cash Services instituted a "sunrise shift" of 14 employees who worked from 4:00 a.m. to 12:00 p.m. to ease the increasing volume of cash in and out of the bank. Since public transportation was not available at those hours, the bank leased a parking lot on the opposite side of Fort Point Channel.

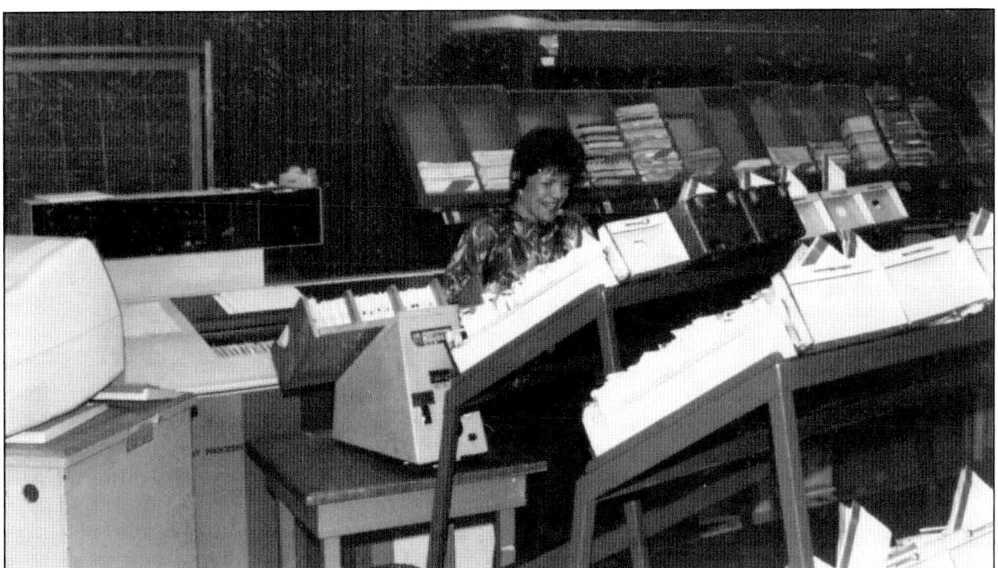

The extended hours were nothing new to Check Collection, which had operated a night force since the 1950s. The high-speed check-sorters crowding the floor lived up to their name: more than one million checks could be processed over the course of a single night shift.

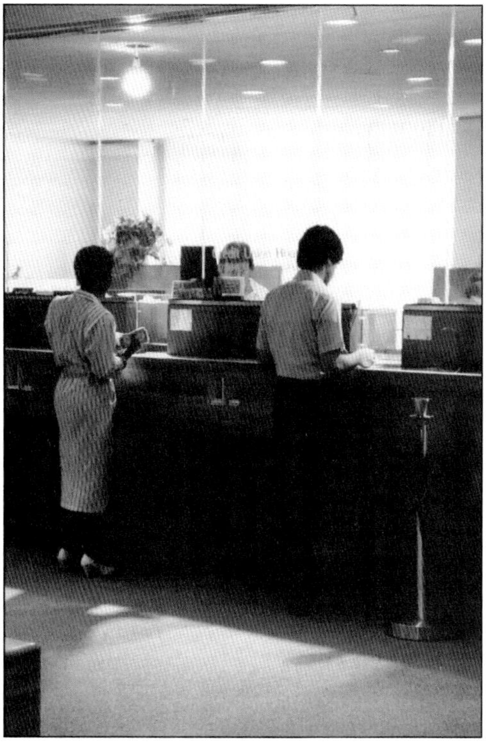

"Credit Union Insolvent" cried a headline in *Breezes* in 1983. A further glance, however, revealed that it was an April Fools' Day prank. Other articles suggested training customers in "Fed Relations," which purported to impart such skills as never asking a Fed employee to identify himself and the ins and outs of being transferred six or more times.

The cafeteria menu for May 1984 seems moderately priced, even for the time. Most likely to induce a nostalgic pang among those who remember 1984 is the $3.95 ticket price of a steamed lobster.

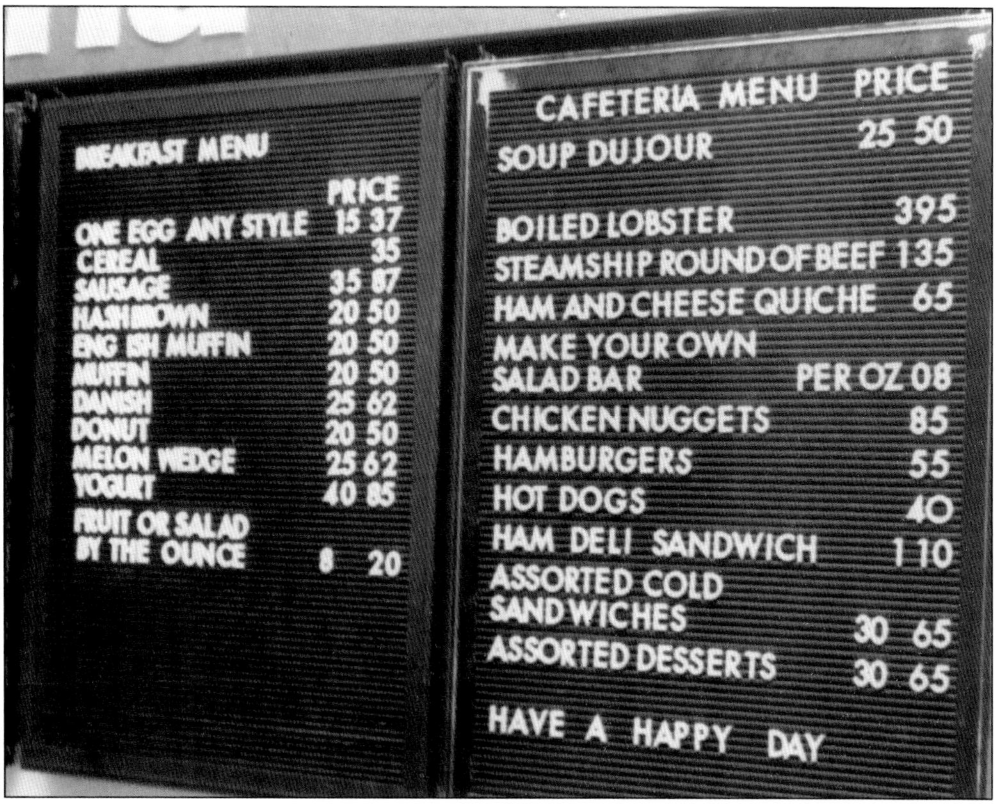

Established in the mid-1970s as part of the bank's overall affirmative action initiative, the Skills Development Center continued to thrive through the 1980s and beyond. High achievers among women and minorities received hands-on, practical business experience as well as training in résumé writing and successful interviewing techniques.

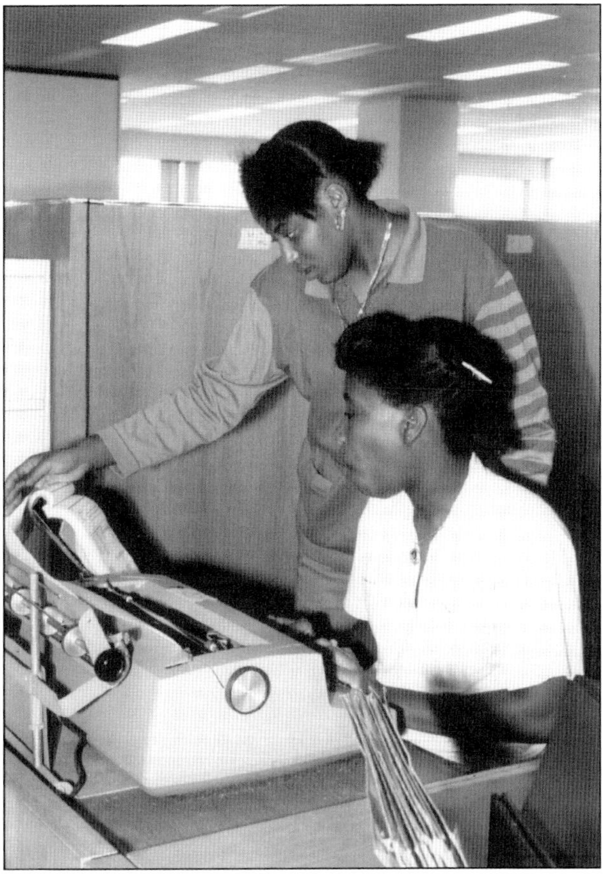

The Three Elements, the geometric sculpture below by Ronald Bladen, had been on loan since 1978 from the Fischbach Gallery in New York and was a fixture on the bank's Dorchester Avenue side. It was sold in 1988 and relocated to a sculpture garden at the North Carolina Museum of Art. The move was handled by the museum, no doubt to the great relief of the property management team.

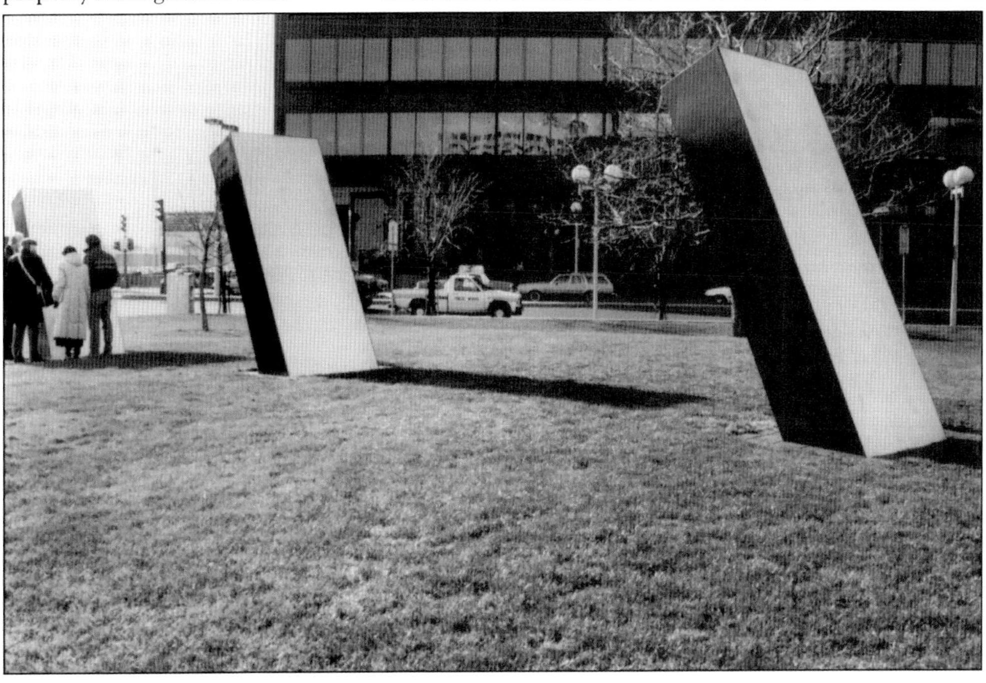

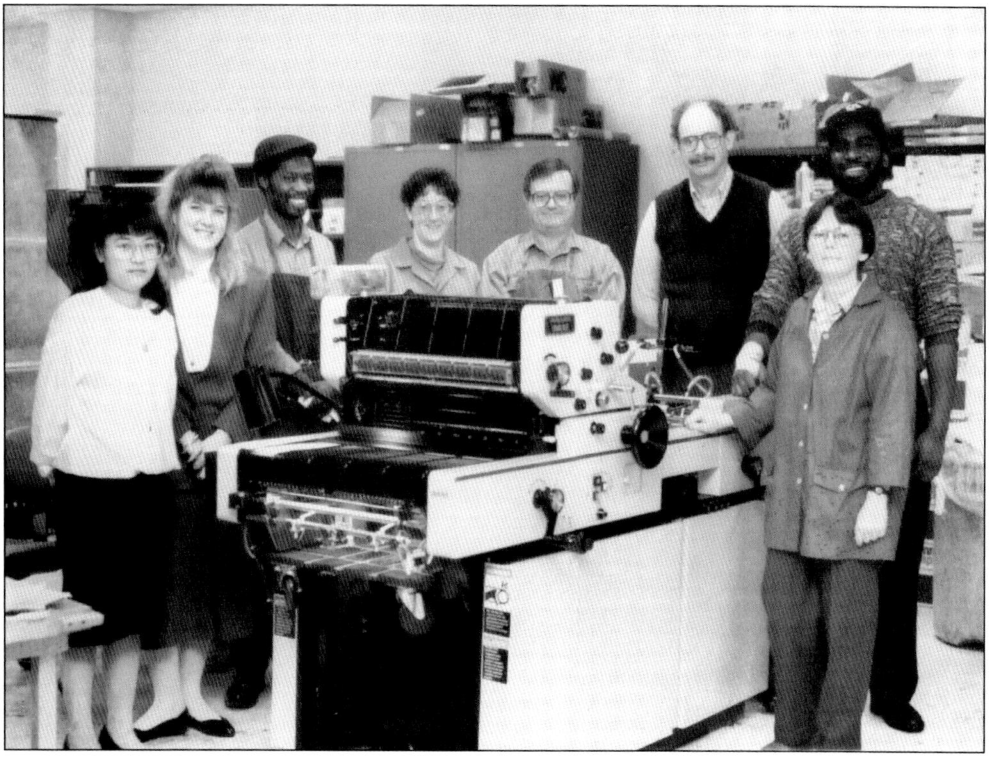

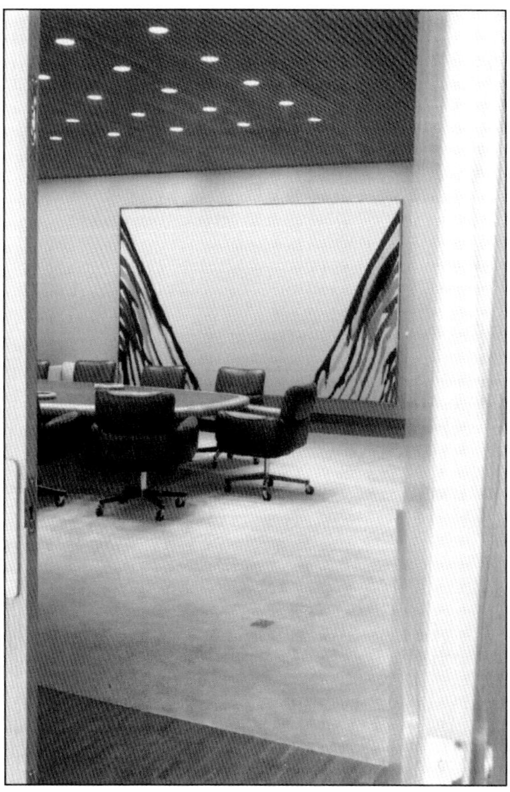

The Printing Department was still fielding a full team in 1989, which handled most of the bank's needs in-house.

When the Atlantic Avenue building was constructed, the bank actively sought to collect appropriate art for the space, concentrating especially on the works of contemporary American artists. In doing so, it established one of the finest collections in the city. *Beta Eta*, by Louis Morris, graced the walls of the boardroom in 1983 and can be viewed today in the Harborview Dining Room.

Eight

TURNING POINTS

The 1990s were an interesting time for New England banking, if the term is used as it is in the famous curse. The Bank of New England (BNE) reached a crisis point in 1990 when the Federal Deposit Insurance Corporation (FDIC) stepped in, seized it, and placed it in Chapter 7 bankruptcy. Boston was called upon to work with regulators to monitor liquidity, provide funding through the discount window, and ensure continuity of payments, among other services. Hard upon the heels of BNE's failure, the Rhode Island banking crisis of 1990–1991 left one in three residents of that state without access to his or her funds. The Boston Fed again stepped in to provide operational support and cash infusions and to ensure that Social Security payments to affected citizens were made in time.

System-wide, the Fed looked to consolidate operations for greater efficiency, and the Boston Fed took on a leadership role, particularly in the payments area. In 1994, the bank became responsible for all retail payment services, including the Automated Clearing House (ACH). In 1995, it joined Cleveland and St. Louis in the handling of system purchasing service; that same year, it took on the Financial Services Policy Committee. In the area of information technology (IT), Boston developed the Integrated Accounting System, a mainframe application that replaced the 12 local systems then in use at each of the reserve banks. Boston IT staff also developed a web-based account management application. At the bank's highest level, the first female assumed leadership as Cathy E. Minehan was appointed president in 1994.

As system efforts expanded, the attention of the general public was focused on the work of the Research Department's study of the Home Mortgage Disclosure Act (HMDA), first issued in 1989 and followed up in 1992, which disclosed a pattern of racial discrimination in lending. In the early 1990s, bank economists were the first to identify the "credit crunch" that resulted from bank failures and its role in deepening the recession, as businesses were unable to borrow sufficiently.

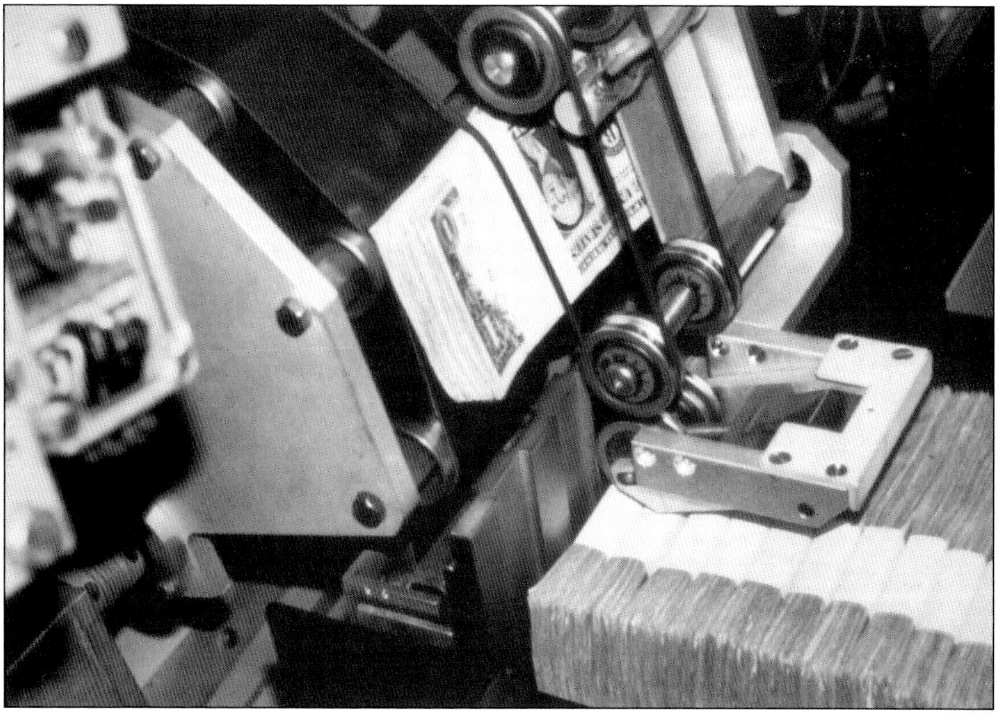

Cash Services added a staff of 145 in 1990 to operate between the hours of 4:00 a.m. and 10:00 p.m. A little-known service provided by the department was the handling of military accounts when Navy vessels docked in Boston Harbor. Cash Services was also responsible for processing food stamps, along with its traditional role of detecting counterfeits and destroying unfit currency.

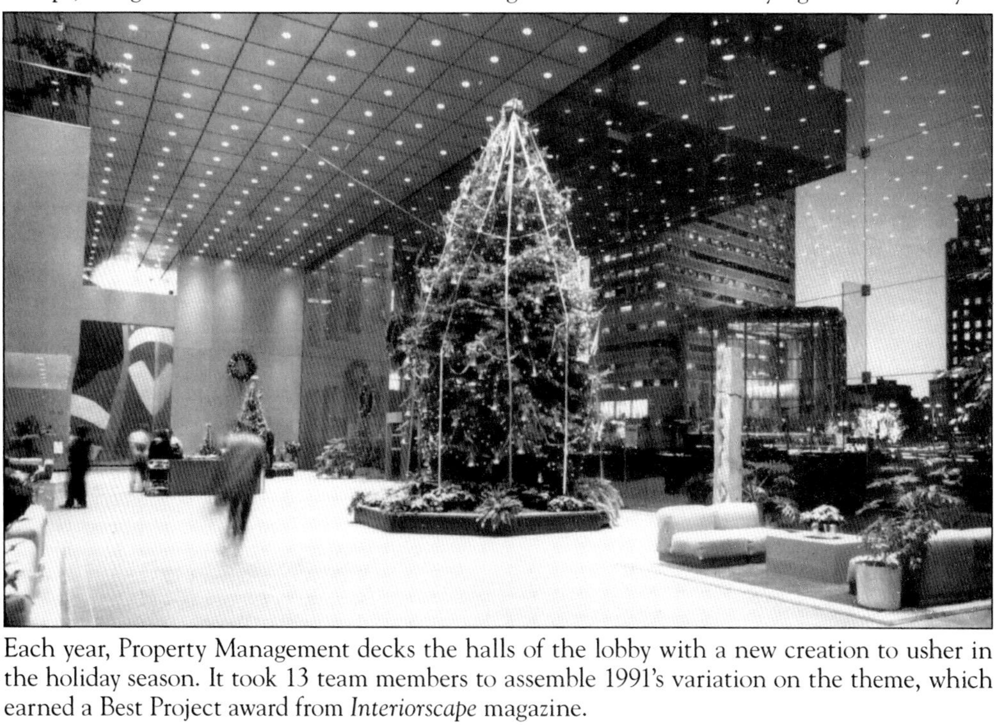

Each year, Property Management decks the halls of the lobby with a new creation to usher in the holiday season. It took 13 team members to assemble 1991's variation on the theme, which earned a Best Project award from *Interiorscape* magazine.

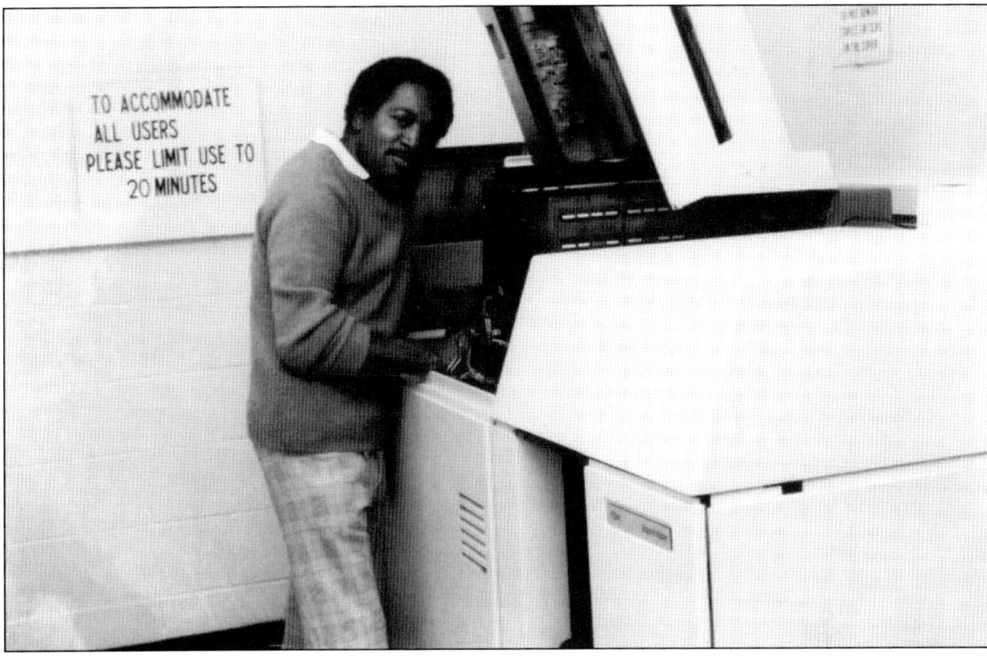

General Services provided (as might be expected) basic services, including purchasing, printing, food services, mail, receiving, and something called addressograph units, which—despite the antiquated name—were still kicking in 1990. That same year, the department hosted a networking fair for minority vendors and members of the New England Purchasing Council. Here, Willie Andrews attends to a printer problem.

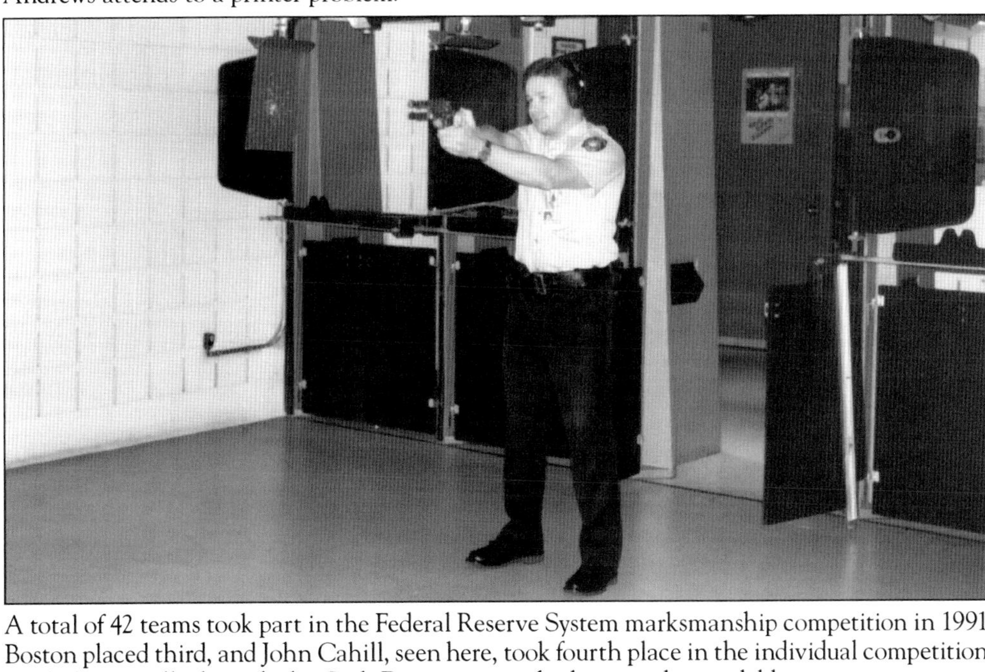

A total of 42 teams took part in the Federal Reserve System marksmanship competition in 1991. Boston placed third, and John Cahill, seen here, took fourth place in the individual competition. Aside from strolls through the Cash Department, which are understandably not easy to arrange, nothing is more popular in guided tours of the building than seeing the Federal Reserve Police's firing range.

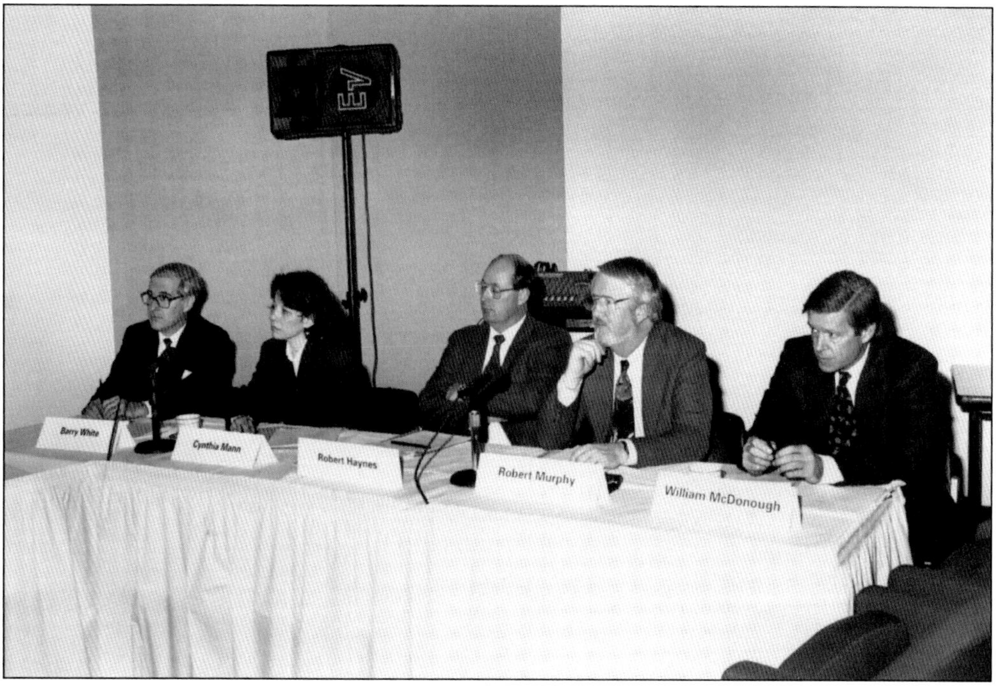

Boston Fed president Richard Syron and general counsel William McDonough joined William Bulger, the Massachusetts State Senate president; Charles Flaherty, the speaker of the Massachusetts House of Representatives; and Rep. Joseph Kennedy on the State Special Commission on Business Tax Policy at a conference held at the Boston Fed in 1992.

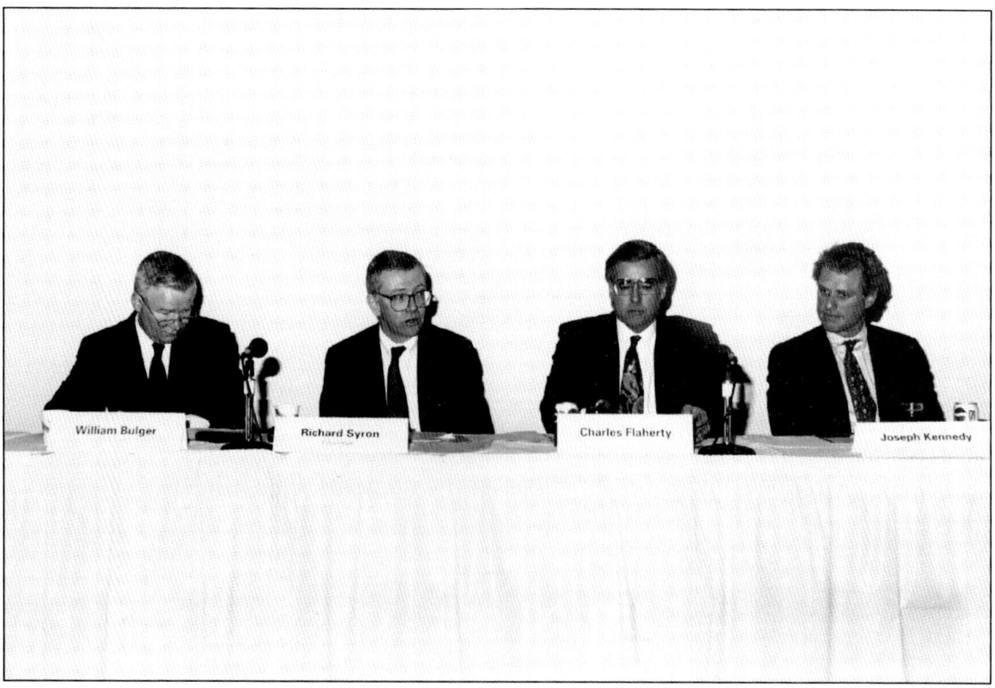

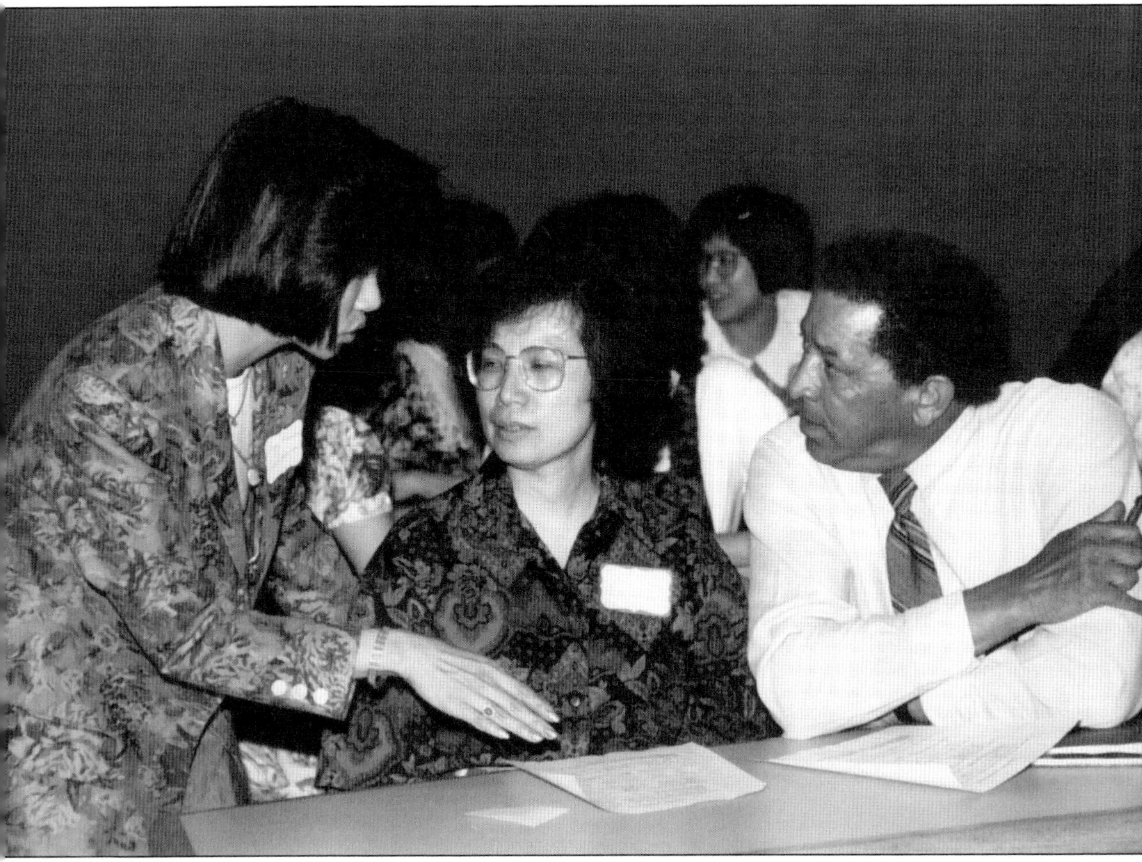

A pilot English as a Working Language (EWL) program was developed for the bank by the Kilmartin Company, specifically for Cash Services, Check Collection, and Fiscal Agency employees. A group of 27 staffers attended the first session, which consisted of two and a half months of classroom study followed by three months of applying their new knowledge on the job and, finally, a return to the classroom to refine the skills they had learned.

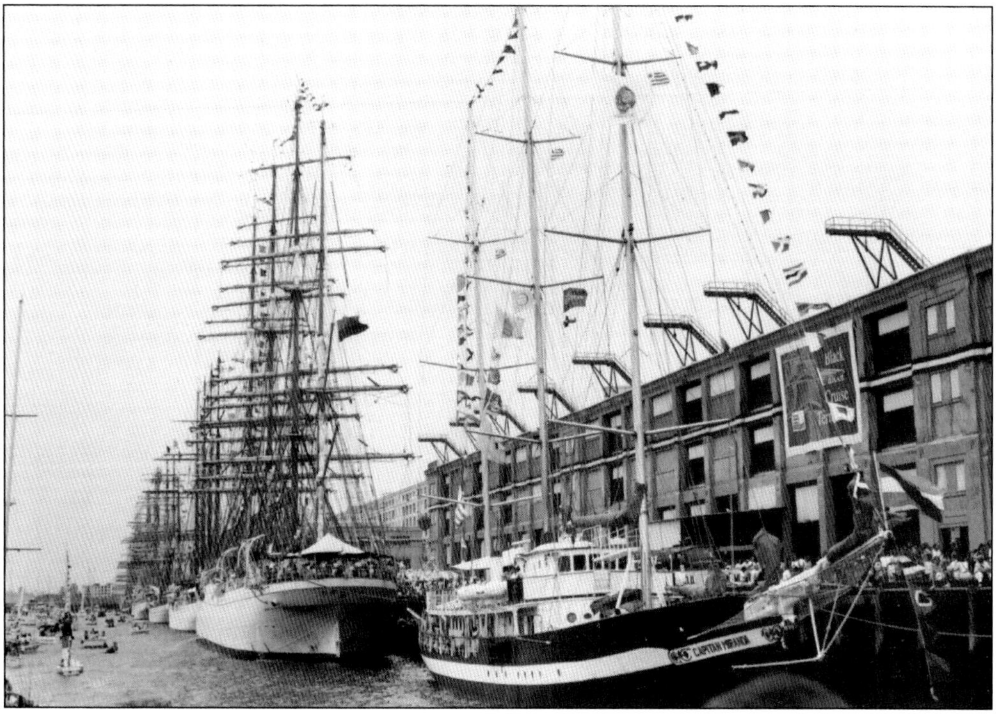

When this group of tall ships made an appearance in 1992, the Fed made an occasion of it, appropriately enough named FedPort. Nearly 4,000 employees and their guests attended a clambake on the roof garden and then took in the parade of sail from chartered harbor cruisers or from the vantage point of the 32nd floor.

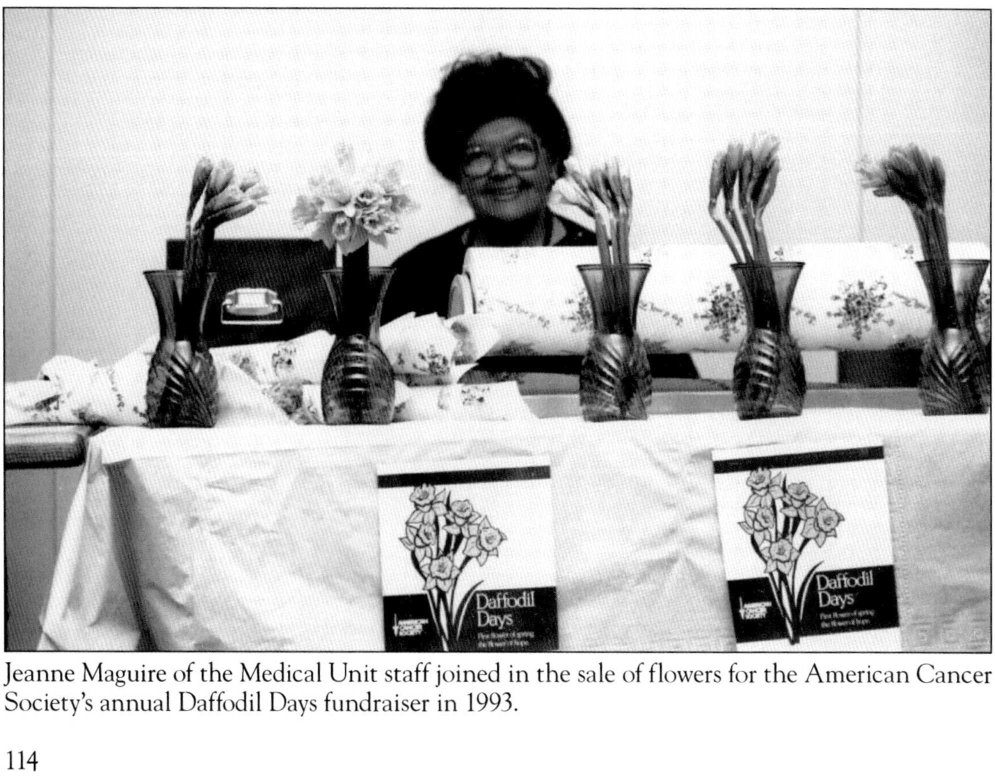

Jeanne Maguire of the Medical Unit staff joined in the sale of flowers for the American Cancer Society's annual Daffodil Days fundraiser in 1993.

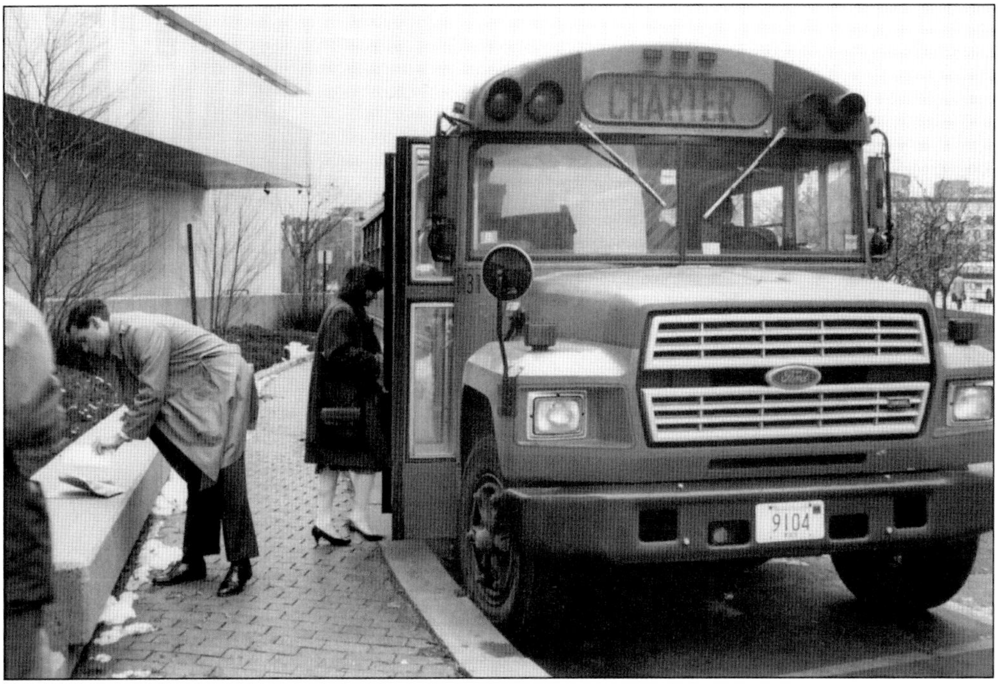

The Books & Kids program established a partnership with Oliver Wendell Holmes Elementary School in Dorchester that continues today. Fed volunteers like the ones above collect books for the school library and send reading enrichment teams to read out loud with students and hopefully instill a love of reading. In 2009, the scope expanded to include Math & Kids volunteers.

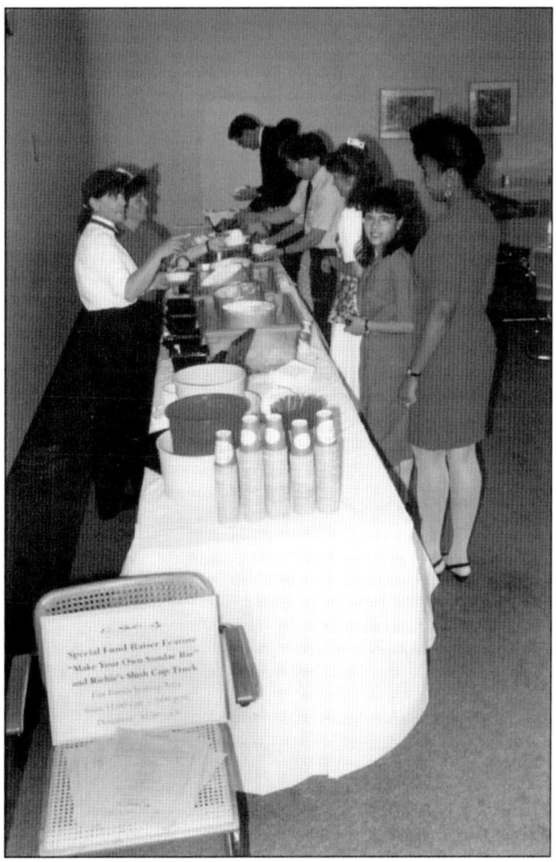

When flooding in the Midwest affected Fed colleagues in St. Louis and Des Moines, Boston responded. Over $4,500 in cash donations was raised through raffles for Red Sox tickets and vacation days and an ice-cream sundae sale. Windsor Locks employees collected much-needed supplies of linens, flashlights, bottled water, and other necessities for eight Des Moines Fed families who had lost everything.

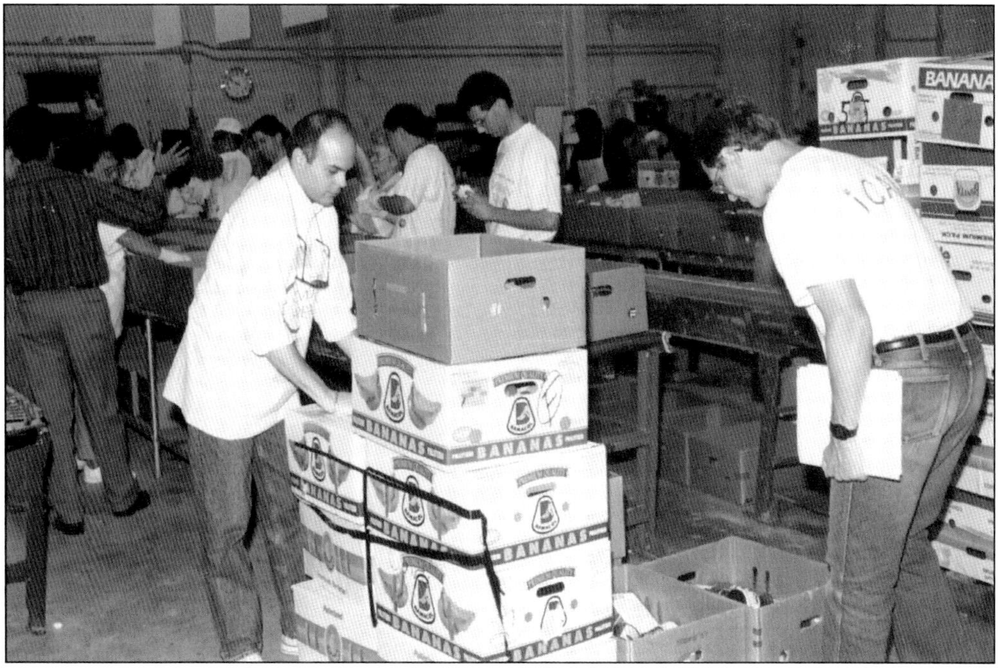

Boston's continued involvement with the United Way added a new feature in the 1990s with Community Care Days, a series of one-day projects that make a lasting difference to one of the many agencies and programs the United Way serves and supports. Among the projects taken on by Fed volunteers in 1994 were assisting in food salvage operations for the Greater Boston Food Bank (above) and painting at Greater Lynn Mental Health and Retardation Association residential facilities (below). The bank typically staffs eight to ten projects each year.

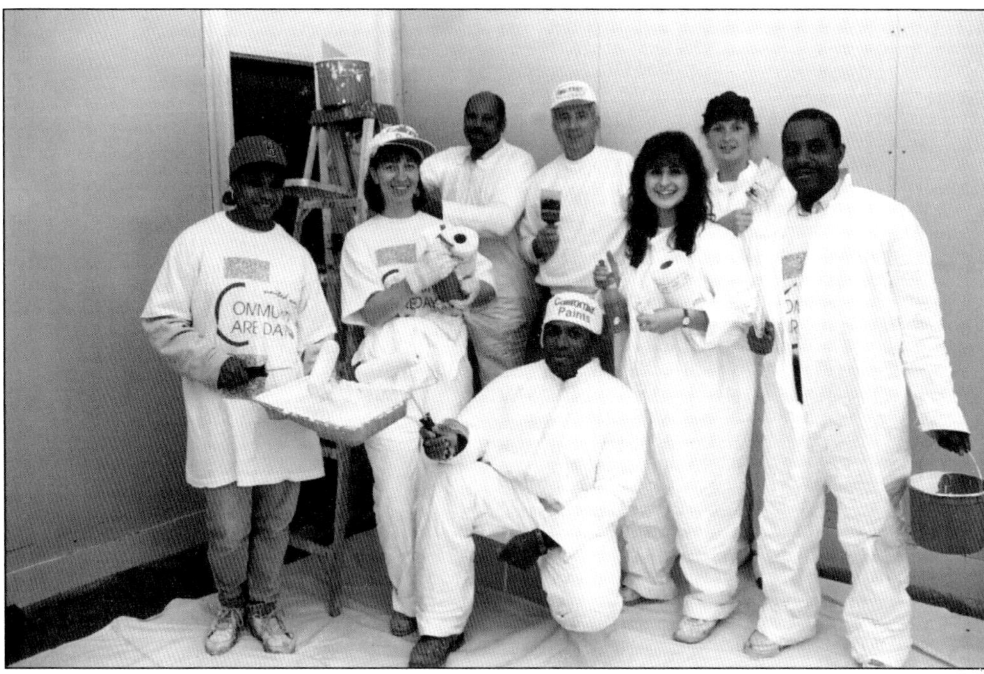

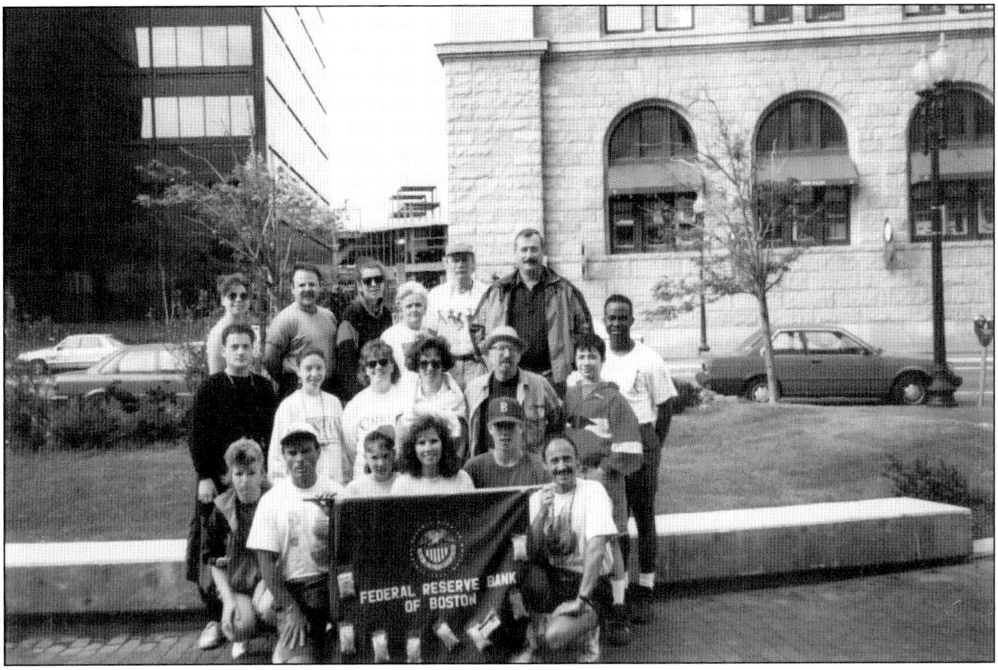

Fed staff, families, and friends raised $3,500 for AIDS research in the 1994 annual Walk for Life, a six-mile course that began at the Boston Common and finished at the Hatch Shell, on the Esplanade. A year earlier, the bank was recognized for outstanding corporate leadership for providing Red Cross HIV/AIDS training in the workplace.

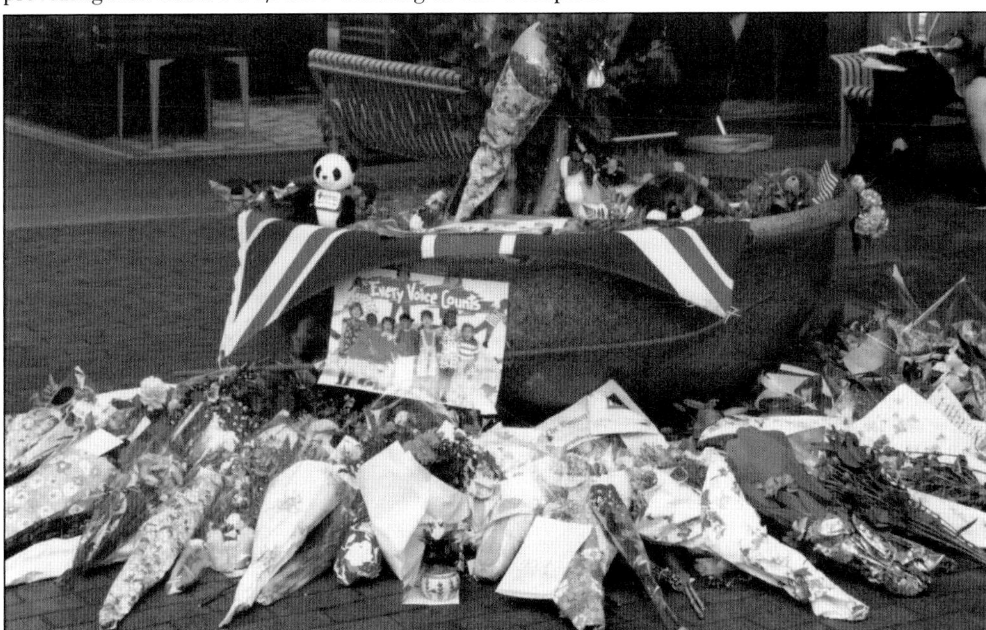

The unexpected death of Diana, Princess of Wales, in 1997 drew crowds of mourners to Federal Reserve Plaza, which was also the home of the British consulate. Mourners stood in line, in some cases for hours, to sign one of the condolence books the consulate provided. Five volumes were eventually filled and sent along to the royal family.

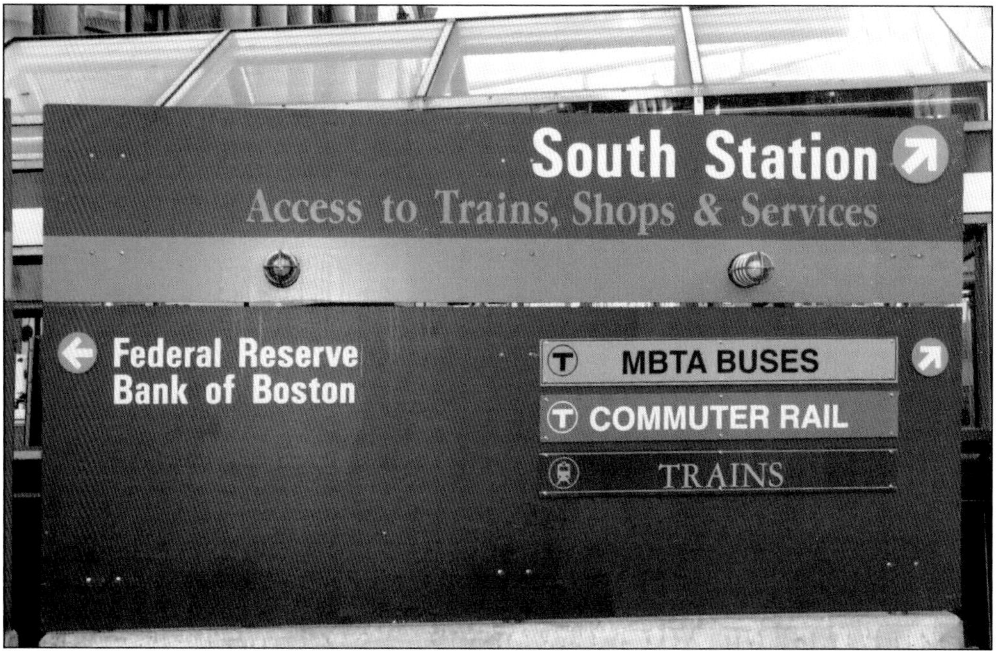

Boston's least favorite public works project, the Big Dig, arrived at the bank's front door in June 1995, necessitating some small adjustments. An optimistic reporter for *Breezes* tried to calmly reassure coworkers that it would be "business as usual," with only minor inconveniences. However, after "business as usual," the list progressed rapidly to "loss of our sidewalk and on street metered parking," "planned power interruptions," "daily movement of construction vehicles," "delays on the T and the street," and, finally, "considerable construction in B-1 [basement floor] and the garage for the next six years."

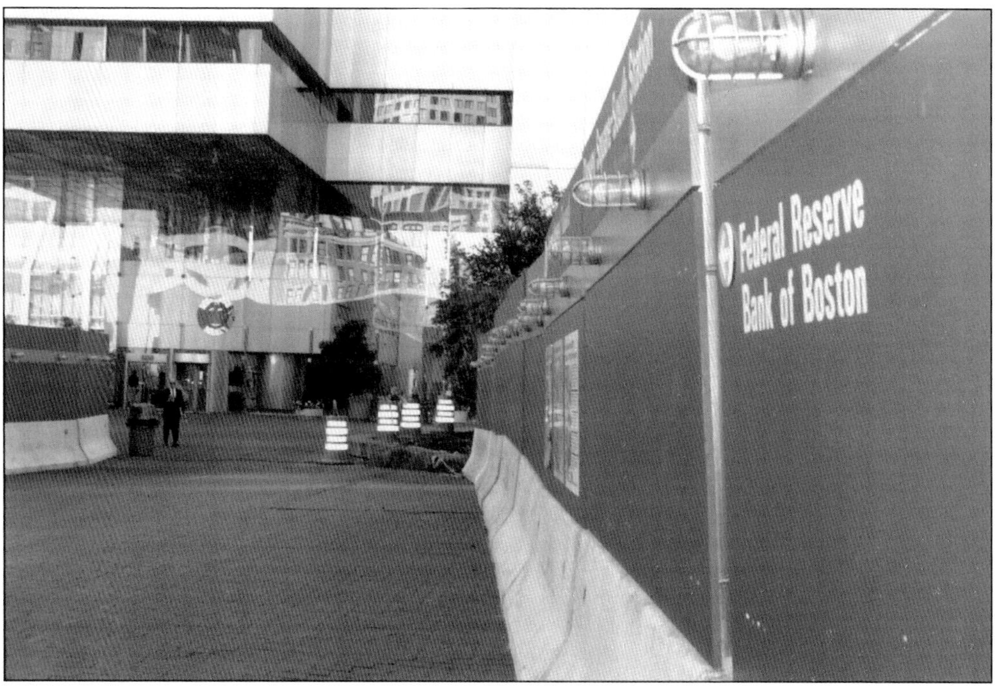

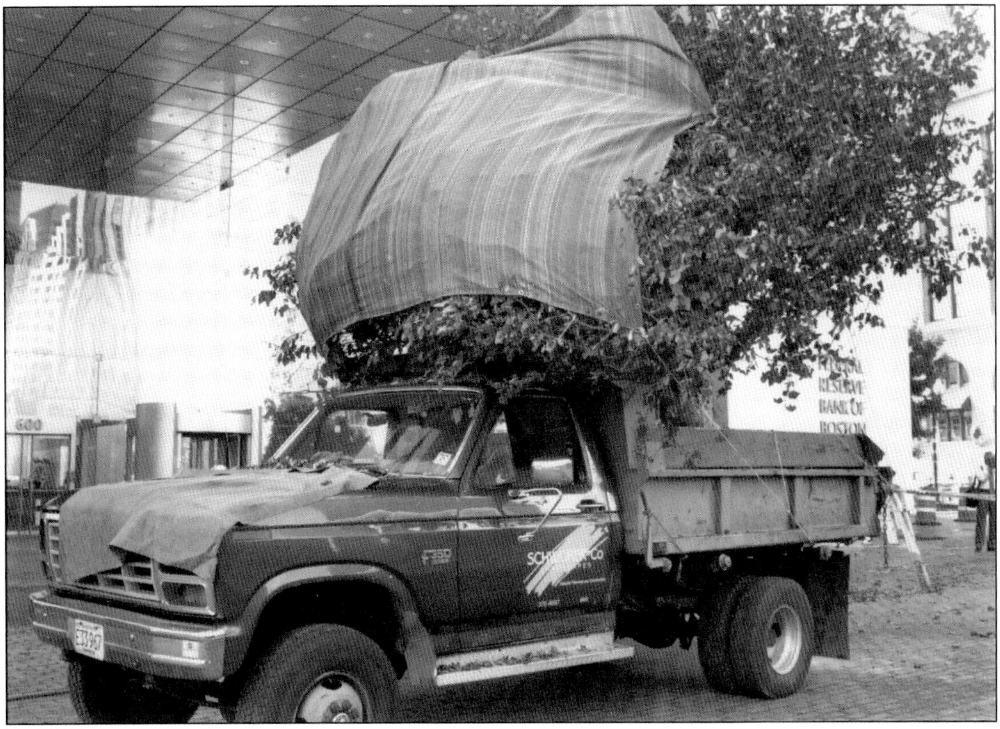

Trees from the plaza area that had to be uprooted did not have to sacrifice their lives to the Big Dig, as the bank's parking spaces had. Instead, through the efforts of Property Management, the uprooted trees were transferred to several Boston Housing Authority sites.

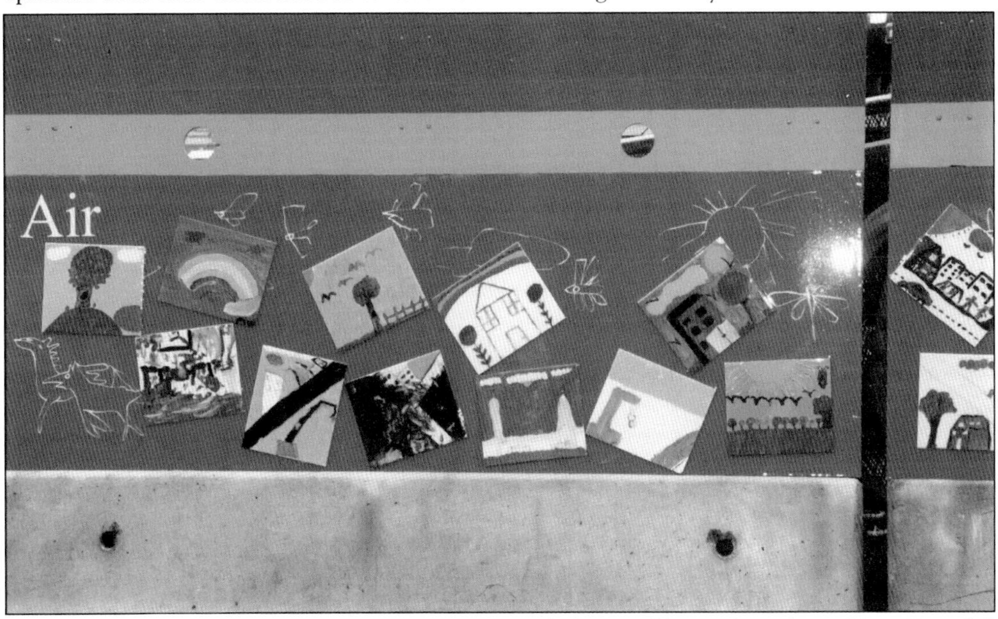

Making the most of an inconvenient situation, murals designed by students from Oliver Wendell Holmes Elementary, South Boston High School, and Dearborn Middle School on the theme of nature and technology graced the construction barriers outside the bank as the Big Dig dragged on.

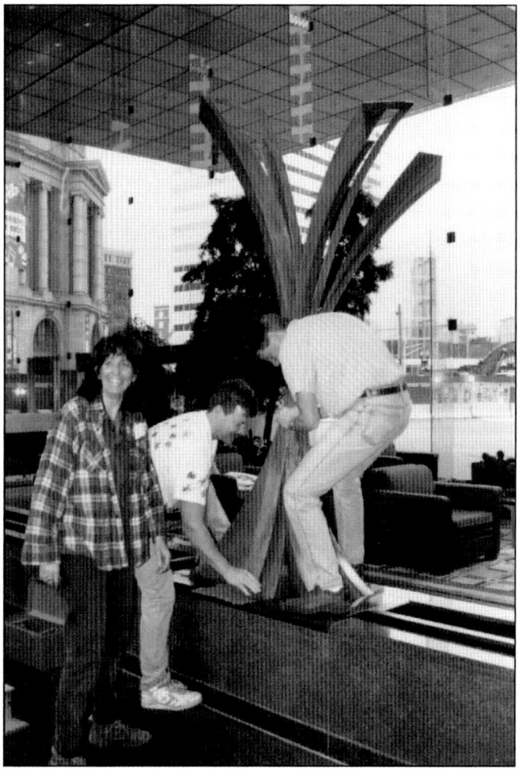

This 10-foot-high aluminum sculpture was installed in the main lobby in May 1992, completing the water element on the north side of the lobby. The sculpture, which took several months to construct, is the work of artist Margaret Swam, who still shows regularly with the Boston Sculptors at Chapel Gallery in Newton. Anne Belson of Cultural Affairs, who coordinated the installation, said, "The sculpture culminates months of work, during which the artist made many visits to the Bank's lobby to study the water element, gain inspiration from the environment, develop ideas, make sketches and construct several small models. One of these small models was selected to become the sculpture, which the artist has named Wellspring because of its water-like qualities."

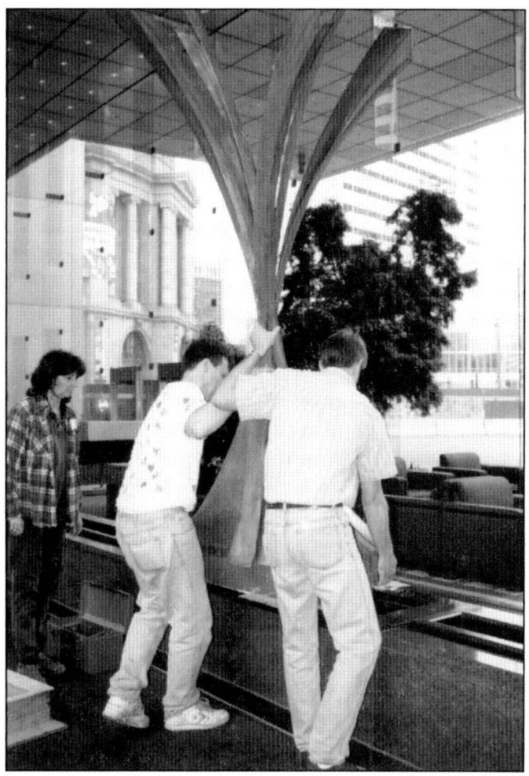

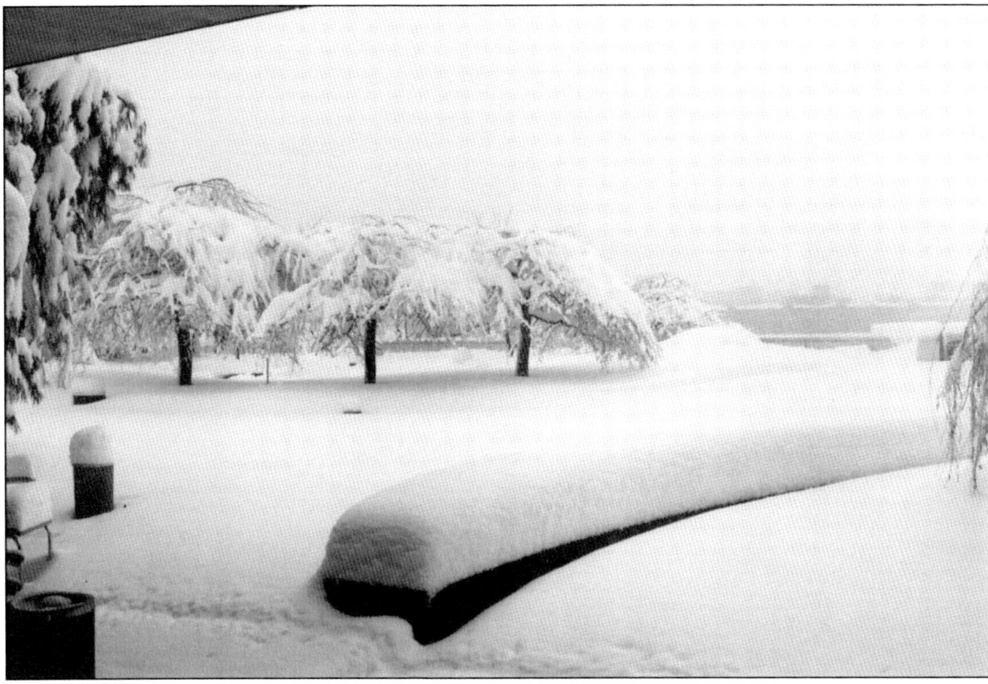

The April Fools' Day storm of 1997 dumped up to three feet of snow around the entire Northeast. It also made for a picturesque tableau on the roof garden.

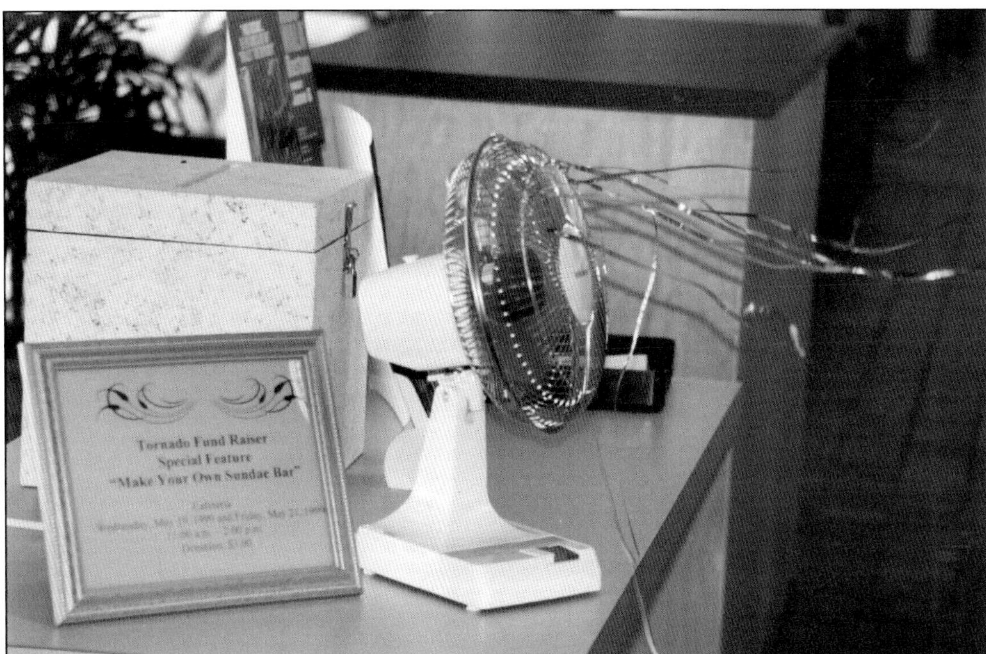

The Boston Fed often supported communities outside of New England. Pictured, the golden fan spreads goodwill towards Oklahoma to aid in relief efforts after the 1999 tornado. There was also a "Make Your Own Sundae Bar."

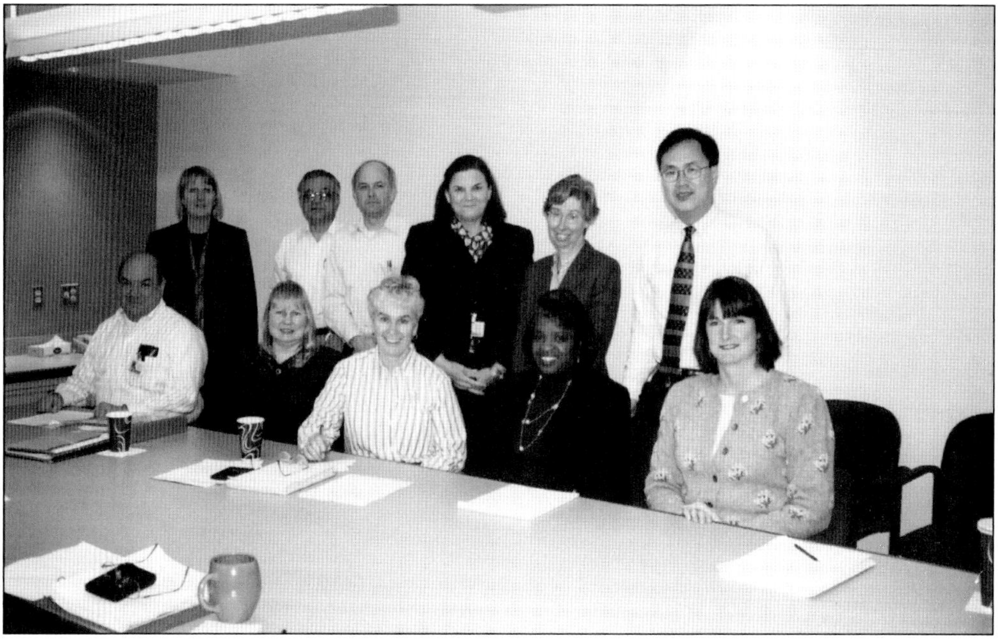

A Diversity Planning Group was formed in 1998 to provide leadership for the bank's diversity efforts. Members were officers and senior staff, representing all groups, and were charged with defining what diversity meant to the bank, refining those objectives, and then recommending procedures on how best to achieve those goals.

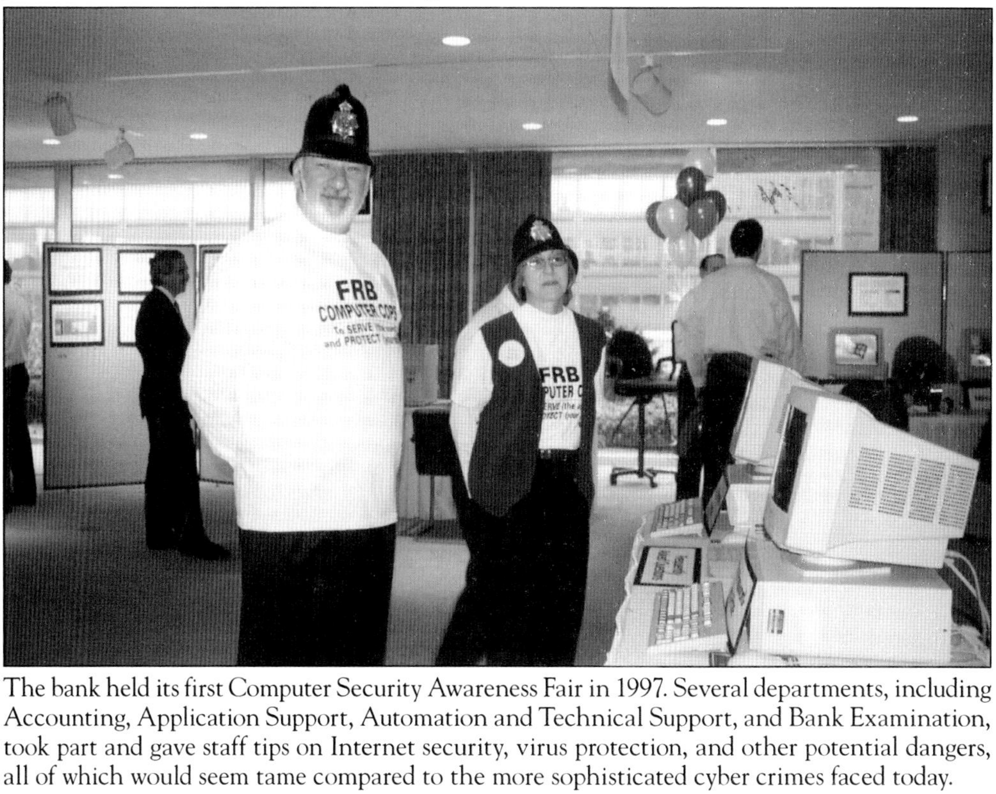

The bank held its first Computer Security Awareness Fair in 1997. Several departments, including Accounting, Application Support, Automation and Technical Support, and Bank Examination, took part and gave staff tips on Internet security, virus protection, and other potential dangers, all of which would seem tame compared to the more sophisticated cyber crimes faced today.

Nine

A New Century

There is often no glory in successfully preventing disasters, especially when success is so complete that even minor inconveniences are prevented. The Federal Reserve System as a whole took the century date change (CDC) issue seriously, and the Boston Fed played a leading role in financial services, in conjunction with the Federal Reserve Board of Governors, in the preparations for the year 2000 switch (Y2K), which were begun as early as 1997. So successful were the efforts that the general consensus of public opinion, unaware of what had been accomplished behind the scenes, was that Y2K fears had been much ado about nothing.

The new century saw the Boston Fed expanding its leadership in system projects, as the bank was selected to implement and manage both the Internet Payment Platform (IPP), as the fiscal agent for the US Treasury, as well as the Stored Value and Eagle Cash Programs, developed for active military personnel. In 2001, Boston began implementing Treasury Direct as one of three system call centers.

In its efforts to expand its services to the community, a major initiative studied the conditions of Springfield, Massachusetts, and sought ways to engage a variety of stakeholders in collaborations that could revitalize the city and, with the lessons learned there, establish the Working Cities Challenge in order to find innovative approaches towards managing the challenges facing mid-sized cities throughout New England. The Fed also increased its efforts in economic education and consumer awareness with the Economic Adventure Program and publications that addressed emerging issues such as identity theft and fair lending practices. In the face of the subprime mortgage crisis, the Boston Fed held two mortgage foreclosure prevention workshops, allowing many borrowers to modify payments and avoid foreclosure. Boston has also taken a lead in so-called green initiatives; it is the first bank in the Federal Reserve System to be granted a LEED-EB Gold designation from the US Green Building Council (USGBC).

As the Federal Reserve System nears its 100th anniversary, the Boston Fed may look back with pride at its accomplishments while also looking forward to its continued evolution in order to meet the needs of the community and the nation.

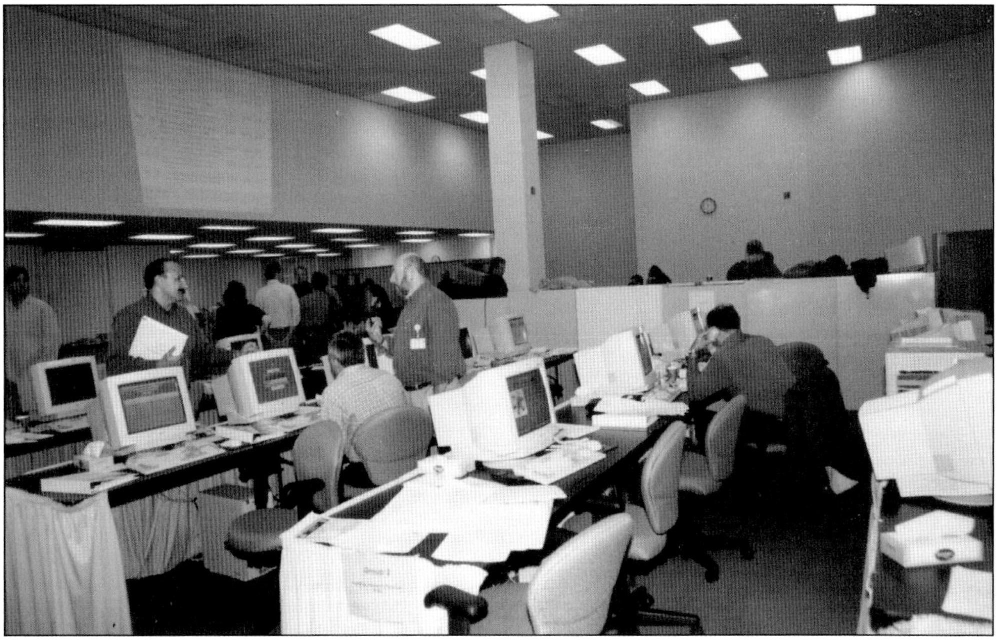

Members of the communication center ran several tests in advance of the century date change (CDC) to prepare for any eventualities. The rollover weekend went smoothly, and the bank's Business Continuity Steering Group, initiated to handle potential CDC issues, became a permanent group.

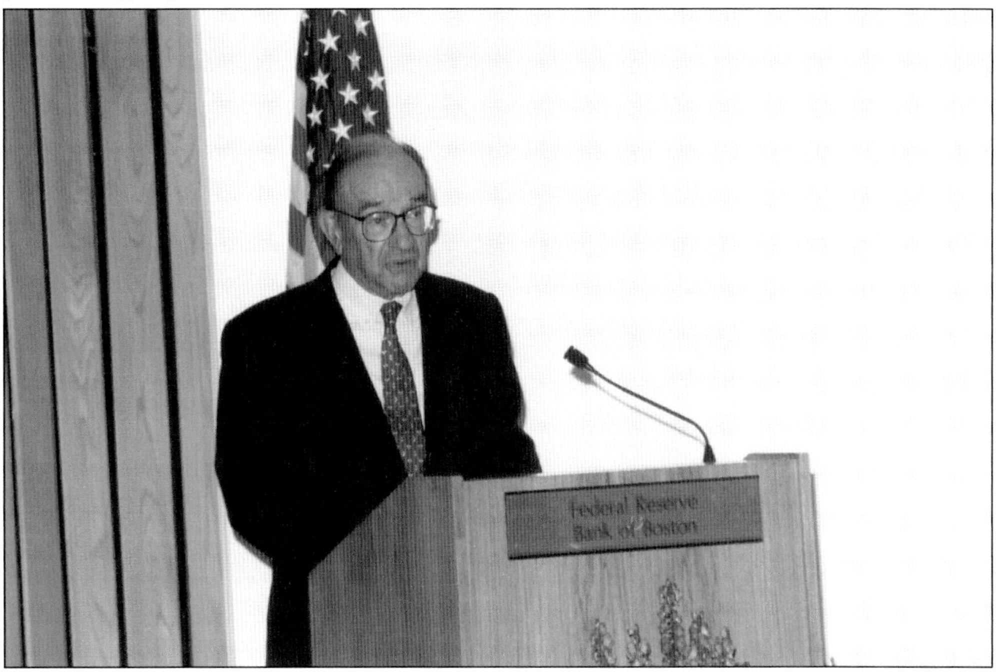

Federal Reserve chairman Alan Greenspan visited Boston in October 2000 in conjunction with the dedication of the bank's auditorium in honor of Frank Morris. Greenspan answered audience questions, which ranged from the expected ("How does the Fed work?") to the not so expected ("Who's your favorite band?"), which, by all accounts, he answered with aplomb.

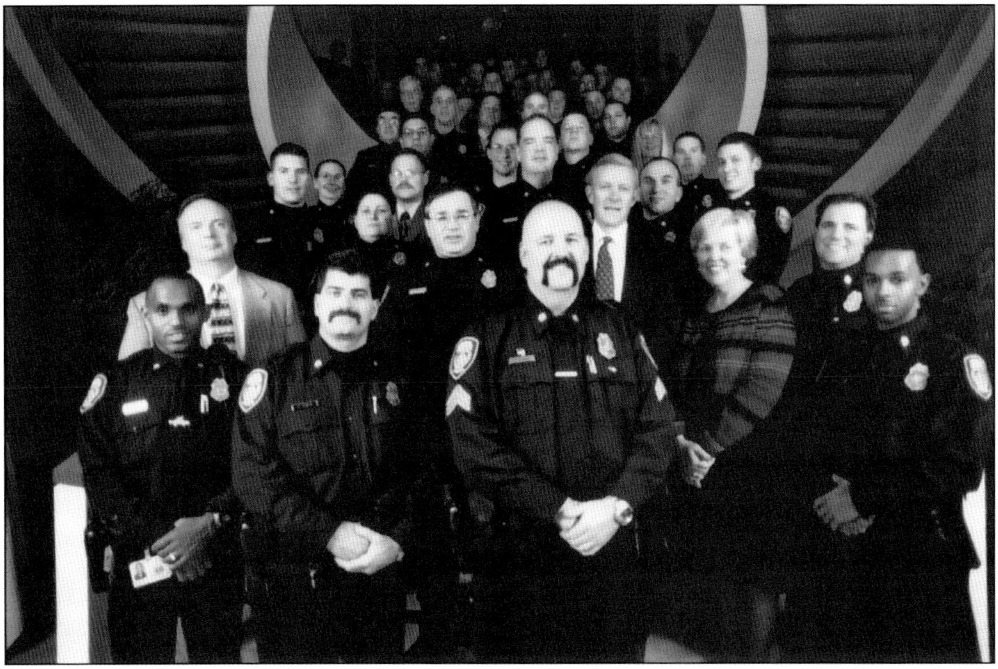

In light of several high-profile incidents, including the Columbine school shooting, 16 members of the bank's Protection Department participated in active-shooter training with the Massachusetts State Police to hone their skills in rapid response to live-fire incidents.

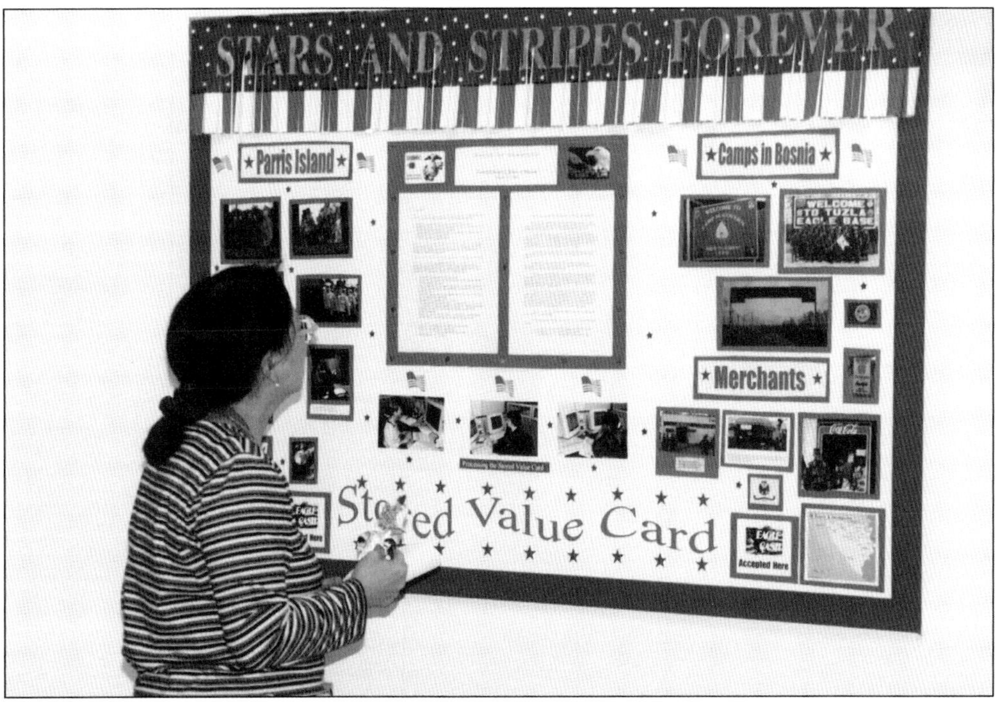

The theme of the 2001 celebration of excellence assembly was "Excellence Through Innovation." Seen here are some of the new initiatives showcased, including the Stored Value Card, designed to support active military personnel.

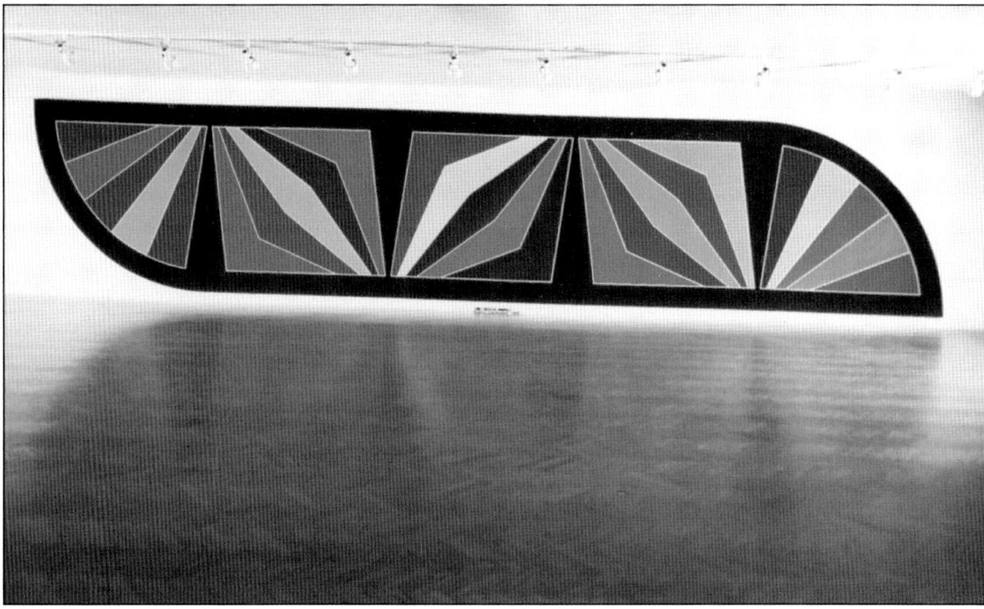

Frank Stella's imposing *Damascus Gate* (above) once hung in the first-floor gallery, but its massive size constricted the flexibility of the space for changing exhibits. Eventually, the painting was acquired by the Museum of Fine Arts, Houston, and carefully rolled out of the gallery (below).

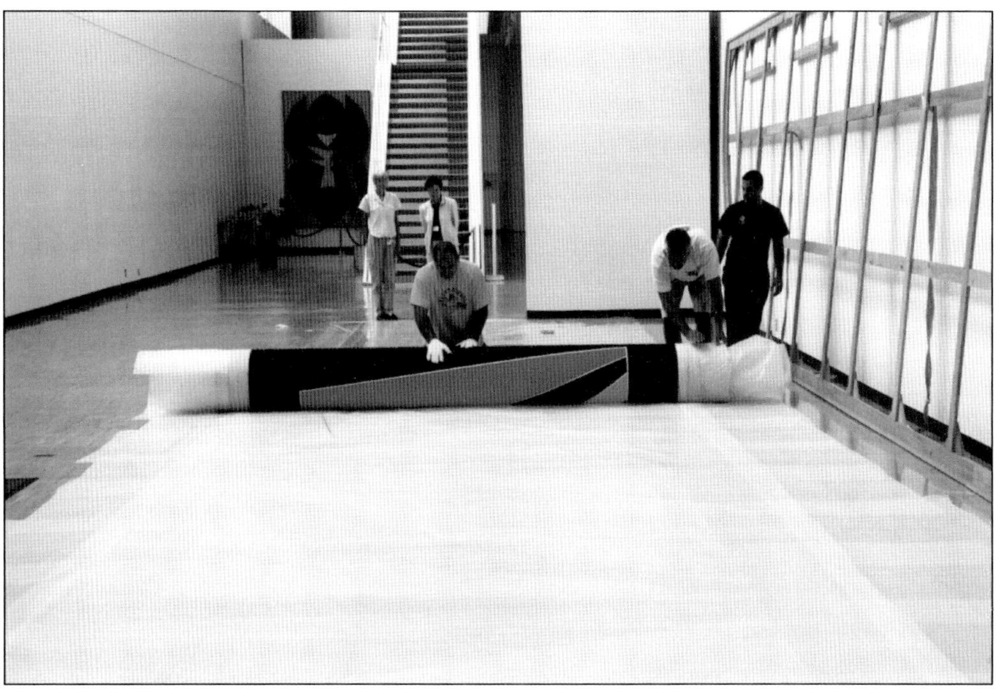

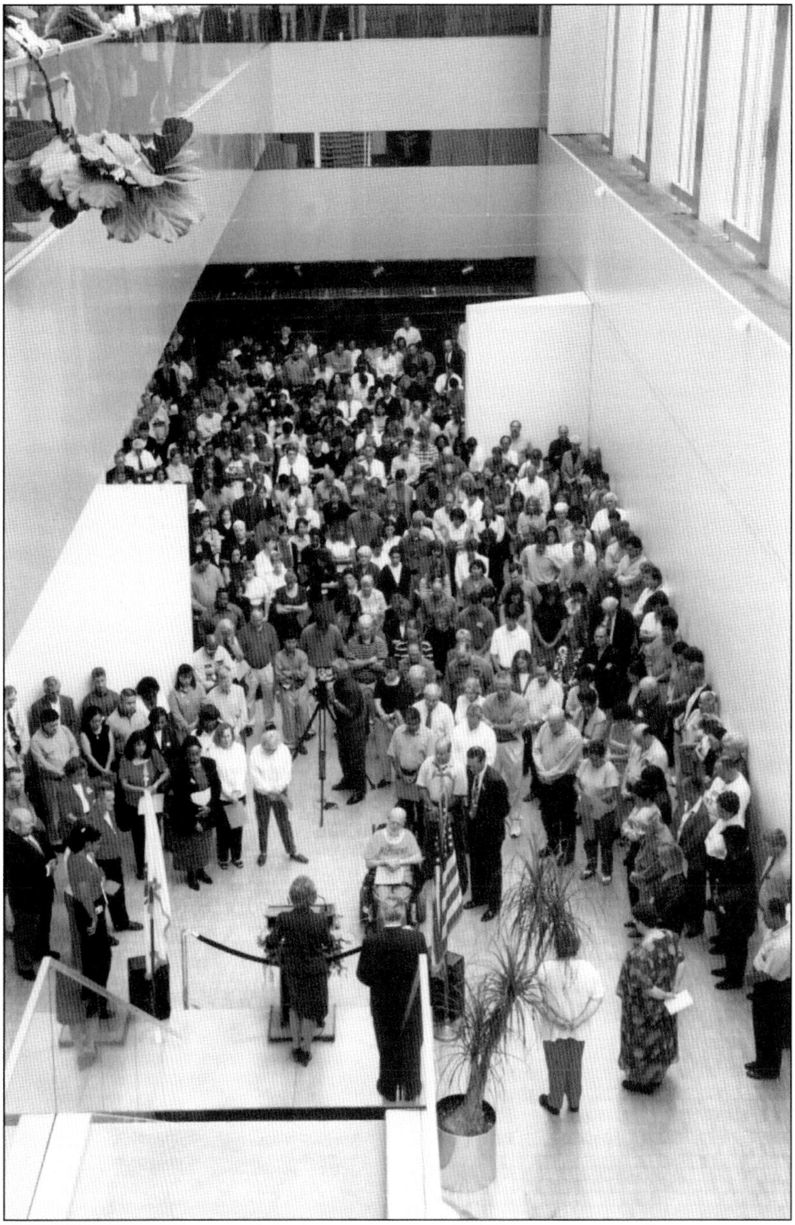

Employees and tenants gathered in the gallery on September 14, 2001, to remember and honor the victims of the attacks of September 11. In the midst of the tragedy, the Boston Fed played an important role in maintaining uninterrupted delivery of critical financial services. As one of two banks in the system responsible for processing off-line transfers, the Boston Fed provided this service to some of the largest financial institutions in the country, whose electronic transfer operations had been disrupted, to the amount of $150 billion in the course of one week. In the chaos and uncertainty of those first hours, perhaps few messages were capable of staving off panic as the simple message released by the Federal Reserve Board of Governors: "For immediate release: The Federal Reserve System is open and operating. The discount window is available to meet liquidity needs."

Consistent with our mission to preserve history on a local level, this book was printed in South Carolina on American-made paper and manufactured entirely in the United States. Products carrying the accredited Forest Stewardship Council (FSC) label are printed on 100 percent FSC-certified paper.

MADE IN THE USA